LATIN-AMERICAN PERCUSSION
Rhythms and rhythm instruments from Cuba and Brazil

BIRGER SULSBRÜCK

English translation by
Ethan Weisgard

DEN RYTMISKE AFTENSKOLES FORLAG / EDITION WILHELM HANSEN

Copyright © 1980 by Den Rytmiske Aftenskoles Forlag.
Copyright © 1982 (English version) by Den Rytmiske Aftenskoles Forlag.
Copyright © 1986 (English revised version) by
Den Rytmiske Aftenskoles Forlag/Edition Wilhelm Hansen, Copenhagen.
International Copyright Secured.
All rights reserved.

Layout: Susanne Brinkø
Front cover layout: Morten Langebæk.
Photo: Ole Haupt (incl. front cover).
Musical notation: Bernard Laux.
Photoset: Bente's Fotosats

Cassettes recorded at Plexus Sound Studio.
Engineered by Ole »Lyd« Rasmussen.

Distributed Exclusively By
BEEKMAN BOOKS INC
845-297-2690
www.beekmanbooks.com

Authors preface to the translated version.

Why does a Danish percussionist set about writing a guide book on Latin American rhythms and rhythm instruments?

I have always felt a great partiality and fascination for these instruments and rhythms, and for the sincerity and helpfulness that is prevalent in the Latin American music scene and environment. The common barrier met in learning Latin American music lies in the large cultural differences. The ways in which the Latin percussionists work with, and especially the way they teach the rhythms can seem strange for the European. For instance, their use of phonetics or verbal interpretations of the rhythms instead of resorting to counting or notation.

The starting point for this book is to begin at a stage where no prior knowledge is necessary or implied, in order to give everyone a chance to get going, and from there to work towards the original culture.

I would like, with this book, to pay my thanks to all the Latin Americans who, through their hospitality and helpfulness, have made it possible for me to feel a part of their music.

Birger Sulsbrück

Copenhagen, May 1982

About the author

Birger Sulsbrück was born in 1949 in Vester-Skerning on the island of Funen, Denmark. He has been a professional drummer since 1971 playing jazz, rock, Latin-American and pop music. He has since 1975 played and taught Latin-American percussion.

Birger Sulsbrück has studied with: Ed Thigpen, Kasper Winding, and Pablo Arosemena. In New York he has studied with Johnny Rodriguez Jr. and in Cuba with Luis Abreu (Los Papines), Tomás Jiméno Diaz, Clemente Balsinde and Rolando Sigler (Rumbavana).

Mr. Sulsbrück is the leader of the Latin orchestra Salsa Na Ma – Europes first Salsa orchestra, which has made a one month tour of Cuba playing the carnivals in 1983.

As a percussionist Mr. Sulsbrück is also working as a studio musician on radio- and TV shows and recording sessions.

Mr. Sulsbrück has formerly worked with bands such as: The Danish Radio Big Band, The Danish Radio Jazz-group, John Steffensens Orchestra, Cox Orange, Blast and with artists such as: Dianne Reeves, Marti Webb, John Tchicai and Bobby Watson.

Concerts and Seminars in Europe and America:
Voss Jazz Festival, Norway. Concerts and seminar for professional musicians (1982).
Venice, Italy. Concert and seminar for professional percussionists (1982).
Trossingen, Germany. Seminar for the International Jazz Federation (1982 and 1984).
Bristol, England. Workshop for International Society for Music Education's conference (1982).
London, England. Workshop for London Jazzcenter (1982).
Tromsø, Norway. Concerts and Salsa seminar, course for Royal School of Educational Studies and Conservatory of Music (1983).
Trossingen, Germany. Seminar for Big Band drummers (1983).
Tübingen, Germany. 2. and 3. International Jazz Workshop (with Jamey Aebersold, David, Liebman, and David Baker, 1984 and 1985).
Bergen, Norway. Concerts at "Nattjazzen" Jazz Festival and Bergen Carnival with the group "Son Mu". Seminar for Royal School of Educational Studies (1984).
Cologne, Germany. Salsa Festival – "Festival de Salsa" – with Salsa Na Ma (1984).
Warsaw, Poland. Jazz Jamboree '84 with Salsa Na Ma.
Dallas, Texas, U.S.A. Concerts and clinic at the National Association of Jazz Educators' conference (1985).

Mr. Sulsbrück has also taught at all the Royal Danish Music Conservatories, most branches of the Royal Danish School of Educational Studies and has taught courses for high school teachers. He has been a teacher at the University of Copenhagen and has held seminars for the Danish Jazz Federation since 1977.

"Latin American Percussion – Rhythms and rythm instruments from Cuba and Brazil" was first published in 1980. The book was translated by Ethan Weisgard and was published in English in 1982. Together with Henrik Beck and Karsten Simonsen, Mr. Sulsbrück has published the book "Salsa Sammenspil" (in Danish) in 1984.

Authors preface

My intention in writing this book is to try and resolve some of the confusion prevalent in the field of Latin American rhythms and rhythm instruments.
From where do the instruments and rhythms come?
How do you use the instruments, and for which rhythms do you use them?
How are the rhythms built up, and how do you distinguish one type from another?

Latin-American rhythms are handed down from generation to generation, not with the aid of written material, but by singing and playing the rhythms together. Since not all of us are brought up in a culture where these rhythms are a part of everyday life, we have to learn them in other ways. The use of notation is, therefore, a necessary evil, but should be used only as a reminder — a sort of stepping stone.
It is of the utmost importance that we listen to, and experience the rhythms. This can be done by listening to a lot of Latin American music, either at live performances or via recordings.
Rhythms are primarily meant to be heard and felt — not to be read.

It is vital to start with a solid foundation. A rhythm doesn't simply develop as a result of feeling, or by showing the whites of your eyes and playing away.
You must make sure that you are playing the rhythm correctly — this may mean that you have to count your way through the rhythmic patterns.
Most people are wary of counting, for fear of losing the rhythm's spontaneity. But understanding the rhythms from the beginning will enable you to play them with more feeling by having learned them correctly.
As with any other musical instrument, practice is extremely important.

I must emphasize that the techniques shown in this book are not of my own invention. I have studied the traditional playing techniques of the various instruments and these are the ones I have described.

Of course, I cannot guarantee that you will become a professional percussionist simply be reading this book, but it will give you the necessary insight and understanding to help you well on your way.

Birger Sulsbrück

Copenhagen, July 1980

Contents

	page
Introduction	8
Notation, »Foot«, Notes	9
The most important notes, rests and signs	10
Preparatory exercises — warming up	12
Practicing the rhythm instruments	14

Part one

Cuban and Brazilian rhythm instruments

Cuban rhythm instruments

Claves	16
Guiro	18
Maracas	21
Cowbell (Cencerro/Campana)	24
Mule jaw-bone (Quijada) and Vibra-slap	28
Bongos (Bongó)	29
Congas (Tumbadoras)	35
Timbales (Pailas)	52

Brazilian rhythm instruments

Surdo	62
Chocalho/Ganza	64
Reco-reco	66
Pandeiro	68
Tamborim (with an »m«!)	70
Ago-go	71
Cuica	74
Pratos (Marching cymbals)	76
Cabasa	77
Triangle (Triangulo)	79
Caixa (Snare- or Marching drum)	82
Caixeta (Wood-block)	83
Apito (Whistle)	84
Atabaque (Brazilian conga drum)	85
Bongos for Samba	90
Caixa de Fósforos	92

Other Brazilian rhythm instruments (not shown with rhythms)	93

Part two

Cuban and Brazilian rhythms

Cuban rhythms

	page
Introduction	96
Rehearsing the rhythms and the rhythm section	99
Cha-cha-cha (rhythm, variations, breaks)	100
Variations on basic conga rhythm	105
Variation for conga and tumba	106
Suggestion for arrangement with rhythm section only — »Descarga«	107
Mambo (two rhythm examples, variations, breaks)	108
Son Montuno (rhythm, variations)	116
Bolero (rhythm, variations)	118
Bongo fills for Bolero	121
Rumba	122
Rumba Popular (three rhythm examples, variations, breaks)	123
Rumba Folklorico (rhythm, variations)	132
Quinto (figures and rudiments)	134
Breaks for Rumba Folklorico	137
Afro-cuban 6/8 (Popular) (two examples, variations)	138
6/8 and 4/4 combined or in continuation	143

Brazilian rhythms

Introduction	144
Rehearsing the rhythms and the rhythm section	147
Samba	148
Samba Batucada (two rhythm examples, breaks)	148
Samba Choro and Samba Canção	155
Samba Moderno (Samba do Salão) (two rhythm examples)	156
Bossa Nova (drum set with variations, percussion with variations)	160
Baion (Baião) (rhythm, variations)	164
Maracatú (two rhythm examples, variations)	169

Calypso from Trinidad (rhythm, variations)	172

Tuning and maintenance of congas and bongos	176
Discography	178
Guide books for drumset	181
Index of terms	182

Introduction

The instruments and rhythms in this book are dealt up into two basic sections: Cuban and Brazilian. There are many rhythms and instruments from other countries in South and Middle America and the Caribbean Islands, but Cuba and Brazil are the two largest suppliers of popular music, although they represent two completely different types of music and musical instruments.

I have chosen the most well known and popular rhythms for this book, but these are just a fraction of what you actually can find in the two countries.

As a single exception, an example of the *Calypso* from Trinidad is shown in the back of the book.

One of the characteristics of Latin American music is that the structure of the music is based on rhythm. The melodic and harmonic elements are secondary in proportion to the rhythm. Without rhythmic stability a *Mambo* will never be a *Mambo* or a *Samba* a *Samba*, no matter how beautiful the melody, or how intricate the harmonic progressions are.
Start by playing with the rhythm section only, using no other instruments. By doing this you will hear the rhythms as music in itself — as something independent.
I can highly recommend anyone who plays a melody instrument to practice playing rhythm instruments and to study the structure of the rhythms. It will give you a rhythmic stability and a greater understanding of the music.

Parts one and two

Besides the division into Cuban and Brazilian sections, this book contains a part **one** and **two**.

In part one each instrument is explained with playing techniques, basic rhythms, and in some cases with alternative patterns.

Part two contains typical examples of the combination of instruments for the rhythms, shown here with alternative patterns that are typical for each style. There are also examples of variations on the basic rhythms, ideas for *fill-ins*, and examples of *breaks* for arranging the rhythms. These may be a bit advanced and require that you are familiar with the fundamental techniques and rhythms first.

It is possible to work with both part one and two at the same time. Practice one instrument from part one and then go on to the combination of instruments in part two.

Before part one and two you will find instructions for studying and practicing the rhythms.
When the rhythms have been learned properly, it is important that they sound right.
The rhythm section must consist of the right instruments and they should be played with the correct technique.

Notation

Many Latin-American rhythms are originally played and written in 2/4.

In this book I have written them in 4/4 — for two reasons: 4/4 is the most common time notation generally speaking, and is the most accessible, and the rhythms shown can be used directly in conjunction with *jazz* and *rock* which are in 4/4 time.

But in order to keep the original feeling of 2/4 I advise that you tap the foot on **1** and **3** instead of on **1-2-3-4** or on **2** and **4**. Try this yourself — and feel the difference.

The same feeling is apparent in rhythms written in »alla breve« – ¢.
»Alla breve« is 2/2. The appearence of the notes are the same as 4/4, but the half note becomes the time unit.

The rhythms that are originally in 4/4 are thus stated in each case. Here I recommend that you tap the foot on **1-2-3-4** or in certain cases on **1** and **3**.

6/8 is explained in part two.

Foot

When the foot is used to keep time (basic pulse), use only a short movement, hitting the ground **on** the counts. Never count when you lift the foot, this will cause tension and it is important to use as little energy in the foot as possible.
Your energy and concentration should be directed towards your instrument.

Which means: keep the heel in place and lift the front of the foot (the toes) slightly, or keep the front of the foot in place and lift the heel slightly.

Use the foot that is most relaxed and change to the other if you start to get tense.

If you play standing up, shoot your hip out slightly, and the leg that you are using to mark time with should be bent slightly.
A rigid leg and a rigid body will only make your playing become stiff.

Notes

One note designates one beat or count. For those who are not used to reading, I have written an explanation over the notes.

Numbers in parenthesis: rest or pause (to be counted).
Numbers not in parenthesis: to be played and counted.

Example:

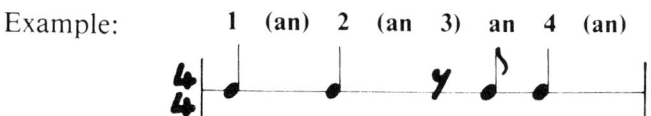

In the text the beats are underlined. Example: **and 2 and**

This book is not meant to be a textbook for reading, so I would recommend people who are not familiar with basic notation and reading to acquire a basic guide book (recommended material page 181).

The most important notes, rests and signs

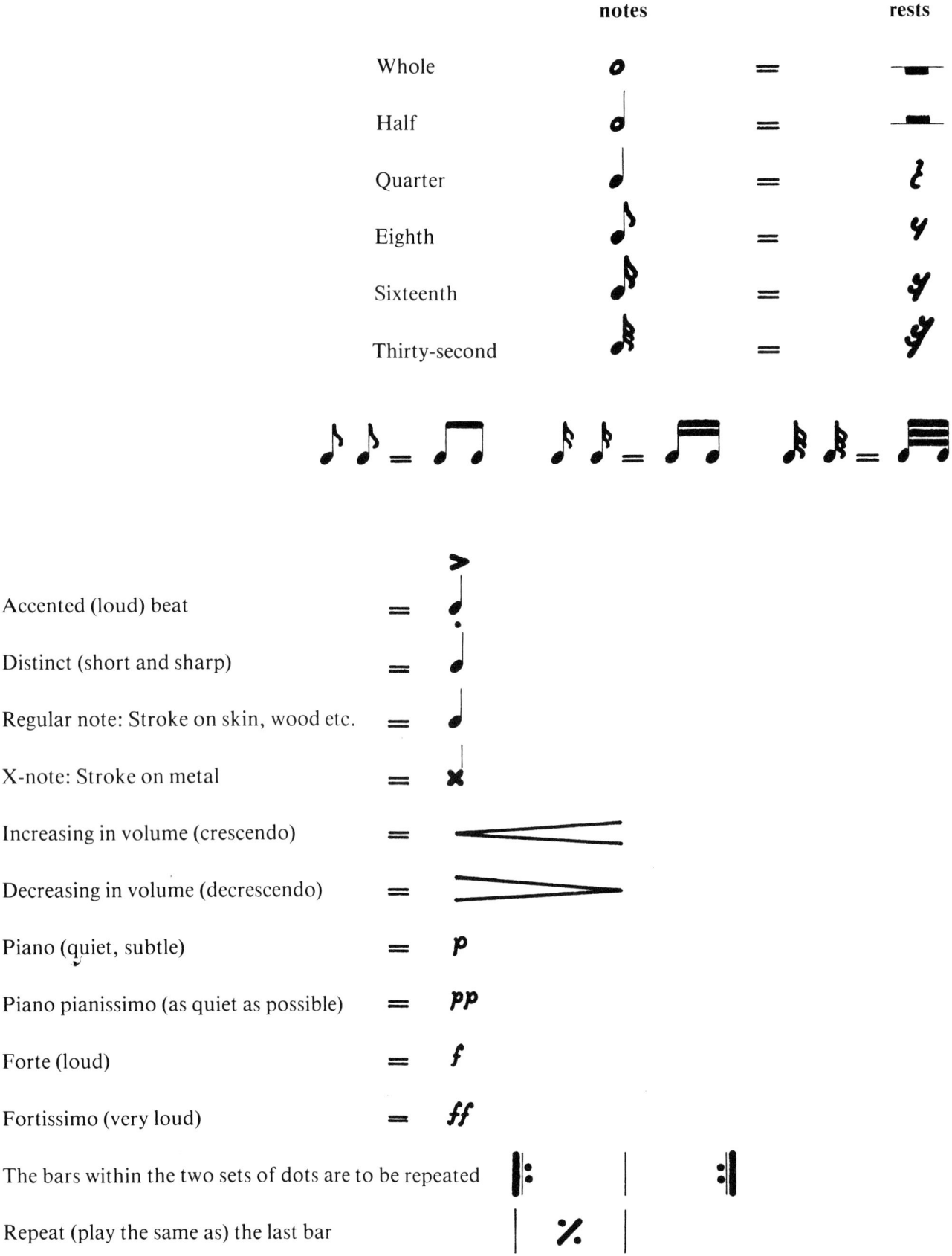

When a rhythm is written on two lines, the highest pitched sound is written on the top line and the lowest pitched sound on the bottom.

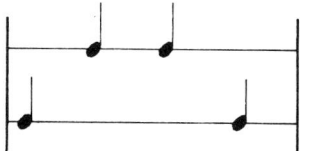

I have NOT used dotted notes

or tied notes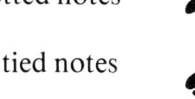

I have only used notes (strokes) and rests.
I have noticed that too many people, in the beginning, become confused when confronted with dotted and tied notes.
Contrary to regular notation, I have used a sign (e.g. ∿∿∿∿) on top of the notes when a sound is to be sustained.

Everything in the book is written for right-handed players. Left-handed players should reverse (R) and (L).

R	right	**R-H**	right hand
L	left	**L-H**	left hand
A , B , C	signs for types of strokes. These are explained with the instruments (*cowbell, timbales,* and *pandeiro*).		
+	»closed« stroke — the instrument is muted.		
o	»open« stroke — the instrument's tone should ring or sustain.		
s	»slap« stroke (shown on conga).		
①	first run-through.		
②	second run-through.		
1	bar number.		
↓ → ♩ ↘	the different arrows are explained with each instrument.		

Preparatory exercises — warming up

It will be easier on your hands and wrists and save a lot of time if you warm up before playing.

1:

This exercise is the mildest. Do not go on to the other exercises if your wrists are sore. Stay with the exercise until you are completely warmed up and slightly tired in your wrists.

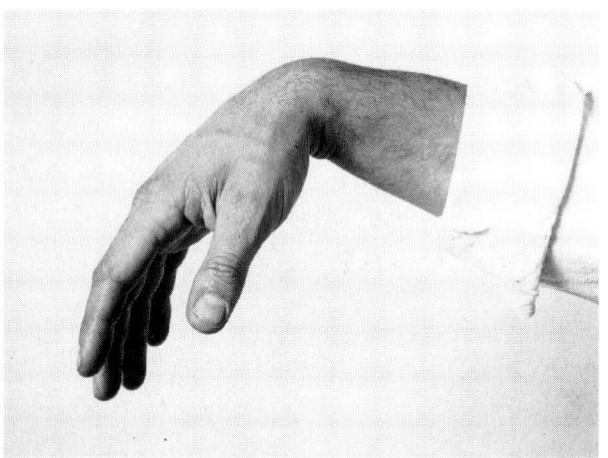 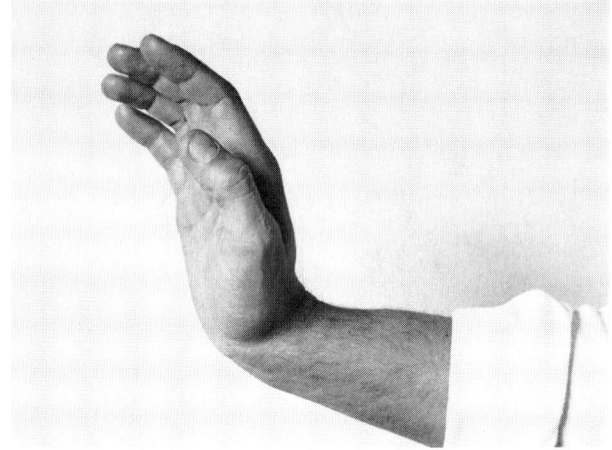

The hand should feel relaxed and heavy. Throw the hand from a hanging position (see photo) all the way backwards (see photo) as in the normal movement of the wrist but with a throwing movement.
To keep balance, use your right and left hand one after the other in fast tempo, completely relaxed.

2:

This exercise is for loosening and warming up the wrists in a sideways manner.

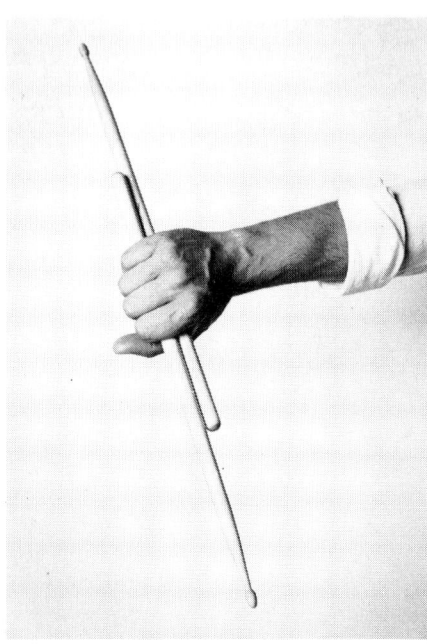 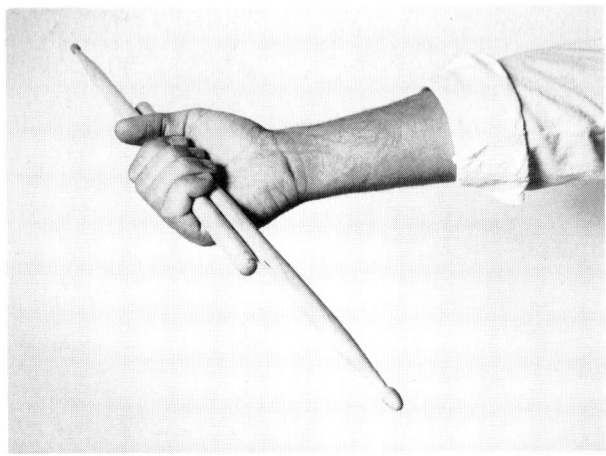

Hold two drumsticks as shown in photo and turn the wrist from extreme right to extreme left. The arm should be positioned horizontally from the body and the exercise performed in fast tempo with one hand at a time.

3:

This exercise should not be used before having performed exercises »1« and »2«.

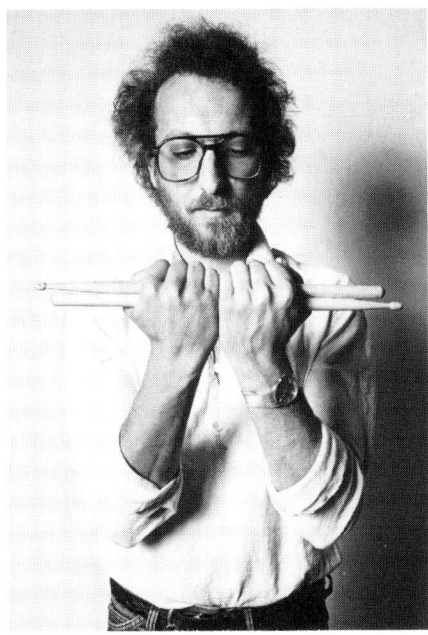

The hands positioned against each other at chin level.

Turn in towards the body, downwards, and out with the arms stretched out and without letting go of the sticks.

Afterwards reach over the head with the arms stretched out and pull backwards several times.

Then go back again without letting go of the sticks.

Repeat exercises »1« and »2« after performing this exercise.

Practicing the rhythm instruments

1: **Count slowly** and do not rush the tempo while practicing because this will cause the tempo to rush while working with the group as well.

2: **Stop** — and set a new tempo. Count the tempo off out loud.

3: Start by singing (mimicking) the rhythm while playing. It is easier to produce the rhythm vocally and it helps the hands.
A short sound should be like: »bák« not »baaaak«.
A deeper, short sound like: »gúng« not »guuuung«.

4: If your hands will not do what you want them to do, then sing the rhythms for a while without playing them — then start again.

5: Remember to revert to a slower tempo again. Practicing at fast tempi is not enough. But starting in a slower tempo does not mean that it will make for easier playing. If you don't keep the tempo straight and steady it will not work.

6: Re-check the rhythm by counting, you may have changed it slightly along the way.

Some people may not find it helpful to count. Omit steps one and two and begin directly with step three: singing the rhythms.
Try both possibilities and choose the method which suits you best.

For really getting the rhythm and the instrument to work, I have realised that you have to go through the following steps:

1: Practice the rhythm and technique slowly. We tend to use too much energy on small movements.
2: Play the same rhythm without variations for a long time, preferably with a group or to a record. After a while you will only be using the necessary amount of energy and will be able to relax and listen to what is going on around you.
3: Relax. When you have gotten to the point where you feel relaxed with the rhythm, you will realise that even the most simple rhythm works.

Use the notes as little as possible. They are only used as a »reminder«.
Sing the rhythms, forget the notes, and listen.

The technical problems with an instrument can often impede the understanding and feeling of a rhythm. Try playing the rhythm on something else: a table, your knee or other hand for instance, depending on which instrument you're practicing.

Try, once in a while, to get the whole rhythm section to sing the rhythm that they are playing (each person their own rhythm) without playing.

To start with, each person should play his/her own instrument and play the same rhythm all the way through the number until he/she takes a solo and can use his/her ideas. Play the rhythms for a long time — this is the best way to allow everybody to relax with his/her instrument.
Practicing in this manner will give you a reserve of strength and enable you to listen more closely.
When everybody is relaxed and playing precisely, the group can start to swing. Then, and only then, will it be possible to play variations and solos.

PART ONE

Cuban and Brazilian rhythm instruments

Cuban rhythm instruments

Claves

Claves play the fundamental beat for the Cuban rhythms.

Claves are two round sticks, 15 to 20 cm (6-8 inches) long and 2 to 4 cm (¾ to 1½ inches) thick, made from hard wood.

The stick that is to be struck is held in the left hand, placed along the thumb and held in place by the other fingers (see photo).

Strike exactly in the middle of the stick, this will give the best and loudest sound.

The two *claves* are of different pitch, so try both of them to find the best sound.

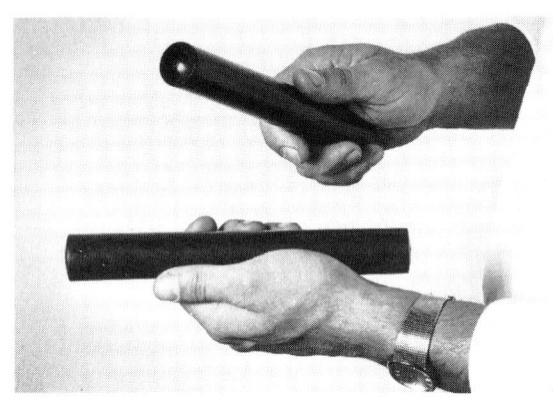

Traditional claves

There is also a model which has one thicker stick with an indentation in its center.

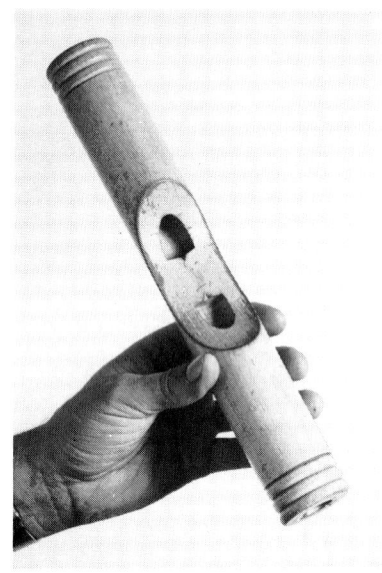

Indentation

For producing the best sound with this type *claves* you have to cup the hand around the indentation (see photo), thus giving them a deeper richer sound.

If you do not have a set of *claves*, you can play the rhythm on anything made of wood (*woodblock*, side of *conga, chair, table* etc.).

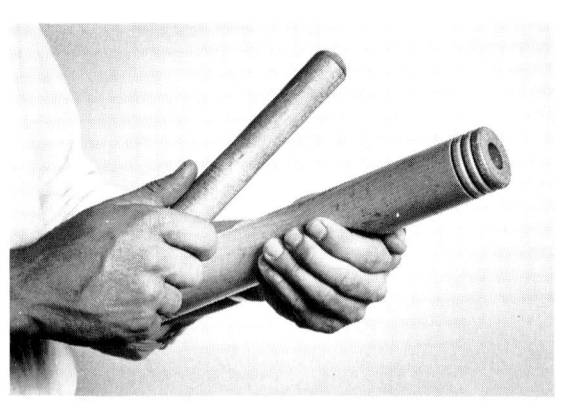

Modern claves »African model«

Clave rhythm

The clave rhythm is the foundation (»KEY«) to most of the Cuban rhythms. The whole rhythm section and music is based on this foundation.

The rhythm has a two bar structure, with three strokes in the first bar and two strokes in the next bar *(3-2)*.

THE CLAVE RHYTHM IS PLAYED WITHOUT VARIATION THROUGHOUT THE WHOLE NUMBER!

Practice the rhythm until it can be played in a relaxed manner. Especially the stroke on **2 <u>and</u>** in the first bar can be very difficult to play precisely in the beginning.

If the rhythm is not steady it will make it impossible for the other instruments to follow it.

3-2 CLAVE RHYTHM:

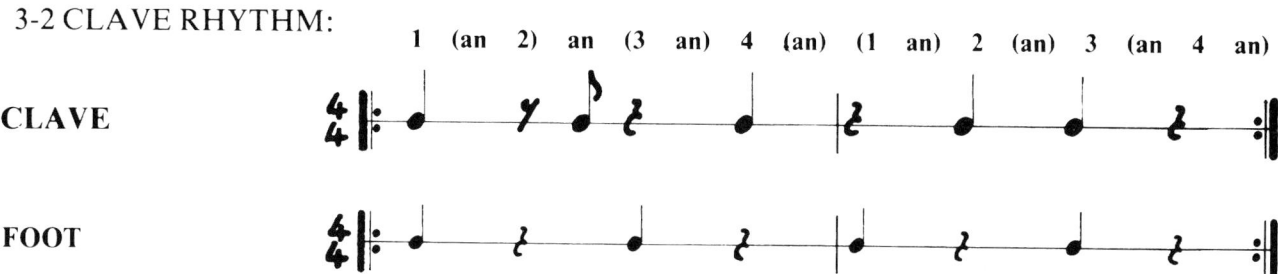

Regarding the »foot« see the introduction.

The *clave rhythm* does not always start with the first bar.
A melody can be written in such a way that the *clave rhythm* fits better rhythmically with the second bar first. This means that the bar with only two strokes is played first and afterwards the bar with three strokes is to be played. This is called *2-3 clave* or *reverse clave*.
The count <u>1</u> in the first bar is now left open which makes it harder but none the less exciting for the other instruments to follow the rhythm.

2-3 CLAVE RHYTHM:

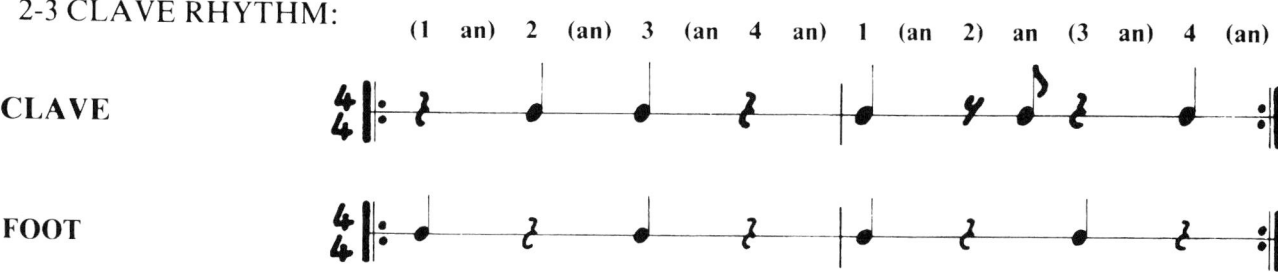

The capability of hearing the correct direction of the *clave rhythm* can be acquired with time, but sometimes even the real masters can be in doubt.
Try playing the rhythm/melody in *3-2 clave* and then in *2-3 clave* to choose which of the two feels right.
REMEMBER when the *clave rhythm* is reversed the *cowbell rhythm* should be reversed along with it (see *cowbell* and *timbales*).

It is a great help to sing the *clave rhythm* while practicing another instrument. It gives the right feeling to the instrument.

Even when not actually played — the *clave rhythm* is implied and felt. The *clave rhythm* is also often used as a *break* in the music.

Guiro

The Cuban *guiro* is made from a dried and hollowed calabash gourd. Grooves, broad or narrow, are filed horizontally down the length of the instrument.

The *guiro* is held vertically in the left hand, gripping with the thumb and index or middle finger (see photo). There are two holes drilled in the back of the instrument for this purpose.

The right hand scrapes the rhythm with a small stick, which should be drawn exactly parallel to the grooves — this produces the best and most distinct sound.

Use a stick 15 to 20 cm (6'' - 8'') long for easiest handling, eg. a shortened *timbales stick* or a chopstick!

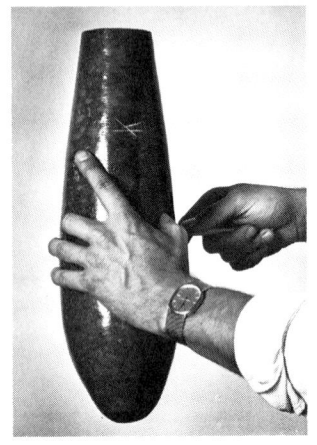

The *guiro* is held vertically because the left hand is in motion when playing the rhythm (moving in the opposite direction to the right hand). This uses less energy and gives a better balance than by allowing the right hand to do all the work.

Cuban guiro

Guiros with finger holes enabling the *guiro* to be held horizontally are usually of the Mexican wood-type. Forget the holes and hold the *guiro* vertically (see photo).

Mexican wood-guiro

Guiro rhythms

Medium tempo

This rhythm is used for *Cha-cha-cha, Mambo* and *Son Montuno*.

The motion of the right hand is always: down-up-down-up... Remember that the left hand moves in the opposite direction to that of the right.

1: a long, drawn out, downward scrape along all the grooves — press
2: a short, sharp, upward scrape
and: a short, sharp, downward scrape
3: a long, drawn out, upward scrape along all the grooves — press
4: a short, sharp, downward scrape
and: a short, sharp, upward scrape

On the short strokes the stick should skim the grooves and be removed promptly afterwards.
The arrows indicate the motion of the right hand.

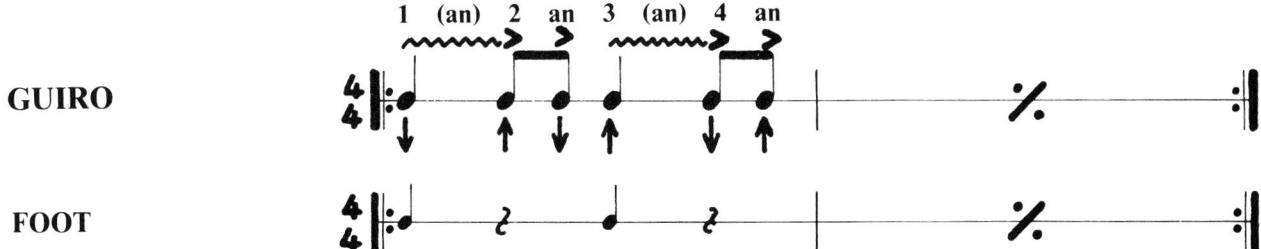

The foot should be tapped to the count of **1-2-3-4** in certain rhythms (refer to rhythms in part two).

Fast tempo

This rhythm is used for *Mambo* and *Rumba*.

Faster tempi will require a more even-sounding *guiro* rhythm.

The motions of the right hand are counted in eighth notes: down-up-down-up... **(1 and 2 and...)**. Remember to move the left hand in the opposite direction.

The movements are alternately: two strong strokes on **and 1** (up-down)
two relaxed strokes on **and 2** (up-down)
two strong strokes on **and 3** (up-down)
two relaxed strokes on **and 4** (up-down)

The arrows indicate the motion of the right hand.

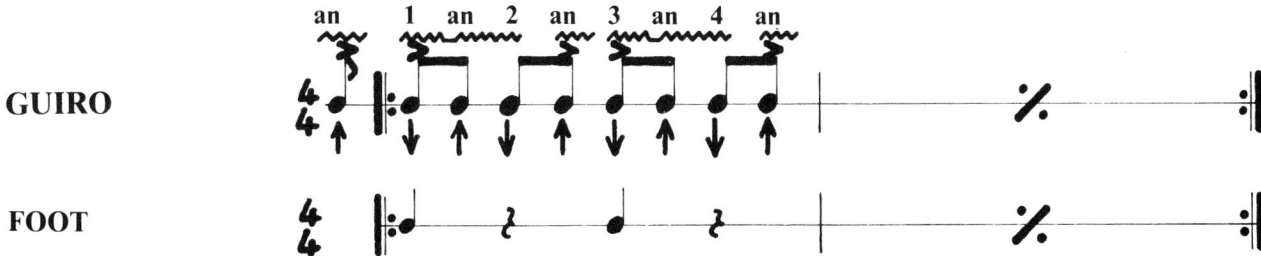

More detailed explanation on next page.

Guiro rhythms in fast tempo (cont'd)

Explanation:

and (before)   **1**: strong upward stroke, the stick should skim the grooves and continue on away from the surface
                1: strong downward movement, stopped after short stroke on the grooves — continued to a...
                and: ... relaxed upward stroke remaining on the surface
                2: relaxed downward stroke. Away from the surface — ready for next stroke
                and: as **and** **1** (**and** before **1**)
ETC.

I recommend starting with the same accent on all the strokes (relaxed). You can gradually start accenting the strong strokes when ready.

Alternative playing technique for medium tempo

The rhythm is actually the same as the first one shown, but this technique gives the rhythm a different flavor. (Stronger accent on **1** and **3**).

The long, drawn out strokes on **1** and **3** are played like this:
A downwards scrape using the wrist (short scrape) which promptly continues in a long, drawn out, upward stroke (↗).

The »sharp« scrapes on **2 and** and **4 and** are: down-up.

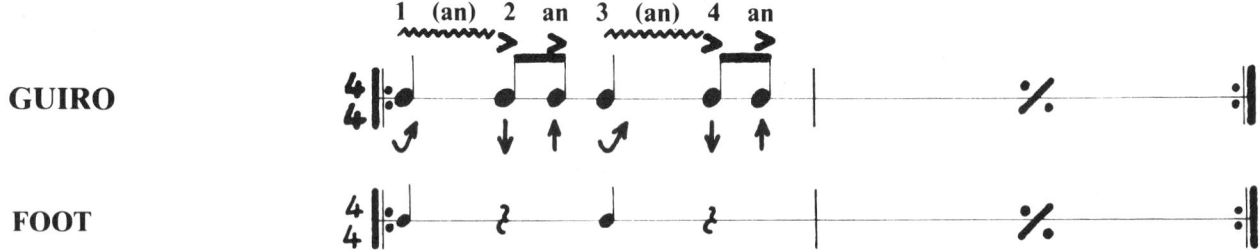

In certain rhythms, the foot should be tapped on the count of **1-2-3-4** (refer to the rhythms in part two).

Maracas

Maracas are two identical round or pear-shaped containers with handles. They are filled with dried peas, fruit pips, or shot.

Maracas were originally made from small, dried gourds, but are now produced from all sorts of materials, among other things: wood, coconuts, leather (sewn together in the correct shape) and a copy of these which is made of plastic.

Maracas made of: wood, coconuts, leather and plastic.

Maracas are often of different pitch but there is no actual rule for which sound is to come from which hand.

The idea is to get the contents of the *maracas* to be pitched forward against the outer wall of the shell with an even sound, without the contents rattling around.

Hold both *maracas* as shown in the left photo – using the thumbs as support.

The elbows are to be held in a relaxed position slightly out to the sides (see right photo).

The movement is, with one hand at a time: starting from the body (see left photo) and forwards to vertical position, and stop (see right photo).
This is done in one movement, starting with the forearm and ending up with a short throwing movement with the wrist ending in a vertical position.
... exactly like throwing custard with a spoon!

Maracas rhythms

The basic rhythm is played as even eighth notes, from hand to hand, starting with the left.
This rhythm should sound relaxed and strong before you start on the other rhythms.

The foot should be tapped on counts **1-2-3-4** in slow tempi.

If you have trouble keeping the beat steady, then try playing the right hand only on counts **1-2-3-4** until you feel at ease. After that you can double up with the left hand on all the off (**and**) beats.

This rhythm is played in all tempi.

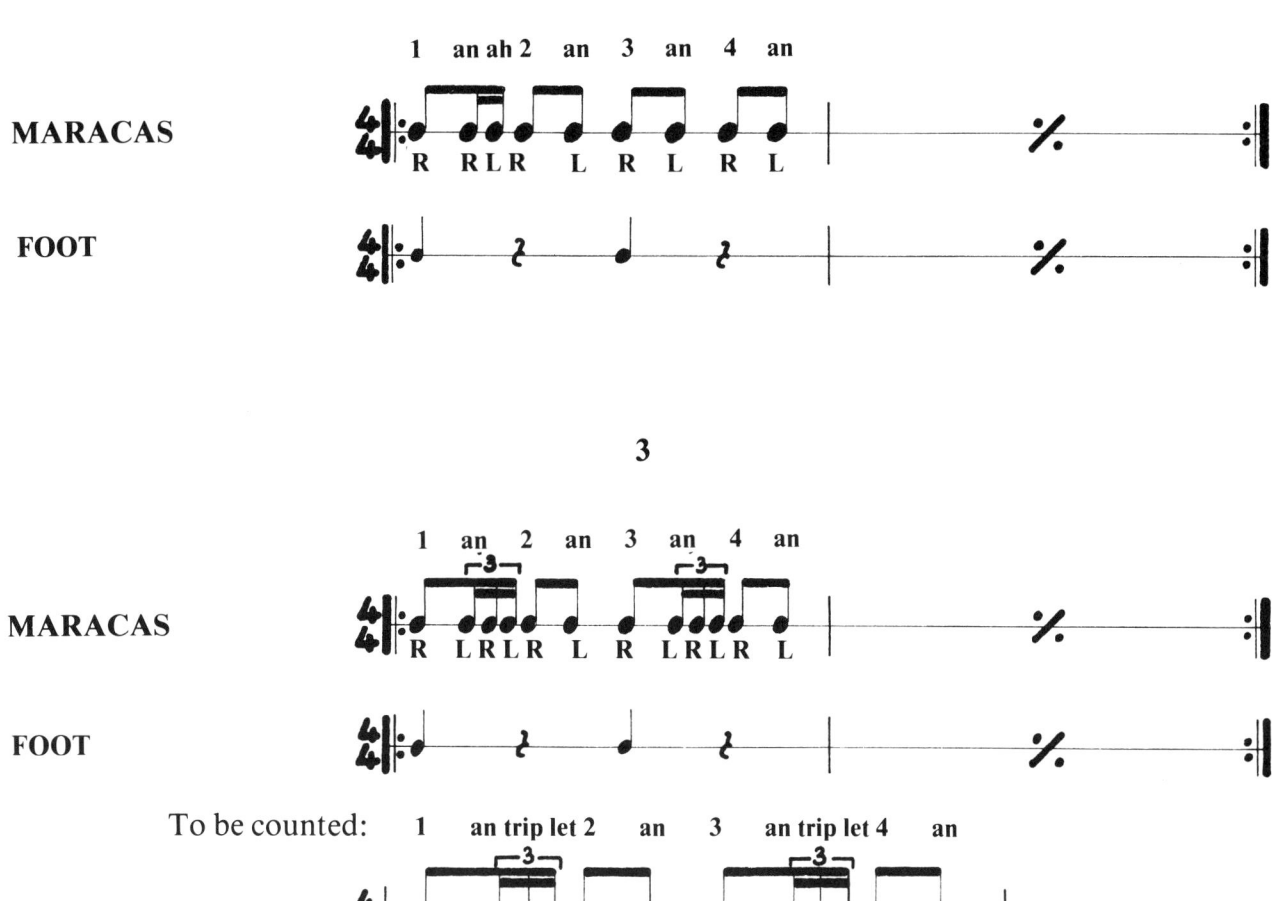

The rhythms are played in all tempi.
Refer to the rhythms in part two.

Cowbell (Cencerro/campana)

The *cowbell* is probably the rhythm instrument that is found in the largest and most varied array of shapes and sizes. You will find that there is a great difference in pitch and tone even within the same model and type of *cowbell*. Try an assortment of the same model when buying.

The *cowbell* is held in the left hand with the mouth of the *bell* pointing away from you (see photo) and the index finger right up by the mouth of the *bell* on the bottom side. (With large *bells* you should hold the bottom of the *bell* with the finger pointing towards the opening.

Muffled stroke (+)
The fingers muffle.

Open stroke (o)
The index finger is lifted.

The muffled stroke (+) is obtained by pressing (muffling) with the fingers.

The open stroke is obtained by lifting the index finger (and if necessary the palm of the hand) from the *bell*.

Use a hammer shaft as a beater, this will give the best balance and the correct »deep« sound. Hold the shaft upside down and strike the *bell* with the thick end.
You can, of course, use a drumstick. Strike with the thick end.

There are two areas of the *cowbell* that you play on:
A: on the rim of the opening with the side of the shaft (see photo).
 The stroke can be either closed (+) or open (o).
B: on the top side of the *bell*, near the closed end with the tip of the shaft (see photo).
 This produces a sharp, high sound (+) or (o).

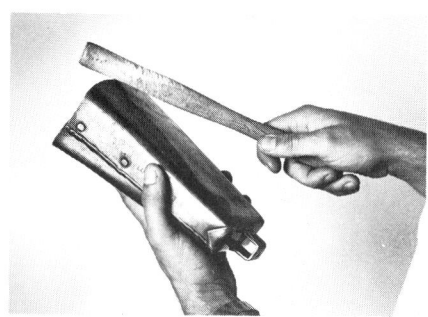
»A«
Stroke on rim,
gives deep sound.

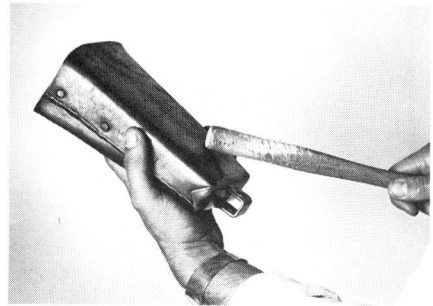
»B«
Stroke near closed end,
gives sharp, high sound.

If nothing else is stated, then play closed strokes (+) on rim (A).

In general, the closed stroke (+) is the most common. Open strokes (o) can be used at your own discretion.

Cowbell rhythms

Most of the rhythms are also explained in the section on *timbales*, but there are various types of Cuban bands that do not use *timbales*, the *cowbell rhythms* being played on a hand-held *cowbell* only. It is also an advantage to learn the rhythms while holding the *cowbell* to start off with.

When playing in a band with *timbales*, the *bongo player* will change to the *hand cowbell* in certain places in the arrangement where the music is to become more intense. The *timbales cowbell* and the *hand cowbell* play different rhythms when played together. (See *Montuno*, page 97 and the rhythms in part two.)

To make things easier, the strokes will only be referred to with their given letters (A and B) as shown under the photos.

The first rhythms are the same in the first and second bar, so the basic *claves rhythm* can be either *3/2* or *2/3* (see page 17).

1

The rhythm is quarter notes on counts **1-2-3-4**.

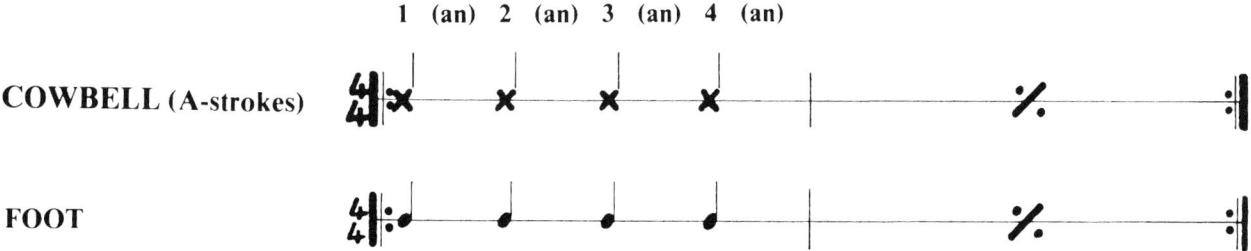

The rhythm can be played for *Cha-cha-cha, Mambo, Son Montuno* and *Guajira*.

2

In this rhythm, both strokes (A and B) are to be used on the *cowbell*.
The highest pitched notes (B) are written on the top line and the lowest pitched notes (A) are on the bottom line. In this case the A-strokes can be shortly open (o).

The rhythm can be played for *Cha-cha-cha, Mambo, Son Montuno* and *Guajira*.

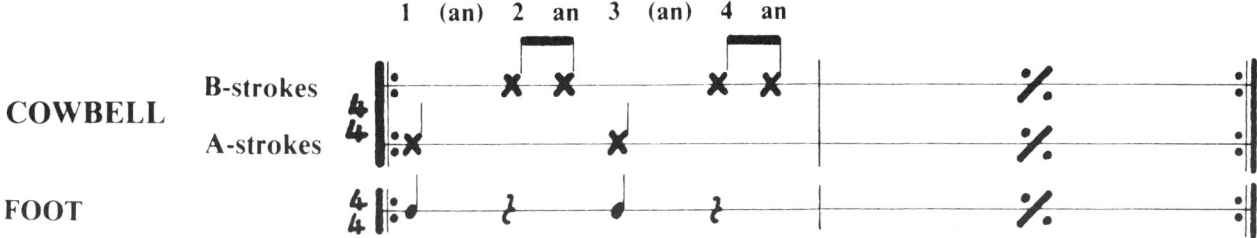

For *Cha-cha-cha* the foot is to be tapped on counts **1-2-3-4**.

3

This rhythm is played on the *hand cowbell* together with the *timbales*, which play a two bar rhythm on either the *cowbell* or the side of the *timbales (Paila)* (see page 57).

This rhythm is a simple version of rhythm number »2«, using only the deeper pitched strokes (A) on counts **1** and **3**.

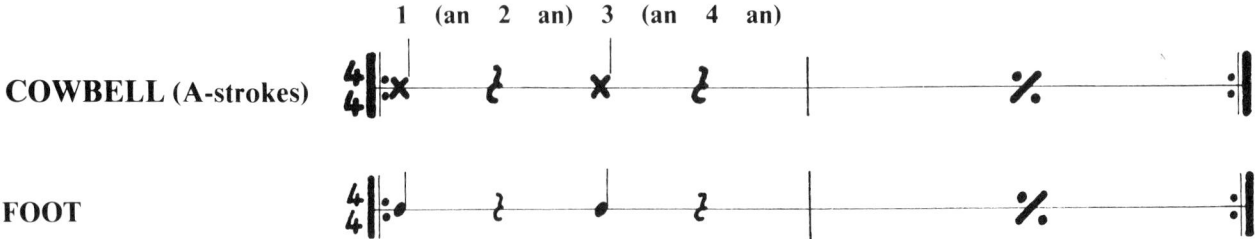

The rhythm can be played for: *Mambo, Rumba* etc. (fast tempi).

Two bar cowbell rhythms

Cowbell rhythms that are played over two bars are based on the *clave rhythm*.
In cases where the reverse *clave rhythm (2/3)* is used, the *cowbell rhythm* must start with the second bar first (see *clave rhythm* page 17).

Rhythm »2« (see previous page) can indicate the direction of the *clave rhythm* by playing one stroke only on the count **2** (not on **2 and**) in the bar with two *clave strokes*. Play: **1** (A) **2** (B) **3** (A) **4 and** (B).
A-strokes = sustained (o). B-strokes = closed (+). See page 113.

4

Play each stroke with equal force (A-strokes).

3-2 clave

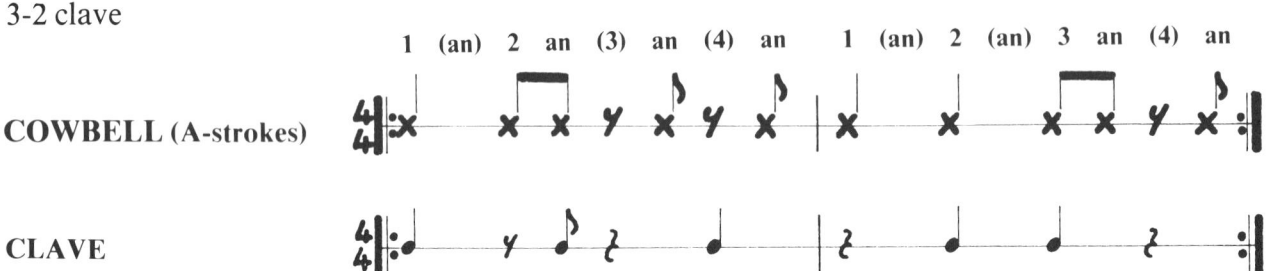

This is the same rhythm, but now played with the *reverse (2/3) clave rhythm*. The *cowbell rhythm* starts with the last bar first.

2-3 clave

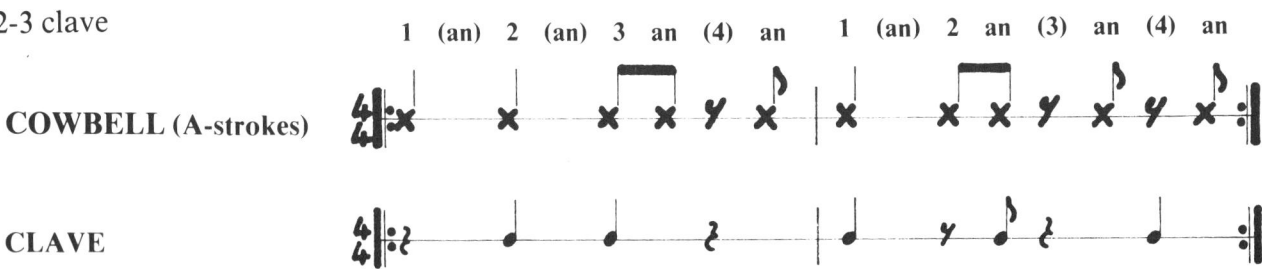

The rhythm can be played for *Mambo*, some types of *Rumbas*, and when the tempo in *Cha-cha-cha* is doubled up *(Ritmo doble)*.

5

Note the accentuated notes (>).

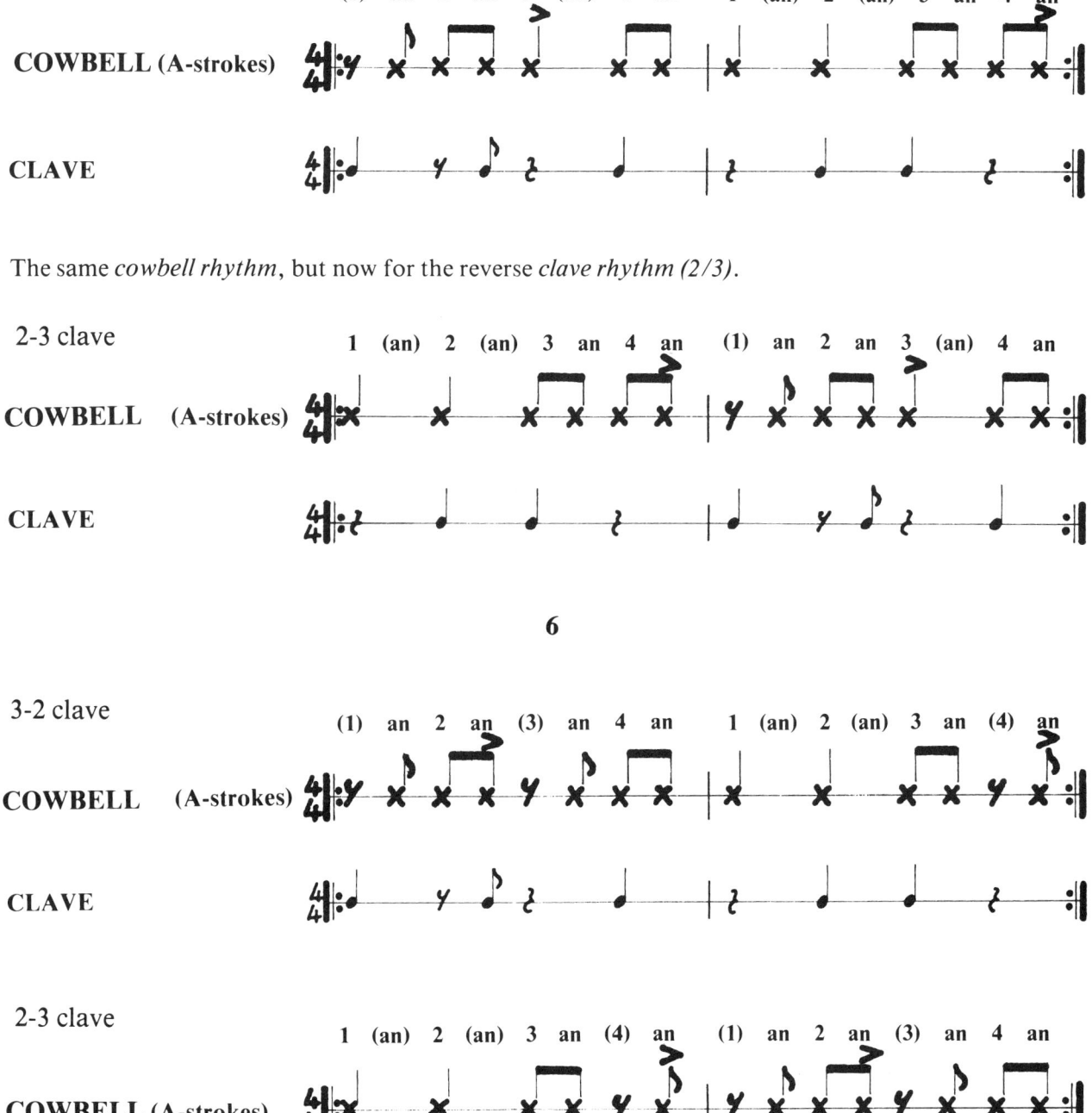

The same *cowbell rhythm*, but now for the reverse *clave rhythm (2/3)*.

6

For other *cowbell rhythms*, see the rhythms in part two.

Mule jaw-bone (Quijada)

By using the jaw of a mule or donkey, with the teeth loosened, you can create a rhythm instrument from a piece of anatomy.

The left hand holds the *jaw-bone* down by the front teeth, and with the side of your fist, strike the broad end of the *jaw-bone* (see photo). This produces a prolonged rattle from the instrument.

Quijada

Vibra-slap

Vibra-slap

The *vibra-slap* is a factory made version of the *quijada (mule jaw-bone)*. It consists of a wooden case mounted on a metal structure with a wooden ball on the opposite end to produce vibrations.
The rattle is produced by metal prongs or teeth inside the wooden case.
Hold the *vibra-slap* at the corner of the metal structure (see photo) and hit the ball with the flat of your left hand. Release the ball from the hand immediately so that the rattle can sustain.

The *quijada* or *vibra-slap* is not a standard part of the rhythm section but is used in arrangements as a special effect.

The *quijada* or *vibra-slap* can either be used in parts of a number or in a whole number, but never in playing *breaks*.

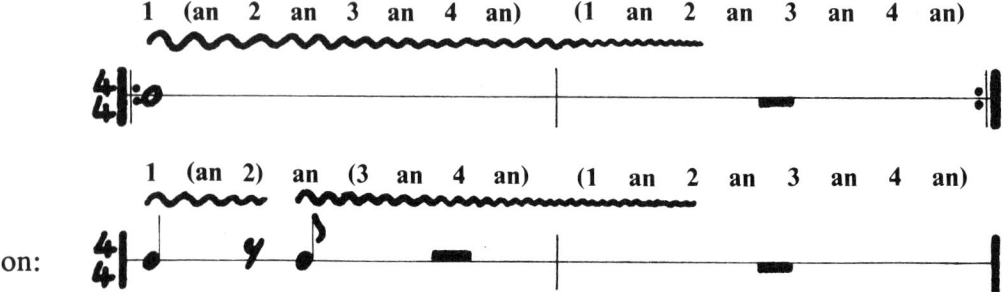

Variation:

Bongos (Bongó)

Bongos are two small hand drums that are fitted together: a small drum (about 17 cm/16¾'' in diameter) and a large drum (about 20 cm/8'' in diameter).

There are many different types of *bongos* — some better than others. I would recommend that you look for the type with hide heads and a thick shell. You should also make sure that there are tuning lugs on the drums, making it possible to tune them with a key.

The heads should be tuned to a high pitch (especially the small one), since the *bongos* are known for their sharp, piercing sound and the way they play »on top« of the rhythm.

The whole idea of having two drums combined as one instrument is that they can »talk« together. A figure that is played on one of the drums is answered in kind on the other.

Apart from playing basic rhythms, the *bongos* are the instrument in the rhythm section that are allowed the most freedom to improvise, playing variations and fills; but not before you are confident with the basics.

The drums are held (hung) between the knees, with the small drum to the left (see photo). Sit with your feet close together under the drums — it gives you a better hold. Be sure not to sit too high.

It is possible to obtain special stands for most of the different types of *bongos* for those who wish to play standing up. Some of the strokes are, however, difficult to play while standing as there are instances where the thighs are used to support the hands.

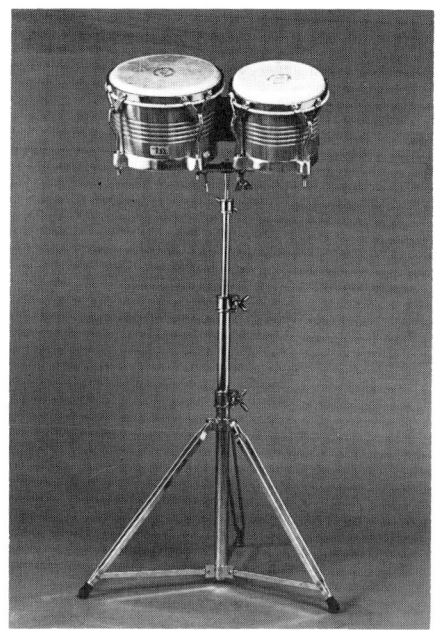

Tuning and maintenance — see page 176.

In the traditional rhythm section the *bongo player (bongosero)* stays on the instrument during the melody, changing to *hand cowbell* in parts where the rhythm section is to be more predominant. (See *Montuno* page 97).
The Cuban *bongo players* call the small drum »macho« (male) and the large drum »hembra« (female).

Cowbell rhythms page 25-26, examples »1«, »2«, »3« and »4«.

The strokes, except the *basic rhythm* for the left hand (refer to left hand on next pages) are played with the index fingers.

All the fingers are stretched out in a relaxed manner, but only the index finger is used to strike the head.

The finger should be removed immediately after striking the head so that it doesn't muffle the tone of the drum.

The feeling of striking the drum can be practiced by »throwing« the index finger forward and downward in the air without hitting the drum.

It is this playing technique that produces the sharp sounds of the *bongos*.
The index finger should hit close to the edge of the head using the fingertip when playing on the small drum.
On the large drum the stroke should be played closer to the center of the head.

The strokes can also be played using the fingertips of the index, middle and ring finger.

This will produce more sound but will also reduce the sharpness of the tone.
This stroke is also used as a variation of the stroke with the index finger alone.

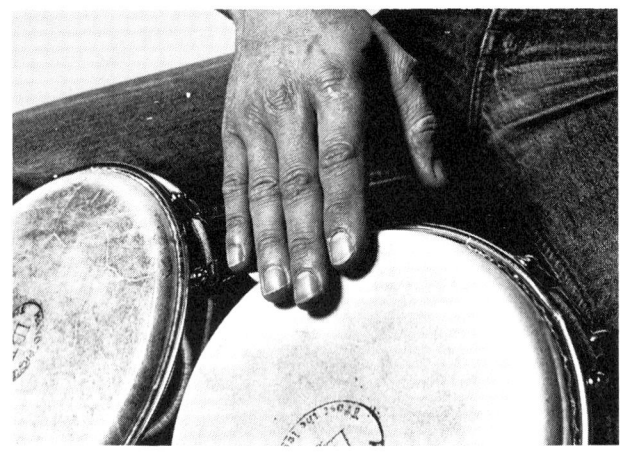

Using sticks, such as shortened *timbales sticks*, is a very nice effect for soloing — but take care of the heads.

Martillo

The basic rhythm of the *bongos* is called *Martillo*. It is used in most of the Cuban rhythms, and is played in all tempi.

Martillo means »the hammer« which refers to the constant beats of the right hand on **1-2-3-4**.

The rhythm is based on eight beats (eighth notes) in each bar, which are played from hand to hand — starting with the right (R-L-R-L-...).

All the beats are accented equally in slower tempi. The faster the tempo the more accentuated the beats on **1** and **3**.

Martillo in slow tempo:

The foot is tapped to the count of **1-2-3-4**.

Martillo in faster tempi:

The foot is tapped on the counts **1** and **3**.

	LEFT HAND	RIGHT HAND
1:	side of thumb muffles in middle of head	hard stroke on small drum
and:	stroke with all finger tips, rotating the wrist	up
2:	up	stroke on small drum
and:	stroke with side of thumb, rotating the wrist	up
3:	the thumb stays on head to muffle	hard stroke on small drum
and:	stroke with all finger tips, rotating the wrist	up
4:	up	stroke on LARGE drum
and:	stroke with side of thumb, rotating the wrist	up

See this rhythm shown with picture examples on the next page!

Martillo explained

LEFT HAND

(4) and

Rotating the wrist. Stroke with side of thumb in the middle of the head of the small drum. The thumb remains on the head to muffle. Use the whole length of the thumb.

(4) AND

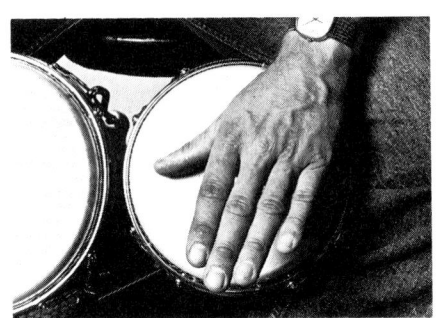

AND

1 and

Rotating the wrist. Stroke with the fingertips in the middle of the head of the small drum.

AND

2 and

Same as **4 and**.

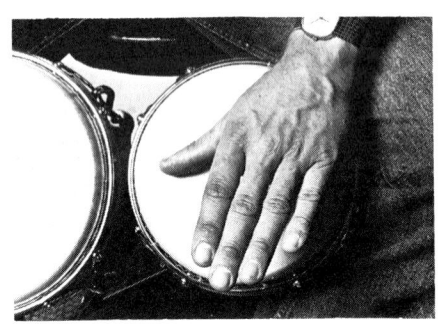

AND

3 and

Same as **1 and**.

4 and (see above)

ore specifically

RIGHT HAND

1 *The rhythm starts on the count of 1

1

The side of the thumb (left hand) is used to muffle the head.

The fingertip (index finger) of the right hand hits the head close to the edge of the small drum.

2

2

The fingertip (index finger) of the right hand hits close to the edge of the small drum.

The drum produces an open tone (the left hand is removed from the head).

3

3

Same as **1**.

4

4

The fingertip (index finger) of the right hand hits close to the edge of the large drum (open tone).

Simplified basic rhythm

It is easier for many beginners to play this version of the basic rhythm.

The rhythm can also be used to practice the original *Martillo*.

The rhythm is played from hand to hand and all the strokes (both hands) are played with the fingertips (see page 30). Start with the right hand.

The counts of **1** and **3** should be accented.

Variations of the *Martillo* can be found in part two.

Bongo playing for *Samba* is shown in the *Brazilian* section.

Congas (Tumbadoras)

The conga drums come in three basic sizes, have three different names and three different functions.

Tumba   conga   quinto

In Cuba the *tumbadoras* are the largest and the next-largest drums in the family — *the tumba* (or *tumbadora*) and *the conga* as we call them. They are the drums used for playing the basic rhythms, and contrary to the *bongos*, they supply the »bass« in the rhythm.

The smallest drum is called the *quinto* and was, in the past, a small wooden box. The *quinto* is used primarily as a solo drum in folk music, where it is used to inspire the motions and steps of one or more dancers.

The barrel-shaped drum shell is made of either wood or fiberglass. One of the advantages of the fiberglass drums is the increased volume and projection – it is easier on the hands.

One of the important factors in acquiring a good sound (»sonido«) is a good quality head. The heads are primarily tanned calf, mule or cow skin, mounted on the drum with tuning lugs that make tuning possible with a key.
Further reference to maintenance and tuning see page 176.

In traditional folk music each person plays one drum. *Conga* and *tumba* each play their own rhythm and the *quinto* plays solo on top of the rhythmic foundation.
Nowadays there is usually only one *conga player* (»*conguero*«) in the band – the *conga* and *tumba* are played by the same person. There are even »*congueros*« that play on three or more drums.
When playing both *conga* and *tumba* at once, the *tumba* is placed to the **right** of the *conga* (see photo).

The Cuban »*congueros*« will often, especially in folk music, use the names »*segunda*« or »*tres golpes*« for the next-largest *conga* drum.
When playing two *congas*, the small drum is sometimes called »*macho*« (male) and the large drum »*hembra*« (female).

Should you play standing up or sitting down?

When you play standing up...
..... the drums produce more sound, but the differences in tone can only be produced by various strokes.
..... the body is free to move more, but make sure that your concentration is on the drums and not on your body.
..... you must stand in a relaxed position in order to keep the basic feeling by tapping your foot. No stiff legs.
..... it makes changing to other instruments easier.

 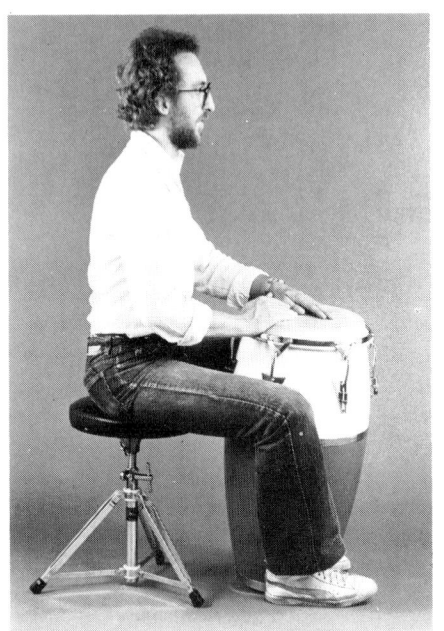

When you play sitting down...
..... the body is not in motion, and it is easier to concentrate on the sound and the strokes to be played.
..... it is easy to keep time with your foot.
..... you can alter the tone of the drum by lifting and tipping the drum with your legs.

Remember to play with the drums placed on a hard surface. It is a good idea to bring a thin wooden board with you to place under the drums for resonance if playing on a carpeted floor. It will save your hands a lot of hurting.

You sit with the *conga* between your legs (see photo). Brace with the thighs and feet.
It is important to feel that you are sitting correctly with the drum.
The drum should be tipped a bit forward and to the right (towards the *tumba*) so the sound is let out of the bottom of the drum.
Sit with a straight back, shoulders relaxed and forearms positioned horizontally – that's where the head of the drum should be positioned.
If the drum is too high you will tend to draw your shoulders up and your neck will become stiff.
If the drum is too low you will hunch downwards. This can cause backache.

Strokes on the congas

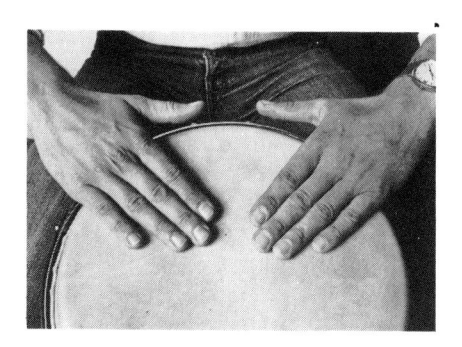

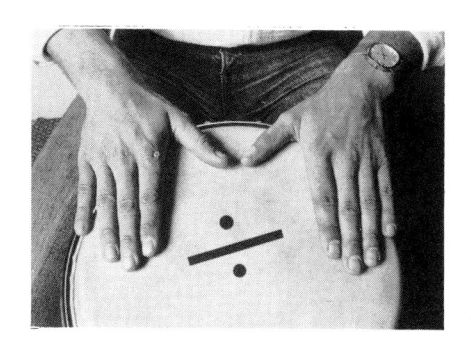

The elbows are positioned slightly away from the body and the hands placed on the drum so that the rim of the drum is situated horizontally under the hands (see photo).
The fingertips should point towards the center of the head.
This is the most relaxed position and it will give you the most precise sound and tone.

The Cuban *conga technique* consists basically of three different strokes:
1:   An open stroke, which produces a sustained tone from the head.
2:   A closed stroke, which produces a muffled tone.
3:   A »slap« stroke, which produces a loud, sharp tone like a shot.
These basic strokes can produce a vast amount of tonal possibilities.

!!! Do not hit hard when practicing strokes and technique. The correct sound cannot be forced. You must practice with wrists and hands completely relaxed. If you practice the technique in a loud and rigid manner, your hands and the rhythm will both suffer from it.
Look at your hands and listen. It is the sound (»sonido«) that is important when learning the technique.

»Open« stroke

(notation: o) Means that the tone is sustained.

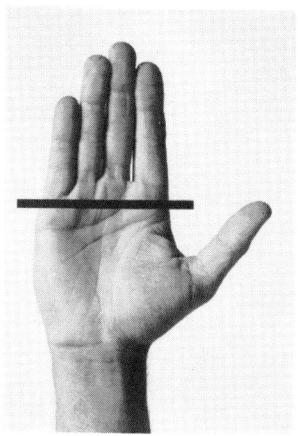

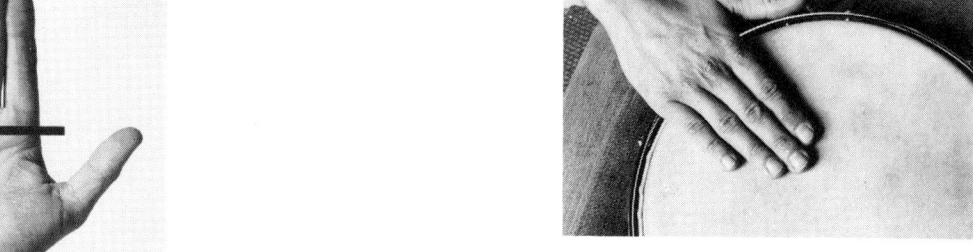

The flat of the hand should hit the head right on the pads (bottom side of knuckles) (see photo).

The fingers should be stretched and close together without being rigid. The thumb should be held slightly out to the side so that it does not hit the edge of the head.

The four fingers of the hand should hit the head in a flat position **(continued on next page)**.

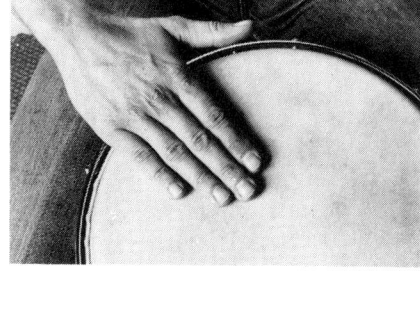

Open stroke continued

Remove the hand immediately, so that the tone is sustained. By hitting with all four fingers at one time you will obtain a clean, open tone from the head. Remember to use the wrist.

Practice the stroke with both hands.

Closed stroke (notation: +)

The muffled sound of »skin on skin« is of great importance for the *conga rhythms*.

The stroke should fall heavily and relaxed in the middle of the head. The palm of the hand should not touch the edge of the head. The whole hand (fingers and palm) is to hit the head simultaneously. The stroke can either be completely flat or with the hand cupped slightly. With the hand flat, the sound will be sharp and distinctly »skin on skin«. With the hand cupped slightly, the sound will be deeper. Practice and use both variations.

When a rhythm is played from hand to hand (R-L-R-L...) using soft closed strokes (+) combined with open strokes (o) and slap strokes (s), all these strokes should be played in the same position: the edge of the head (see photo).
The hands should only be moved to the center of the drum when using accentuated (>) closed strokes or if playing several closed strokes one after the other. This occurs in, for instance, *Rumba* and *Afro-Cuban 6/8* (page 125-142).

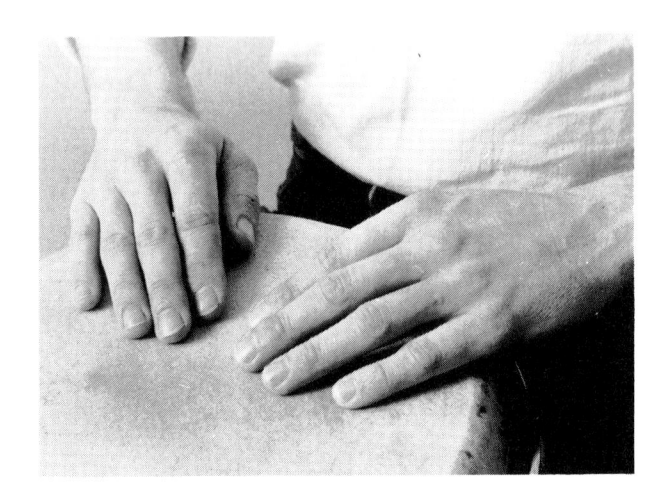

The closed strokes can also be played by making a light, tapping stroke using a flick of the wrist and hitting with the fingertips. This technique is shown and explained on pages 85-89 *(Samba)*.
This technique is also used for the Cuban rhythms.

Notice: There is a special technique in which the left hand plays two closed strokes one after the other. This technique is explained in *basic conga rhythm – Tumbao* (pages 41-43).

»Slap stroke
(notation: S)

The »slap« stroke has a loud and sharp sound (crack or shot) which is of great importance for rhythms and soli.

The »slap« stroke is the most difficult stroke to play, and the correct sound can only be achieved when the hand is relaxed completely. But it is well worth the effort to learn it.

The left hand muffles the head (some photos do not show the left hand, in order to show the right hand to more advantage).

The hand in motion towards the head: the hand is open and relaxed and the thumb is held alongside the hand throughout the whole stroke.

Hit with the hand relaxed (see photo).

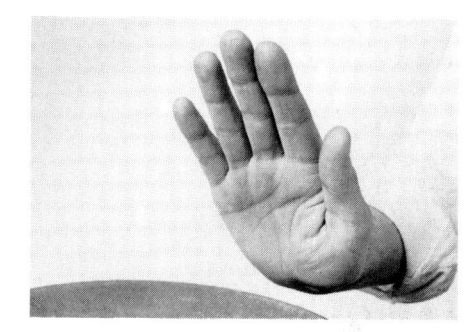

The palm of the hand hits the edge of the head further in than in the »open« stroke (see photo).

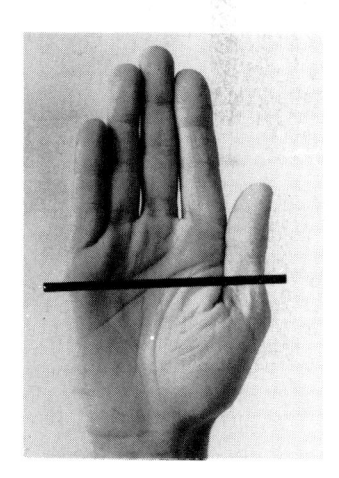

The palm of the hand hits the edge of the head. Not too hard, but enough to support the hand (see photo).

The fingers of the hand strike the head immediately afterwards. There should be no tension in the fingers.

The underside of the fingertips (excluding the thumb) hit the head at the same time. Using a short movement the fingers »grab« the head, to make sure that they don't bounce up off the head after striking (see photo). The weight of the hand should be put into the fingertips; the palm of the hand resting on the edge of the head.

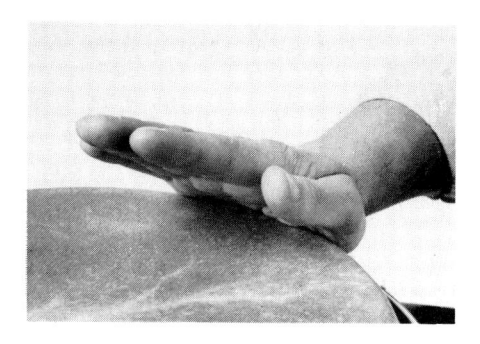

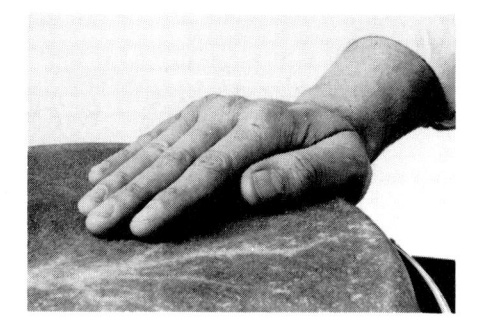

(See practicing of the »slap« stroke on next page).

Practicing the »slap« stroke

Place the hand on the drum with the edge of the head horizontally positioned under the hand and with the fingers pointing towards the center of the head. The palm of the hand is resting on the edge a bit further towards the center than when playing the open stroke (see photo on preceding page). The thumb should be held alongside the hand.

Draw the fingertips 1 cm outwards towards the edge where the hand is resting. When drawing the fingertips outwards, grabbing the head, be careful not to cup the hand too much. This will cause the hand to strike with the actual tips of the fingers instead of the underside of the fingertips, and will not produce the required sound.

Lift the fingers back to the head again and repeat the process for a couple of minutes – at least.

Strike with the underside of the fingertips. The fingers should be stretched out without being taught or rigid.
The palm of the hand should stay on the edge of the head during the exercise.

Now lift the open hand a few cm over the head of the drum.
Drop the palm of the hand onto the edge of the head (not too hard), and then let the underside of the fingertips drop down afterwards, using no tension, and perform the grabbing motion.

Practice this for a good length of time alternating hands, playing gradually louder and louder. Remember to use the wrist.

The correct motion for the »slap« stroke can be practiced by »throwing« the fingertips in a downward motion into the palm of the same hand.

The »slap« stroke played with either hand

The motion in which the fingers grab the head results in the muffling of the head by the fingers themselves. The left hand is now not used to muffle and the stroke can, after a bit of practice, be played with either hand.

The open »slap« stroke

The open »slap« stroke is often used in solos and fills.
The hand movement is the same as the closed »slap« stroke except that the fingers do not remain on the head to muffle the stroke. This technique still creates the snap of the »slap« stroke but produces a more open tone. The open »slap« stroke is used especially for fast figures, for instance:

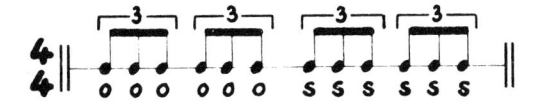

Refer to the *quinto figures* on page 135 and 136.

Basic conga rhythm — Tumbao

The conga is used as the basic drum in most of the modern Cuban rhythms.

The conga drum plays »tumbao«, which is the basic pattern that the other drums base their rhythms upon. The secondary rhythms of the other drums will not function without this basic rhythm, but »the tumbao« is often used on its own as an independent rhythm.

The tumba is used as the basic drum in the old, and in several of the modern types of *Rumba*. The *tumba* plays the *tumbao* as the basic rhythm and the other drums base their rhythms upon the *tumba* pattern. This is explained later on (see *Rumba* page 51, and the rhythms in part two).

When playing solos and fills, the strokes should be played from hand to hand: R-L-R-L...
This method is also used in rhythms but not in the *basic conga rhythm*.

In the *basic conga rhythm* the left hand plays the »closed« strokes (+), the strokes that produce the distinctive »skin on skin« sound, and keep the tempo steady.
The right hand plays the accentuated strokes, »open« (o) and »slap« (s).
Do not underestimate the importance of the left hand. You should use the same amount of strength in the left hand as in the right in order to keep the tempo steady.

In order to get used to the »slap« stroke, the stroke on **2 and-** should be omitted.

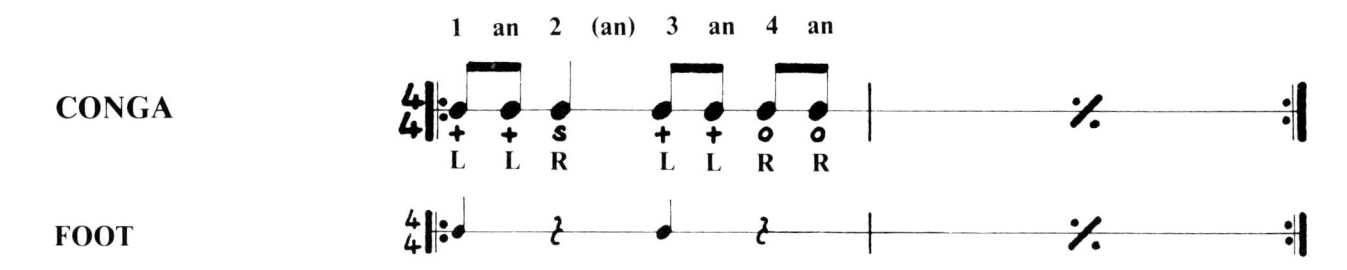

CONGA

FOOT

The foot should be tapped to the count of **1-2-3-4** in slow tempi.

	LEFT HAND	**RIGHT HAND**
1:	closed stroke (+) (tipped upwards)	
and:	closed stroke (+) (stays on head to muffle)	
2:	muffles	»slap« stroke (s)
and:	up	
3:	closed (+) stroke (tipped upwards)	
and:	closed stroke (+) (then remove hand from head)	
4:	up (off head)	open stroke (o)
and:	up (off head)	open stroke (o)

Refer to the rhythm shown with pictures on the next page.

42

LEFT HAND

Conga

Starting point:
The left hand is held in a relaxed position over the center of the drum.

1

1 → **1 and**

»Closed« stroke (+) in the center of the head. The stroke should be applied with the entire hand, putting weight on the heel of the hand. As soon as the hand strikes the head, it is tipped upwards by using the rebound from the head, while the heel of the hand remains on the head.

»Closed« stroke (+) number 2.
The fingers are tipped downwards again and strike the head with the hand lying flat.

The hand should stay on the head and muffle.

3

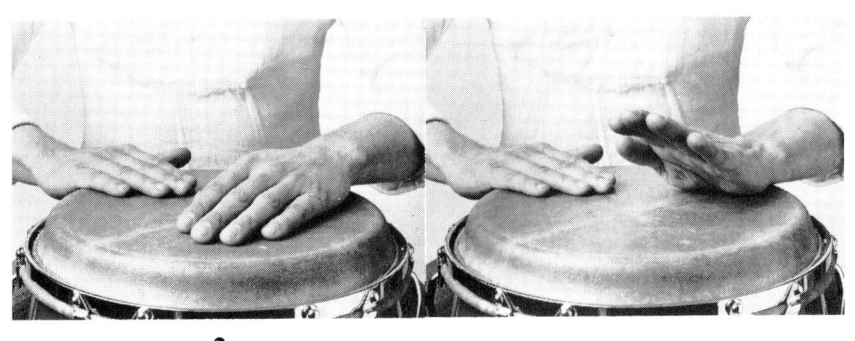

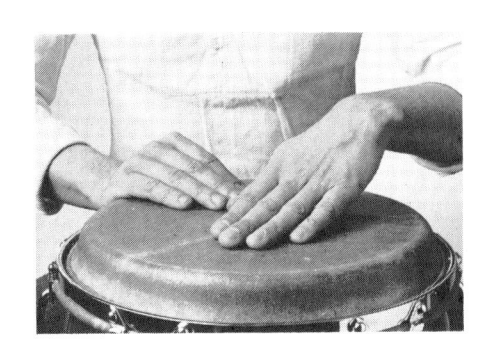

3 → **3 and**

»Closed« stroke (+).
The hand is tipped upwards as on the first beat of the bar.

»Closed« stroke (+).
The fingers are tipped downwards and strike the head, but this time with the fingertips only and with the heel of the hand off of the head. After the stroke, the fingers should be removed promptly — the whole hand is now off the head.

basic rhythm

RIGHT HAND

2

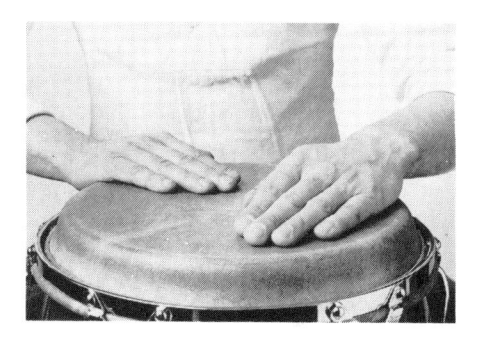

2

»Slap« stroke (s) (the left hand muffles the head).

→   No stroke on **2 and**

4

4

»Open« stroke (o).
The hand should be removed promptly to let the head sustain.

→   **4 and**

»Open« stroke (o).

43

Basic conga rhythm with all eighth notes included

The stroke on the count of **2 and** means that all the eighth notes are to be played which will give the rhythm a more steady feeling.

The stroke is to be played with the right hand and should sound like a »closed« stroke (+).

The hand should be cupped in the same manner as when finishing a »slap« stroke, and the hand should bounce slightly, the stroke being played in the same position as the »slap«, but with a muffled tone (+).

The entire hand should hit the head at the same time (see photo).

The entire rhythm, with the exception of this stroke, is played as shown in the pictures on the previous page.

Now each hand will be playing two strokes.

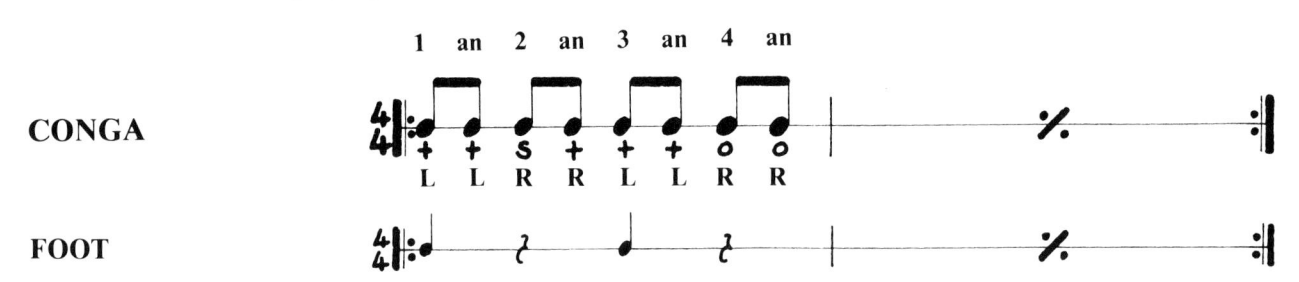

CONGA

FOOT

In slow tempi the foot should be tapped to the counts of **1-2-3-4**.

	LEFT HAND	**RIGHT HAND**
1:	closed stroke (+) (tipped upwards)	
and:	closed stroke (+) (stays on head to muffle)	
2:	muffles	»slap« stroke (s)
and:		closed stroke (+) (as explained)
3:	closed stroke (+) (tipped upwards)	
and:	closed stroke (+)	
4:	up (off the head)	open stroke (o)
and:	up (off the head)	open stroke (o)

Alternative playing technique for basic conga rhythm

In this variation, which gives the conga rhythm a different feeling, the »closed« stroke on **2 and** is played with the LEFT hand. This means that all the »closed« strokes are now played with the left hand.

The strokes on the counts of **1** and **3** have the weight concentrated in the heel of the hand and the strokes on **2 and 3 and** are played with the fingertips, while lifting the heel of the hand.
On the count of **1 and**, the stroke should be played with the hand flat in order to help muffle the next »slap« stroke.

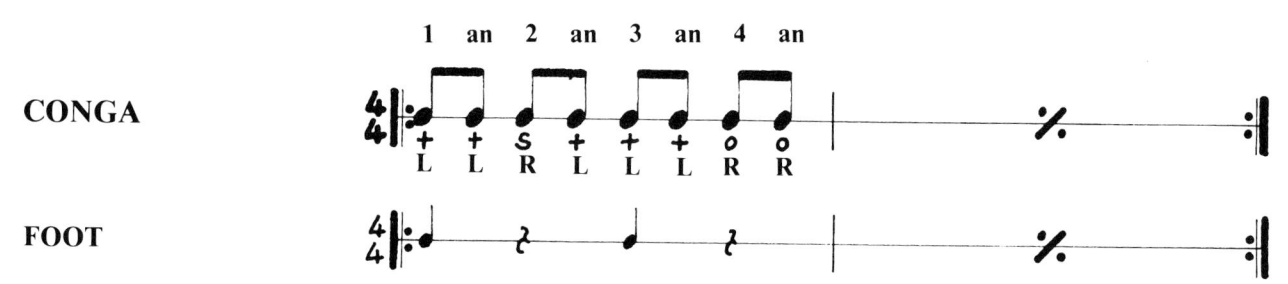

```
              1  an 2  an 3  an 4  an
CONGA         +  +  S  +  +  +  o  o
              L  L  R  L  L  L  R  R

FOOT
```

	LEFT HAND	**RIGHT HAND**
1:	closed stroke (+) with weight on heel of hand, hand tipped upwards from head.	
and:	closed stroke (+) with flat of hand	
2:	muffles	»slap« stroke (s)
and:	closed stroke (+) with finger tips, the heel of the hand off the head	
3:	closed stroke (+) with the heel of the hand	
and:	closed stroke (+) with fingertips, the heel of the hand up off the head	
4:	up off the head	open stroke (o)
and:	up off the head	open stroke (o)

In playing the rhythm the left hand is lifted off the head to the count of **4 and**, in order to let the head sustain.

The tipping motion of the hand when playing the »closed« strokes should NOT be applied as a bounce or hop of the hand from the head.

I recommend learning both playing techniques. There is no certain rule for when the two techniques are to be used – it is completely up to the individual.

For the rhythms and variations shown later on in the book, I have written: (v) for variation, thus making it possible to use either technique.

Variations of the *basic conga rhythm* are shown on page 105.

Conga and tumba played by two persons

In the first rhythms, the *conga* and *tumba* are played by two persons. Later on, the rhythms are shown with one person playing both drums.

> In Cuban folk music, each person plays one drum only. I have used the same idea for the rhythms here in order to give a better understanding of how to combine the rhythms and to make room for more people in a practice situation.

The first *tumba* rhythms are meant to be played together with the *basic conga rhythm*. They are meant **only** for this purpose.

Cha-cha-cha

The tumba rhythm for *Cha-cha-cha* is played from hand to hand (the right hand starts).

All the closed strokes (+) are played in the center of the head.

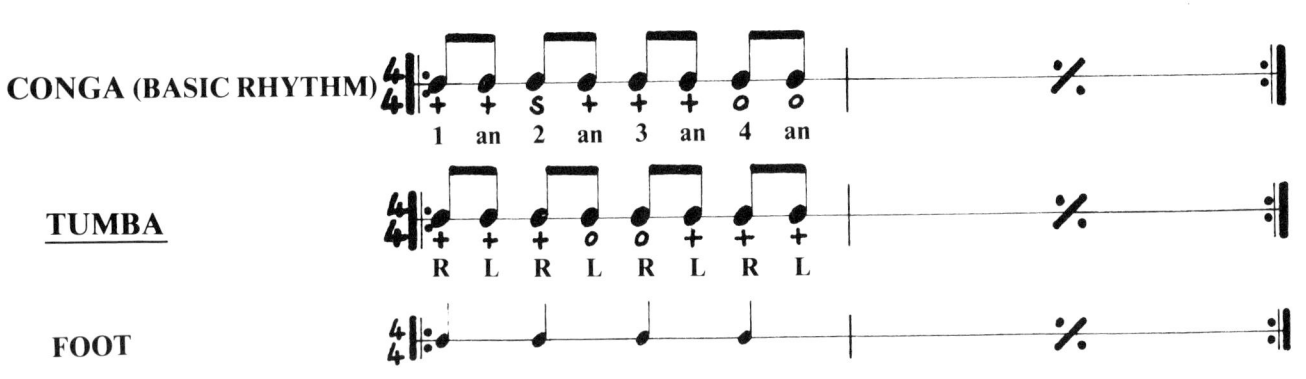

CONGA (BASIC RHYTHM)
+ + S + + + o o
1 an 2 an 3 an 4 an

TUMBA
+ + + o o + + +
R L R L R L R L

FOOT

	LEFT HAND	RIGHT HAND
1:		closed stroke (+)
and:	closed stroke (+)	
2:		closed stroke (+)
and:	open stroke (o)	
3:		open stroke (o)
and:	closed stroke (+)	
4:		closed stroke (+)
and:	closed stroke (+)	

Notice the way the open strokes (o) are placed in conjunction with each other: *tumba:* **and 3** - *conga:* **4 and**.

The same rhythm is used for:
Medium slow: *Guajira*
Medium tempi: *Son Montuno, Mambo* and *Bossa Nova*

In all tempi for *Rock* rhythms

The next *tumba* rhythm (together with *conga*) is *Mambo*.
This rhythm is also used for *Cha-cha-cha* in cases where playing the »open« (o) *tumba* strokes in each bar may tend to sound too cluttered.

Mambo

The rhythm is played over two bars.

In the first bar *the tumba* plays only »closed« strokes (+).
In the second bar, *the tumba* should play the same strokes as in *Cha-cha-cha:* »open« strokes (o) on counts **and 3**, the rest »closed« strokes (+) (see previous page).

This means that *the conga* plays the »open« strokes in the first bar.

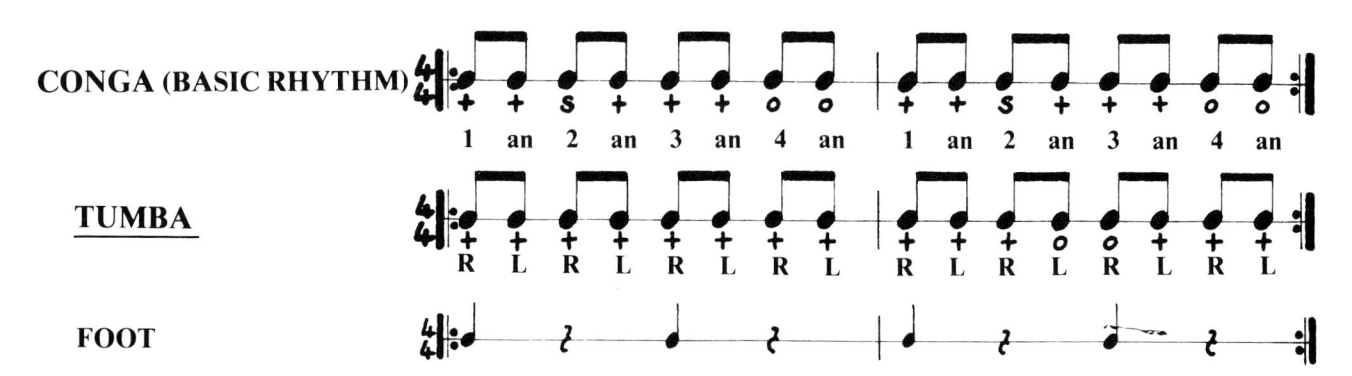

CONGA (BASIC RHYTHM)

```
+ + S + + + o o | + + S + + + o o
1 an 2 an 3 an 4 an  1 an 2 an 3 an 4 an
```

TUMBA

```
+ + + + + + + + | + + + o o + + +
R L R L R L R L  R L R L R L R L
```

FOOT

The tumba plays:

	LEFT HAND	**RIGHT HAND**
1:		closed stroke (+)
and:	closed stroke (+)	
2:		closed stroke (+)
and:	closed stroke (+)	
3:		closed stroke (+)
and:	closed stroke (+)	
4:		closed stroke (+)
and:	closed stroke (+)	
1:		closed stroke (+)
and:	closed stroke (+)	
2:		closed stroke (+)
and:	open stroke (o)	
3:		open stroke (o)
and:	closed stroke (+)	
4:		closed stroke (+)
and:	closed stroke (+)	

This conga/tumba rhythm is the most common rhythm for two drums.

The same rhythm is used for:
Medium tempi: *Cha-cha-cha* and *Son Montuno*.
Fast tempi: *Rumba* that has a *Mambo*-like character.
In all tempi for *Rock* rhythms.

Conga and tumba played by one person

When *the conga* and *tumba* are played by one person, the basic rhythm is played on *the conga*. This rhythm on *the conga* is only broken when going from *the conga* to *the tumba*.
The »open« strokes (o) from *the basic tumba rhythm* (see *conga/tumba for two persons* page 46) are used — after which *the basic conga rhythm* is continued.

All the strokes on *the tumba* are played with the right hand, since *the tumba* is placed **to the right**.

Cha-cha-cha

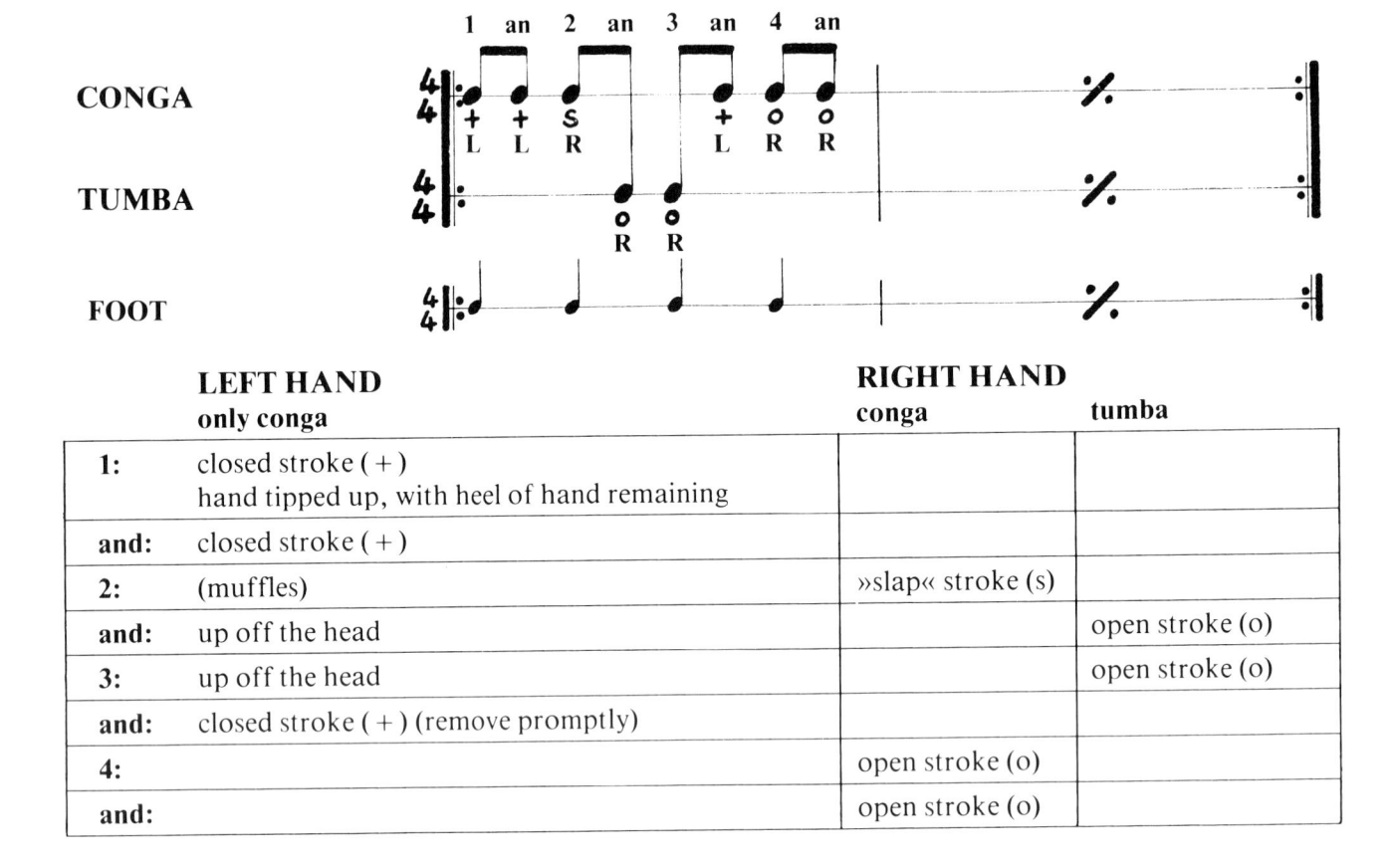

	LEFT HAND only conga	**RIGHT HAND** conga	tumba
1:	closed stroke (+) hand tipped up, with heel of hand remaining		
and:	closed stroke (+)		
2:	(muffles)	»slap« stroke (s)	
and:	up off the head		open stroke (o)
3:	up off the head		open stroke (o)
and:	closed stroke (+) (remove promptly)		
4:		open stroke (o)	
and:		open stroke (o)	

Mambo

The first bar of the rhythm is only played on *the conga (basic rhythm)*.
The second bar is the same as *Cha-cha-cha*. *The tumba* strokes are in the second bar only.

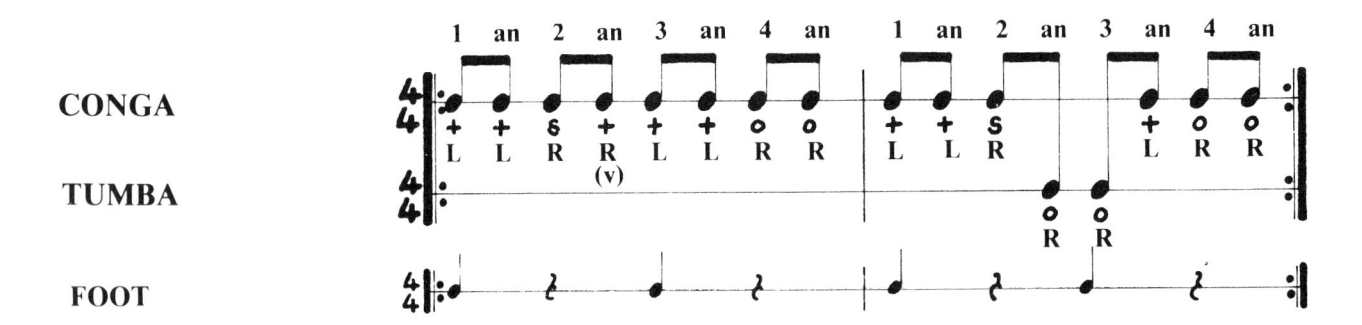

See the comments as to »*Mambo played by two persons*« page 47.

Conga rhythm for Bolero (slow tempi)

The conga rhythm for *Bolero* (one drum) is played together with *the bongo rhythm* — »*Martillo*« (see page 31).

The characteristic sound of this rhythm is produced by the »open« strokes on **3 and 4 and**. The strokes have a deep sound in comparison to *the bongo strokes*.

The bongo stroke on the large drum should be played on the count of **4**, between the two deep tones played on *the conga*.

This »gung«-»ging«-»gung« pattern is played without variation through the entire number. The foot should be tapped on counts **1-2-3-4** in *Bolero*.

Conga rhythm (basic Bolero rhythm)

The three first strokes are the same as in the *basic conga rhythm*.

On **2 and:** the left hand is tipped upwards after having muffled the »slap« stroke, and plays a stroke with the finger tips (»closed« stroke (+) as on **3 and** in *basic conga rhythm* — see page 41).
  3: »closed« stroke (+) with the flat of the hand. The hand should be removed from the head promptly after playing the stroke to give way for an »open« stroke with the right hand to be played directly afterwards.

See the whole rhythm in the example here:

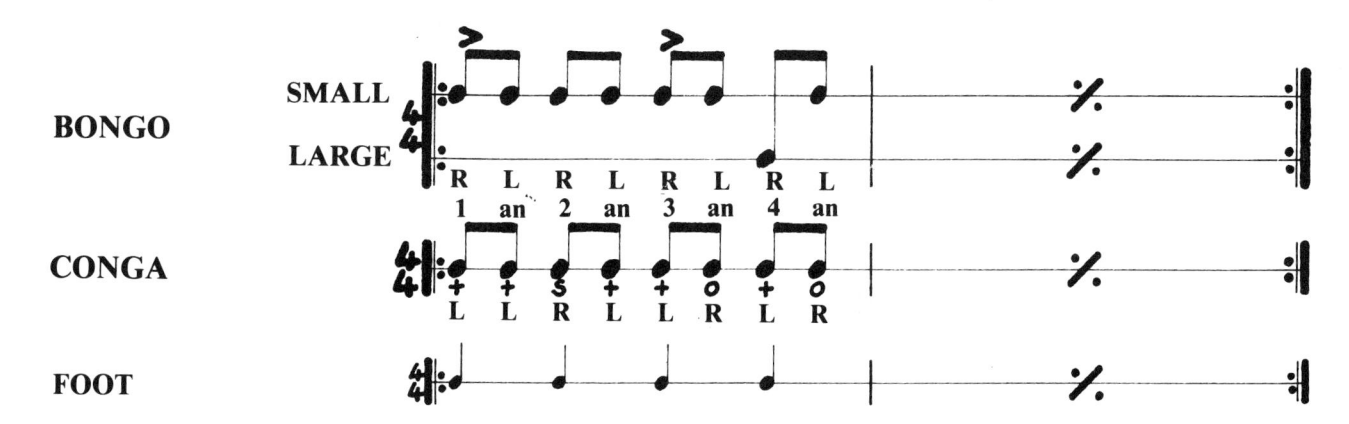

	LEFT HAND	**RIGHT HAND**
1:	closed stroke (+) hand tipped upwards with heel of hand remaining	
and:	closed stroke (+) stays to muffle head	
2:	muffles	»slap stroke (s)
and:	closed stroke (+) stroke with fingertips only, heel of hand is off of head	
3:	closed stroke (+) flat of hand	
and:	up off head	open stroke (o)
4:	closed stroke (+) flat of hand	
and:	up off head	open stroke (o)

Conga/tumba for Bolero

played by two persons

When *Bolero* is played on *conga* and *tumba*, the *bongos* are allowed to play more freely, since they do not have to play the basic rhythm.

The conga replaces the role of *the bongos* by playing an »open« stroke on the count of **4**. *The conga* now plays *the basic conga rhythm* but with **only** one open stroke on **4**.

The regular »open« stroke on the count of **4 and** can either be omitted completely or played very softly as a »closed« stroke near the edge of the head.

The tumba plays the same rhythm as when *the conga* plays alone with *the bongos* (see page 49).

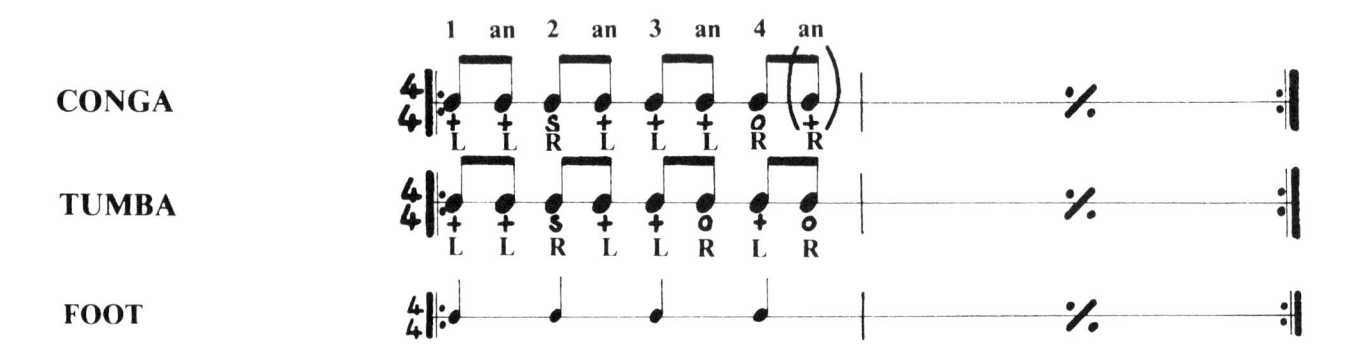

The conga-stroke on the count of **2 and** can also be played with the right hand.

Played by one person

The rhythm is the same when one person plays both *conga* and *tumba* as when *the conga* is played alone with *the bongos* — except:

The open stroke of the right hand (**and 4 and**) which is now played on *the tumba* (to the right), and the stroke of the left hand (on **4**) which is usually »closed« (+), is now played as an »open« stroke (on *the conga*) with the left hand.

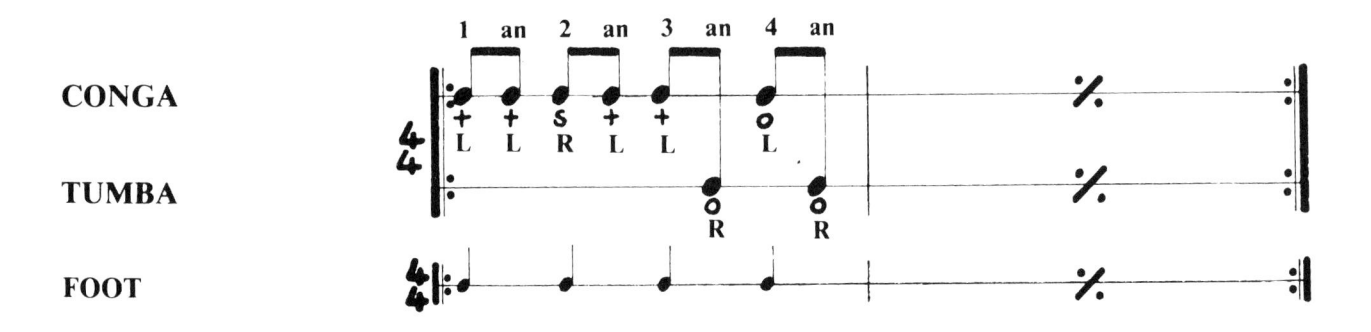

Alternative rhythm for Bolero

This figure is used as a basic rhythm or as a variation of the *basic conga/tumba rhythm for Bolero*.

1: »closed« stroke with the flat of the hand. The hand is tipped upwards while the heel of the hand remains on the head.

1 <u>and</u>: the fingertips fall back onto the head for a »closed« stroke. They are lifted promptly off the head again, leaving the heel of the hand on the head.

1 and <u>ah</u>: another »closed« stroke with the flat of the hand. The hand remains on the head to muffle for the »slap« stroke on the count of **<u>2</u>**. From here on, the rhythm is played as *basic Bolero*.

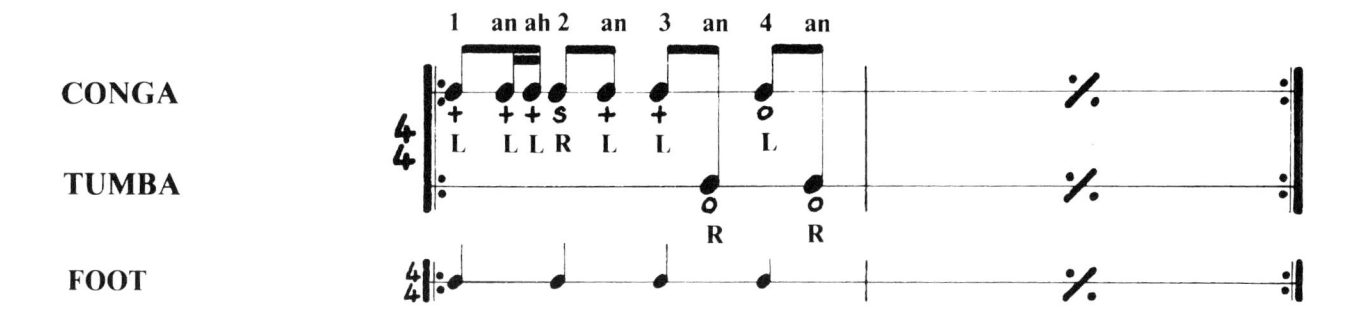

Rumba

The tumba plays the basic rhythm *(tumbao)* in *Rumba*.
This means that the rhythm can be played without other drums (see page 41).
When *the quinto* and *conga* are included, their figures are structured on *the BASS rhythm of the tumba*, and will not sound right without this.

The left hand plays »closed« strokes (+) in the center of the head on the counts of **<u>1</u>** and **<u>3</u>** (the foot should be tapped on the same counts).
The right hand plays one »open« stroke (o) on the count of **<u>4</u>**.

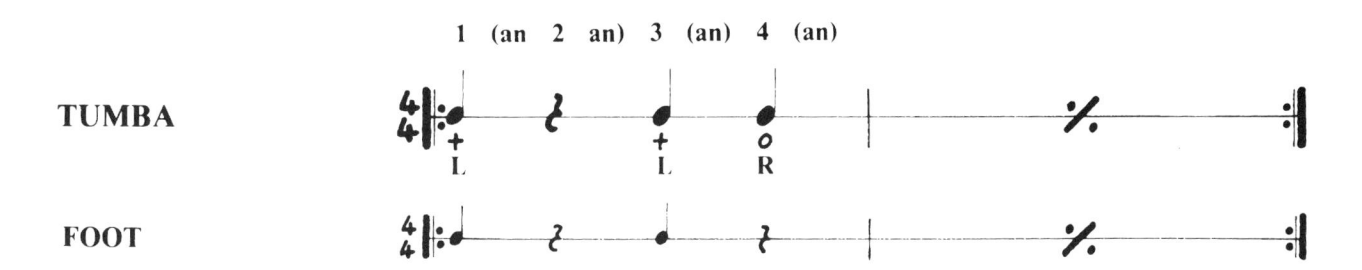

The conga and *quinto* figures that fit *the tumba rhythm* are shown under »Rumba« in part two (from page 122).

The tumba rhythm is also used for: »*Conga*« (the Cuban rhythm) and »*Calypso*« (Trinidad).

There are certain variations and figures later on in the book that are not introduced here in part one, but with the information supplied so far this should not cause any problems.

Timbales (Pailas)

The timbales consists of two single-skinned, metal-shelled drums.
The shells are made of either brass or steel.
The drums are set on a stand, and as opposed to almost all other drums, the LARGE drum is placed to the LEFT and the SMALL drum is placed to the RIGHT, as seen from the person playing.
The diameter of the head of the large drum is normally 14'' (approx. 35 cm) and the small drum 13'' (approx. 33 cm).
Some models are slightly larger, usually used for large bands, and some are smaller, called *timbalitos*.
The cowbells are placed on a holder on the front side of *the timbales*, between the two drums. *The large cowbell* is set up with the mouth pointing to the right.
This bell is called the »*Mambo cowbell*«.
The small bell is placed on top of *the large cowbell*, pointing to the left.
This bell is called the »*Cha-cha-cha cowbell*«.

The timbales are played with sticks.
(Notice the basic rhythm with the left hand, though.)
The sticks are of a type without tips, and can be found in a variety of sizes.

The sticks are used with a *matched grip* (see photo). The thumb presses the stick against the first joint of the index finger and the strokes are played using the wrists.

The right hand plays the basic rhythm on either one of the *cowbells*, or on the side of *the small timbale*.

The left hand plays on the head of *the large timbale*.

Sometimes both hands play on the sides of *the timbales* (left and right).
Playing on the side of *the timbales* is referred to as *PAILA* or *CASCARA*.

The timbales can be played either sitting or standing, whichever is most comfortable.

In some cases, Cuban »*timbaleros*« will use the word »*Pailas*« for *the timbales* and »*cascara*« for playing on the sides of the drums.

Strokes on the timbales

Left hand

+

Muffled stroke with the fingertips in the middle of the head. The hand remains in position to muffle the head after striking.

o

»Open« stroke with the fingertips in the middle of the head. The hand is removed from the head after striking to let the tone of the head sustain freely.

Cross-rim

When playing cross-rim, the end of the stick is held with the heel of the hand on the drum thus muffling the head.
It is only the thumb and index finger that hold the stick, striking the rim of the large timbale.

Try moving the stick about in order to find the best sound (a hollow click).

»Open« stroke in the middle of the head.

The stick should be lifted promptly after striking in order to let the head sustain its tone.

You may choose at your own discretion whether to play the left hand strokes with a stick or without, but the rhythm being played by the left hand should not be too dominating.
Cross-rim = muffled stroke with fingertips (+).
»Open« stroke with stick = »open« stroke with fingertips (o).

When the left hand stick is not in use, it should be placed on *the small timbale* for easy access when playing fills. (Shown with pictures on the next page.)

Right hand

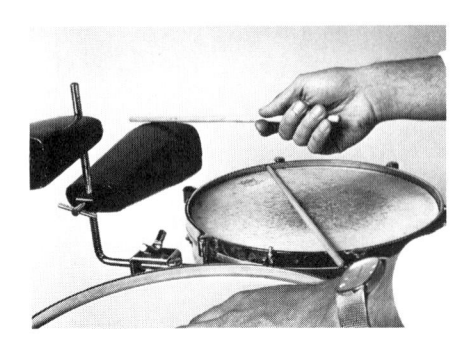

»A«
Stroke near the mouth of *the bell* with the side of the stick, producing a deep tone.

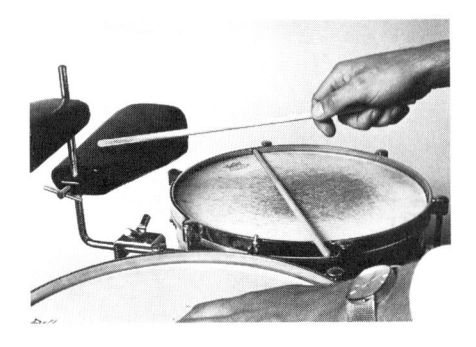

»B«
Stroke on the closed end of *the bell* with the tip of the stick, producing a high-pitched, sharp tone.

»C«
Stroke on the middle of *the bell* with the side of the stick.

Paila/cascara
Stroke on the side of *the timbales*, the right hand on the shell of the small drum.

When nothing else is stated, use strokes »A« or »C«.

Paila/cascara with both hands

Paila is also on occasion played with both hands. The right hand on the small drum and the left hand on the large drum.

Rim-shot

The stick should strike the rim of the drum and the head, close to the edge, at the same time.

This produces a sharp, metallic sound.

This stroke can be played with both hands and is used for solos and fills.

Abanico

Abanico means »*fan*« in Spanish and is also the name of a special *timbale-figure* used as a signal for changes and breaks in the rhythm being played.
The figure consists of one or more strokes, a roll and another stroke.
Abanico is also used as a pick-up to a rhythm, to be played in tempo in front of the rhythm.

1

The fundamental *Abanico-figure* consists of:
A rim shot on the count of **3**, a double-stroke roll ($\equiv$) on the count of **4** and another rim-shot on the count of **1** (the first beat of the bar), after which the rhythm continues on *cowbell* or as *Paila*.
All the strokes are played on the *small timbale*.

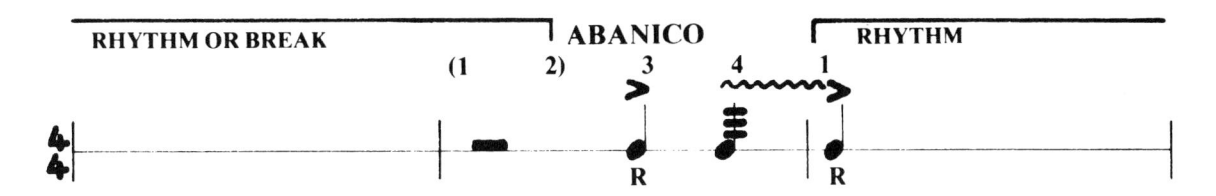

If the rhythm is played in *2-3 clave*, the first stroke can be played on the count of **2 and** instead of **3**.

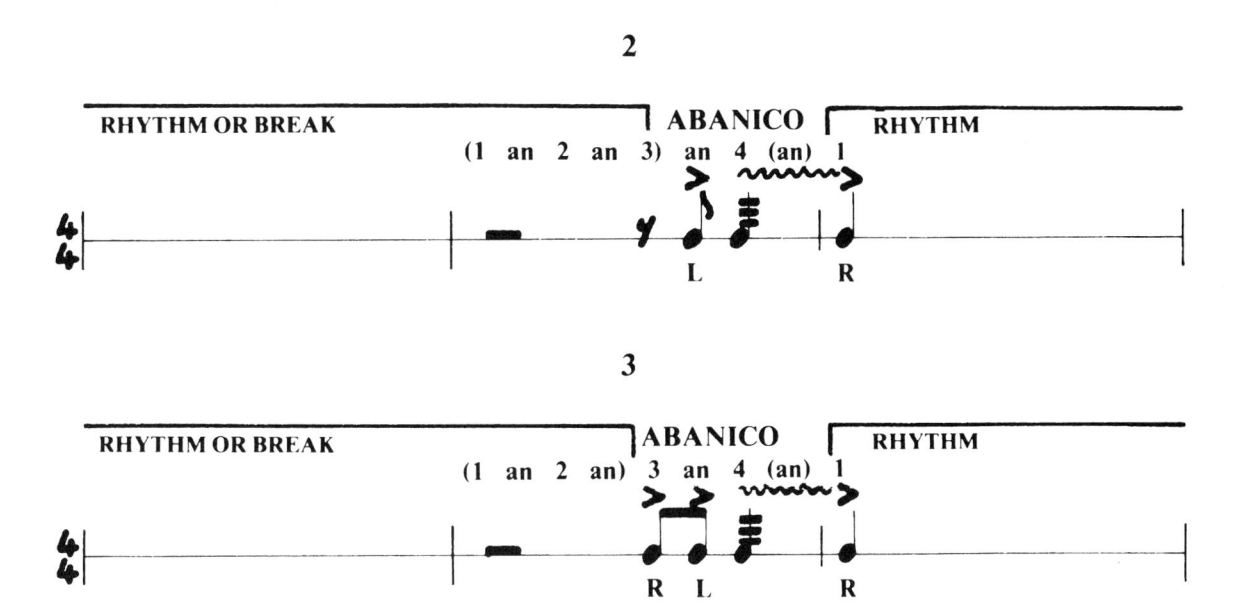

2

3

Timbales rhythms

To make things easier, the strokes on the *cowbells* will only be refered to with the notation (A, B, C and Paila) that is shown below the pictures.

To make playing the rhythms easier in the beginning, I can recommend holding the *large cowbell* in the left hand instead of having it set up on *the timbales*. It will be easier to coordinate the hands when the right hand rhythms are understood properly.

The number of the rhythms are the same as the rhythms refered to under »*hand-cowbell*« (pages 25-27).

> In all the rhythms, unless *Paila* or *cowbell* is indicated for both hands, the left hand should play the strokes on *the large timbale* either with or without the stick (see page 53).
> The rhythm is played with a muffled stroke (+) on the count of **2** and an »open« stroke (o) on the count of **4**. This rhythm is used to balance the timing of the right hand rhythms.

The first rhythms shown are identical in the first and second bars, the rhythms are not influenced by the direction of *the clave: 3/2* or *2/3* (see page 17).

Cha-cha-cha

1

The right hand should play C-strokes (or A-strokes) on *the small cowbell* in this rhythm.
The rhythm is played as quarter-notes on the counts **1-2-3-4**.

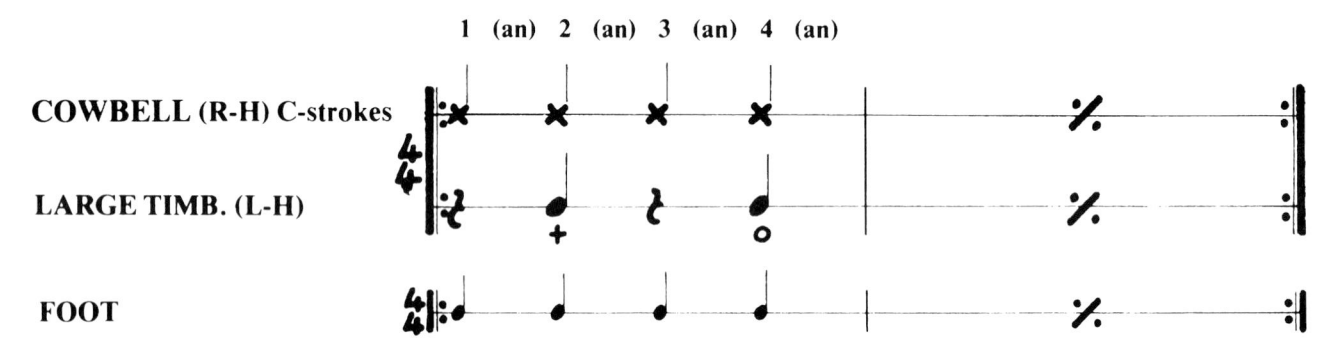

The same rhythm can also be used for *Son Montuno* and *Guajira*.

2

There are two different strokes on *the cowbell* in this rhythm. They are A- and B-strokes and can be played on *the large* or *small cowbell*. Refer to the variations on page 102.

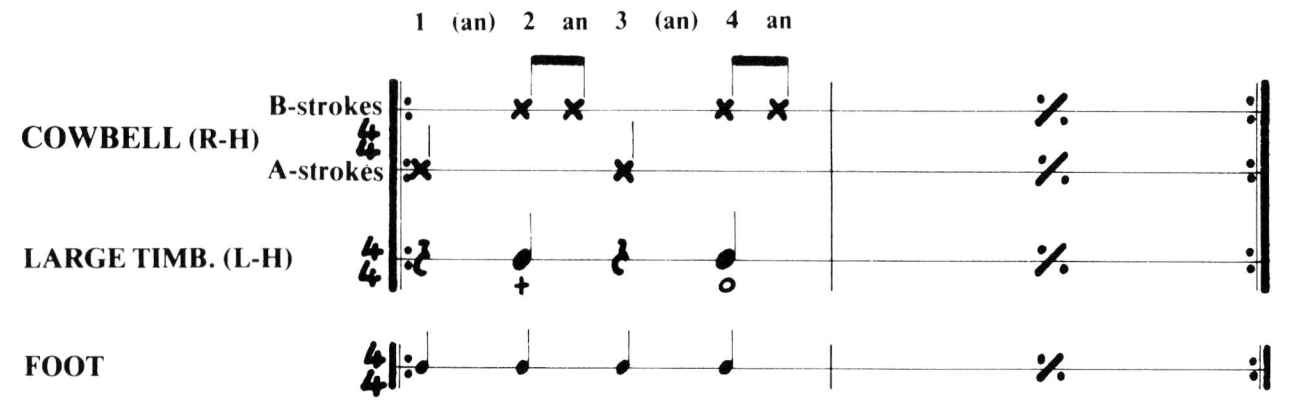

The same rhythm can also be used for *Mambo*, *Son Montuno* and *Guajira*.

Mambo

Rhythm number »2« (see *Cha-cha-cha*) can also be used for *Mambo*.

Rhythm number »3« is played on *the hand cowbell* (see page 26), when *the timbales* play a two-bar rhythm.

The next rhythms shown are two-bar rhythms, that are based on *the clave rhythm (3/2)*.

In cases where *the clave rhythm* is reversed *(2/3), the cowbell rhythm* must be reversed accordingly (see *clave rhythm* page 17).

The right-hand rhythm is either played on *the large cowbell* or on the side of the *small timbale (Paila)*.

Paila is often used in the beginning of a number and in places where the rhythm section should not be too loud, when accompanying a singer, flute or piano.

The cowbell is used mostly when the rhythm section should be more predominant.

4

Right hand: C-strokes or *Paila*. All strokes are to be accented equally.

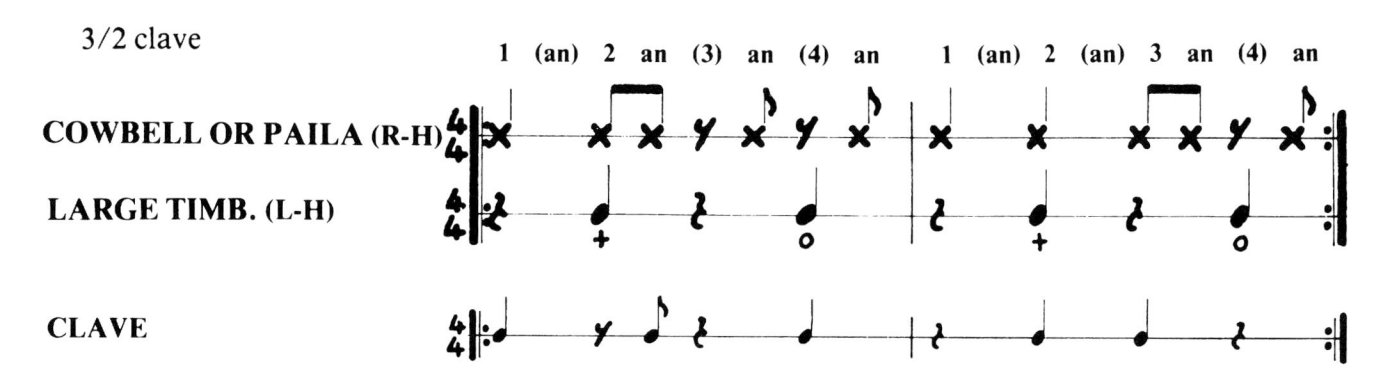

[Musical notation: 3/2 clave pattern for Cowbell or Paila (R-H), Large Timb. (L-H), and Clave]

This is the same rhythm but now played with *reverse (2/3) clave*.
The cowbell rhythm should now start with the last bar first.

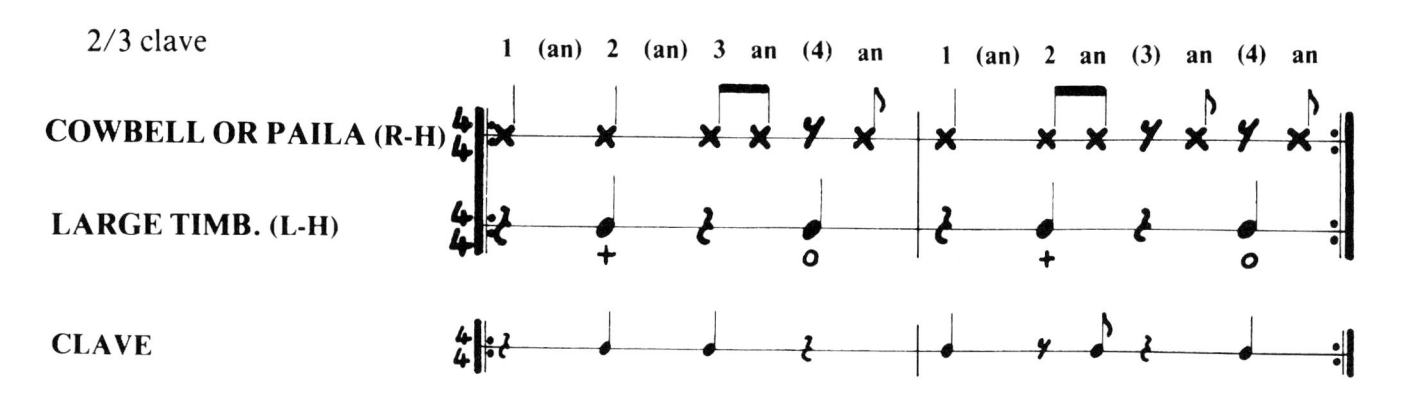

[Musical notation: 2/3 clave pattern for Cowbell or Paila (R-H), Large Timb. (L-H), and Clave]

This is the most common *cowbell* or *Paila rhythm* —
not only for *Mambo*, but for certain types of *Rumba*, and when playing *Cha-cha-cha* in double tempo *(Ritmo doble)*.

5

This rhythm is often used as a *Paila rhythm* in the beginning of a number. When the rhythm section plays a more predominant role, the *large cowbell* is taken into use.
The rhythm played is either the same as *the Paila rhythm,* or as rhythm number »4«.
All the strokes on *the cowbell* are played as C-strokes, or the regularly accentuated as C-strokes and the accentuated (>) as A-strokes.

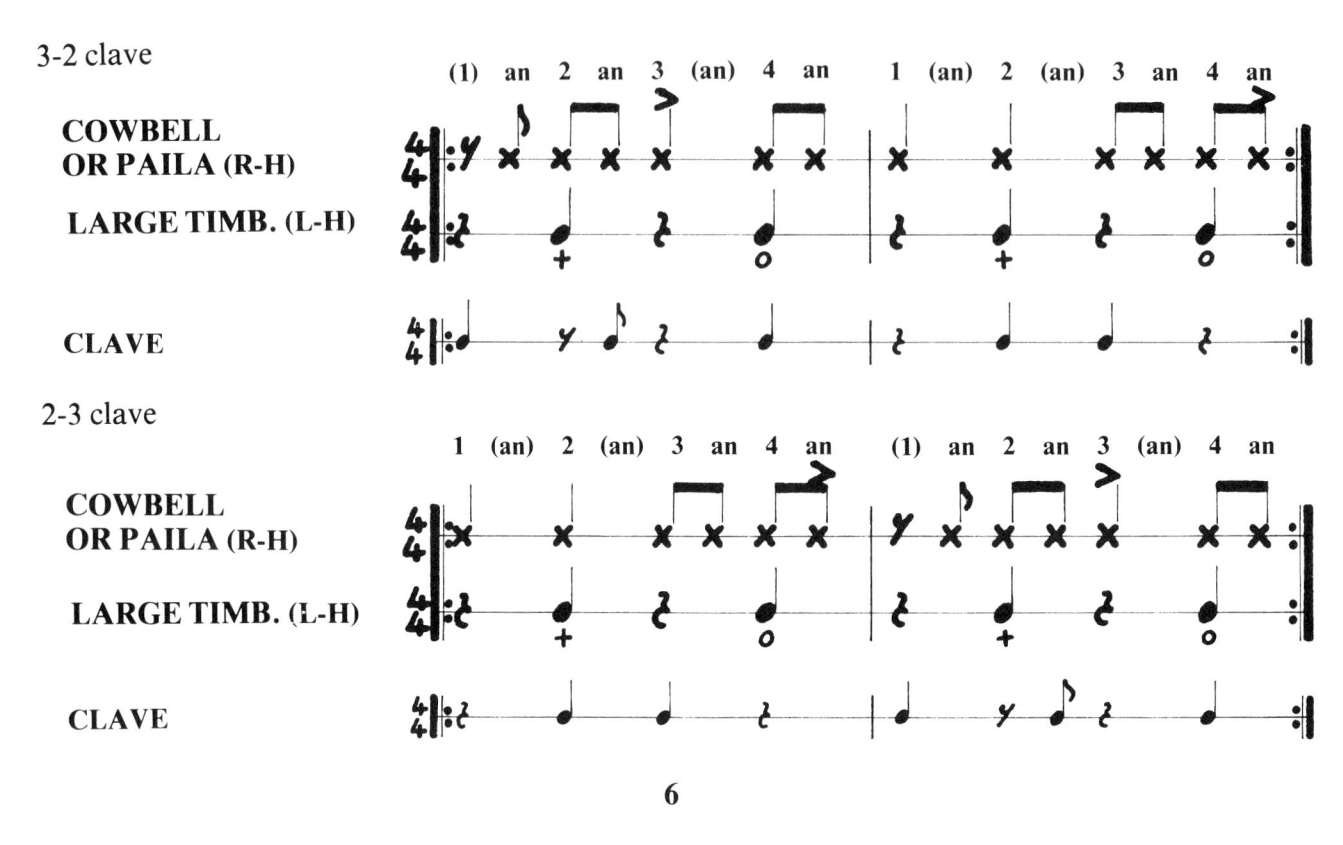

3-2 clave

2-3 clave

6

All the strokes on *the cowbell* are played as C-strokes, or alternatively the regularly accentuated strokes as C-strokes and the accentuated (>) as A-strokes.

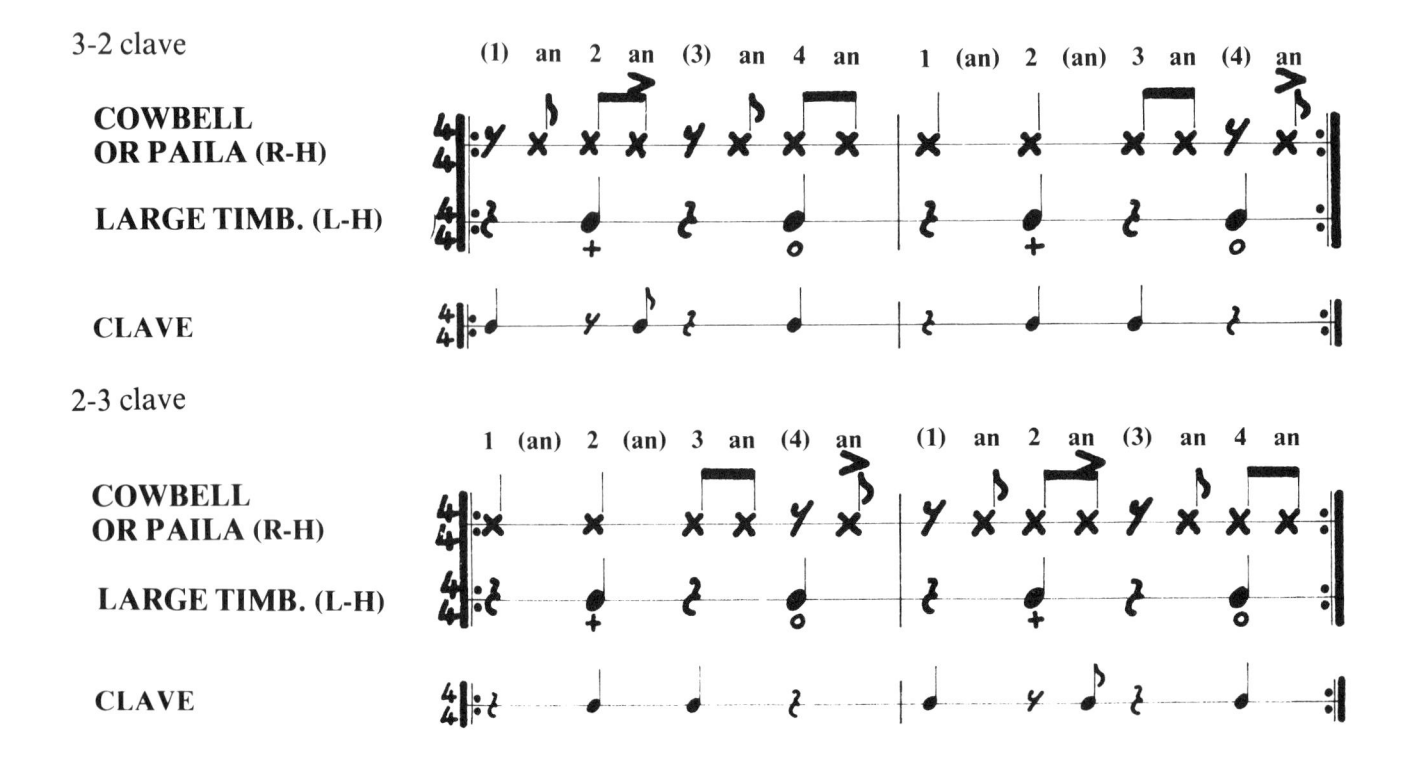

3-2 clave

2-3 clave

Bolero, Rumba, Guajira and Son Montuno

When playing *Bolero* and some types of *Rumba*, the sticks are played on the sides of both drums (*Paila* with both hands).
When playing together with *maracas, the timbales* and *maracas* play the same rhythm.
In *Guajira* and *Son Montuno* the *Paila rhythms* shown here are often played in the parts of the arrangements in which the rhythm section is to play a less predominant role.

7

The basic rhythm is eighth notes played hand to hand, starting with the right. This rhythm should feel relaxed and steady before progressing to the other rhythms.

Important: The foot should be tapped on the counts **1-2-3-4** when playing *Bolero* in slow tempi. When played in faster tempi *(Rumba)*, tap on counts **1** and **3**.

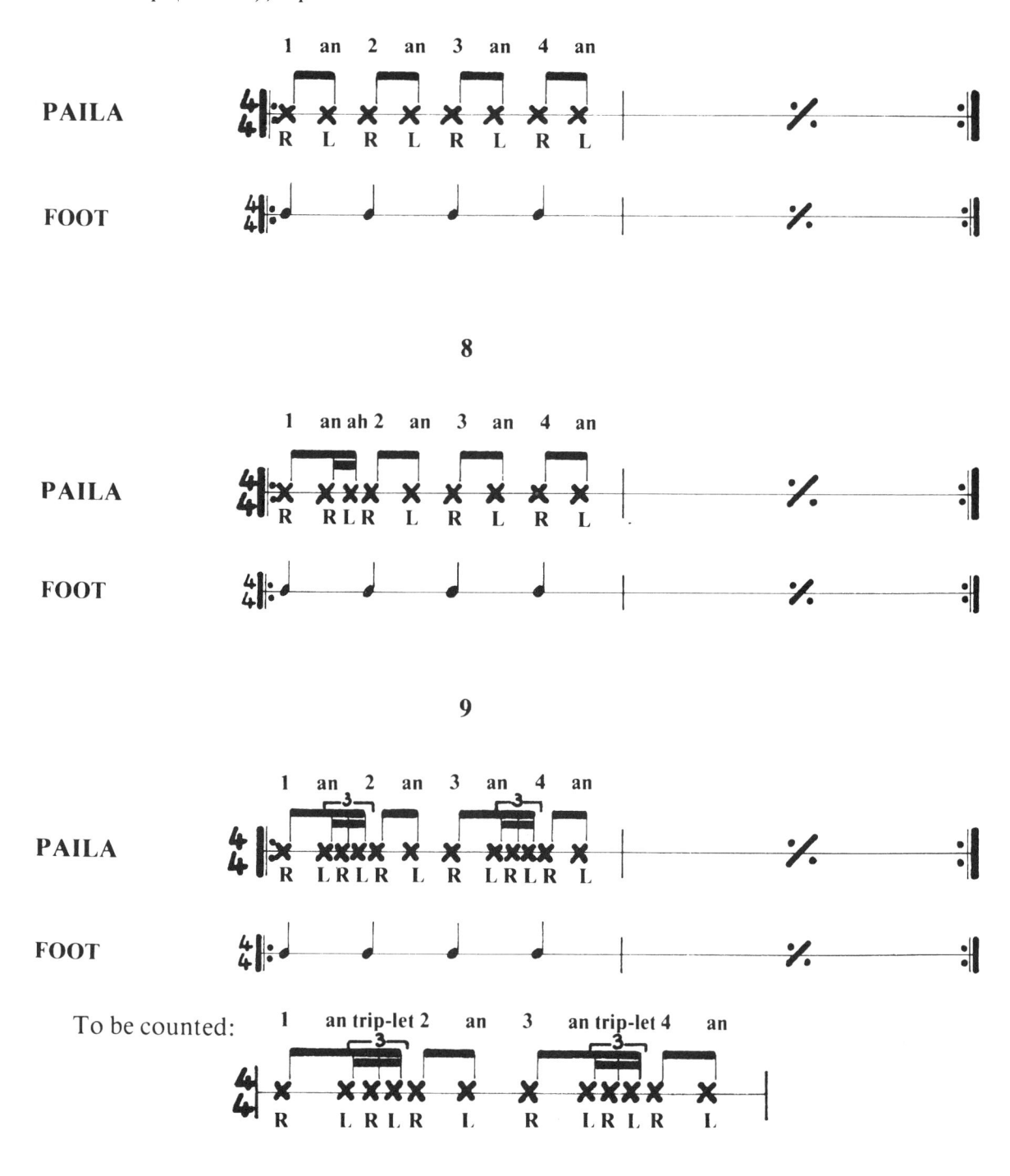

Brazilian rhythm instruments

When studying the Cuban rhythm instruments, we have noticed that they all have the *clave rhythm* as a foundation.
Another characteristic is the accentuated <u>2</u> and <u>4</u>, or <u>2</u> and <u>4 and</u> feeling.
This means that the rhythms are not generaly based on <u>1</u> and <u>3</u>.

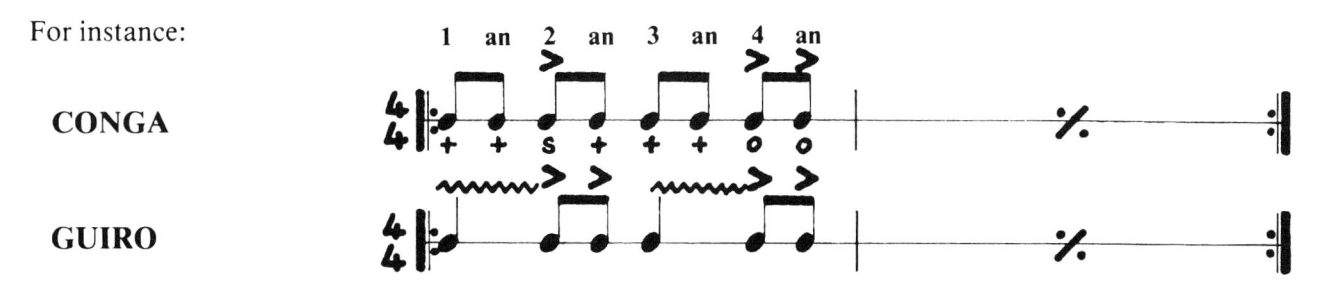

For instance:

CONGA

GUIRO

But contrary to the Cuban rhythms, the Brazilian rhythm foundation is based on the counts <u>1</u> and <u>3</u>.
There is no basic *clave rhythm*, but an equivalent basic pulse constructed by various instruments.

Samba is the most well-known of the Brazilian rhythms, so the following chapter will deal basically with this rhythm. There are many different types of *Samba*, but they all have the same basic pulse or feeling. The different types of *Samba* are explained in part two of the book.

Basically, *Samba* is split up into three parts or functions:
1: »**basic**« **rhythm.** Rhythms that accentuate the counts of <u>1</u> and <u>3</u> or **and** <u>1</u> and **and** <u>3</u>.
2: »**balance**« **rhythm.** Rhythms that accentuate the counts of <u>2</u> and <u>4</u> in order to balance and stabilize the rhythm.
   The »basic«- and »balance« rhythm combined produce the »basic pulse« or feeling.
   The strokes on the counts of <u>1</u> and <u>3</u> are more heavily accentuated than strokes on the counts of <u>2</u> and <u>4.</u>
3: **The third part** of the rhythm is the various types of instruments that play **rhythms that span over two bars**. These rhythms have no value without the »*basic pulse*«.

The flow of the melody can sometimes require the two bar figures to start with the second bar followed by the first bar, just like when playing the Cuban rhythms. This type of rhythmic adjustment can be acquired with practice, but sometimes even the real masters can be in doubt.

Surdo

Surdo is the bass drum that is used to keep the rhythm together and to provide the deep bass tones.

The drum is usually made of metal and fitted with a top and a bottom head.

The surdo is carried by a shoulder strap.

The right hand uses a large beater to play the rhythm, and the left hand is used to play the muffled (+) strokes.

A large *floor tom-tom* can be used as a substitute for *the surdo*.

When using a *floor tom-tom* in place of a *surdo*, it is best to use a felt-tipped mallet or the blunt end of a drumstick to strike with.

The rhythm of *the surdo* consists of two different strokes:

Muffled stroke (+)
The left hand muffles the middle of the head — strike with the right hand.

»Open« stroke (o)
The head is allowed to sustain. Strike with the right hand in the middle of the head, promptly removing the stick afterwards to let the head sustain.
The left hand is off the drum.

Samba

1

The basic rhythm on *the surdo* consists of a muffled stroke (+) on the count of **1** and an »open« stroke (o) on the count of **3**. The left hand should muffle the head on the count of **4**, but this should not be regarded as a stroke.

Basic rhythm:

2

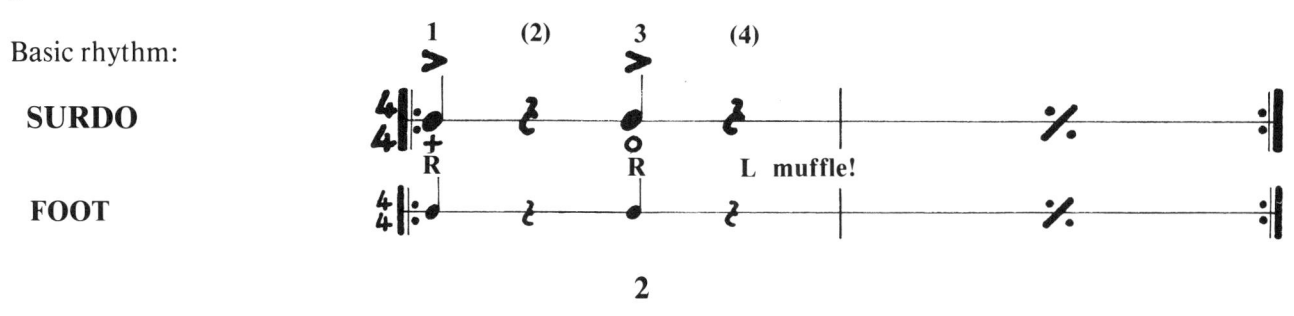

The strokes in this rhythm are played with both hands.
The left hand plays the stroke with the flat of the hand an eighth note before (upbeat) the accentuated stroke with the right hand. The right hand still uses a beater.
The left hand remains on the head to muffle when the right hand is to play muffled strokes (+).
The left hand is removed from the head after playing the upbeat when the right hand is to play »open« strokes (o).

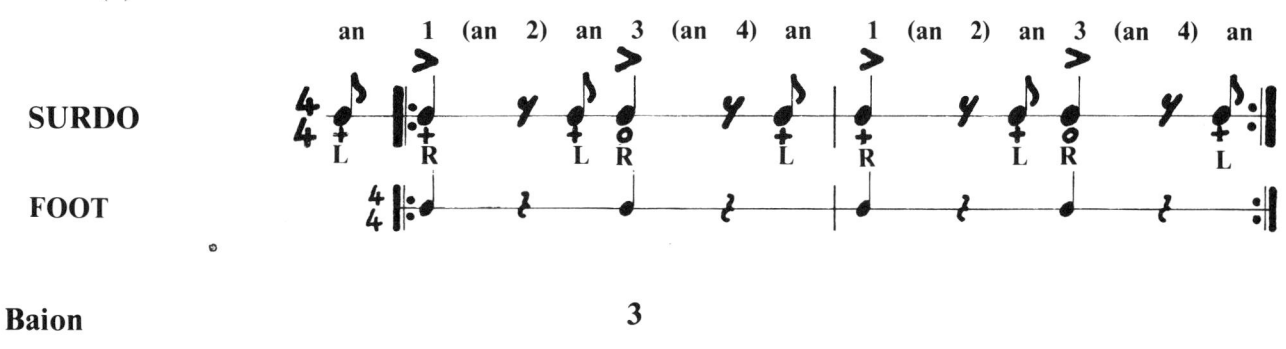

Baion

3

The basic rhythm for *Baion* is an accentuated muffled stroke (+) on the count of **1** and an accentuated »open« stroke on the count of **2 and**. Both strokes are played with the right hand. The left hand muffles the head on the count of **4**.

Samba and Baion

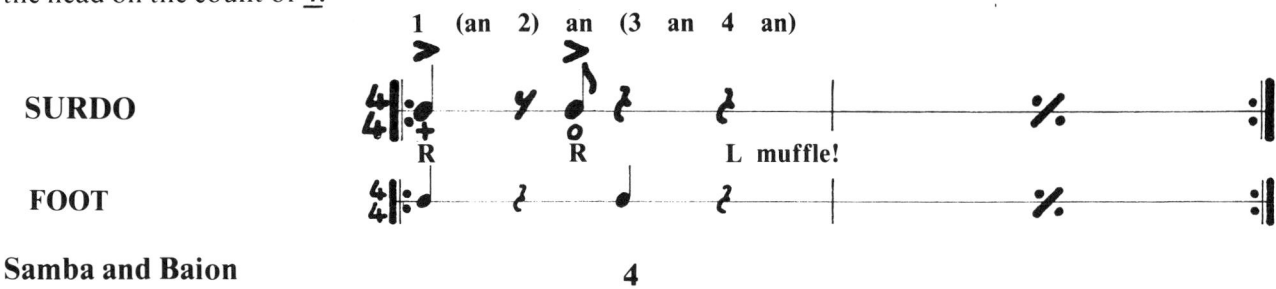

4

This rhythm is used either as a basic rhythm throughout an entire number, or as a varation of the rhythms shown. This rhythm is for *Samba* or *Baion*.

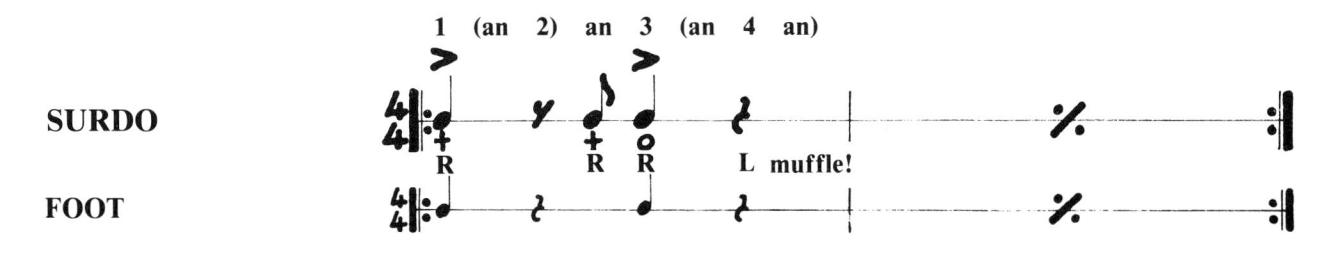

For other variations, refer to the rhythms in part two.

Chocalho/Ganza

Chocalho and *Ganza* are both names for the same instrument.

The instrument consists of a cylinder, 30-50 cm (12-20 inches) long, usually made of metal (tin). The cylinder is filled with sand or shot, and in many of the more imaginative models made, two or more cylinders are fixed together in parallel (see photo).

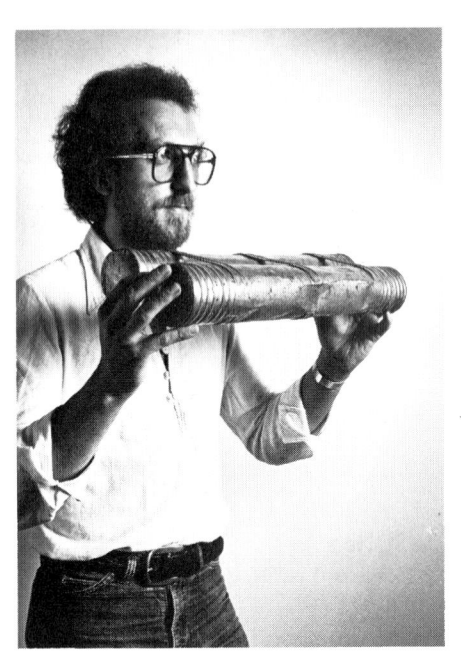

The *chocalho* is held with both hands at a height that feels comfortable – approx. chin height (see photo).

The basic rhythm of *the chocalho* is played by moving the instrument away from the body and back towards the body again, using even eighth notes (unaccentuated), causing the contents to be shaken back and forth.
When the basic movement feels comfortable, the accentuated strokes can be played by tossing the contents of *the chocalho* against the inside of the instrument with a quick motion of the hands, stopping abruptly to make the contents strike the shell. The tossing motion is done with the arms and the stopping motion with the wrists and hands.

Samba

When playing *Samba*, the basic rhythm of *the chocalho* is played on the eighth notes with accents on the counts of **1** and **3**.

CHOCALHO

FOOT

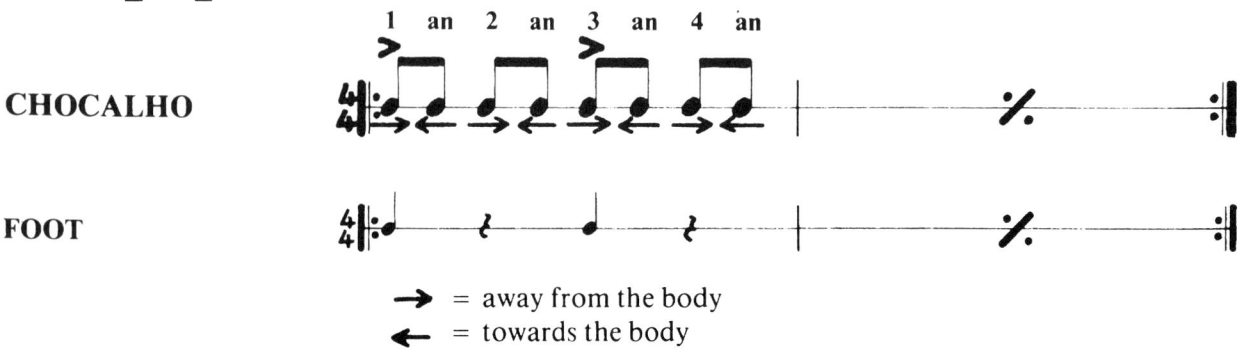

→ = away from the body
← = towards the body

2

The basic rhythm can be varied by playing the eighth notes <u>before</u> counts **1** and **3** as accentuated strokes. BUT do not do this until the basic rhythm can be played steadily.

and:	(upbeat) vigorous movement towards the body
1:	vigorous movement away from the body
and:	light movement towards the body
2:	light movement away from the body
and:	vigorous movement towards the body
3:	vigorous movement away from the body
and:	light movement towards the body
4:	light movement away from the body
and:	vigorous movement towards the body

3

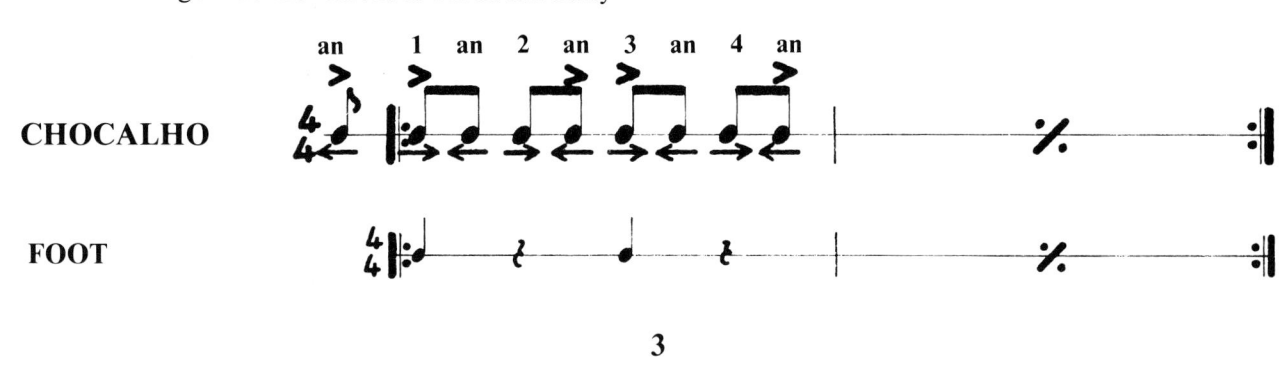

Samba, Bossa Nova and Baion

This *chocalho rhythm* is used in various Brazilian rhythms.
The accentuated strokes are played on the counts of **2** and **4** now *(The »balance« rhythm)*.
Make sure to coordinate the tapping of the foot on counts **1** and **3** and the accentuated strokes on the counts **2** and **4**.

This rhythm is used for *Samba* in cases where there are many instruments playing on the counts **1** and **3**.

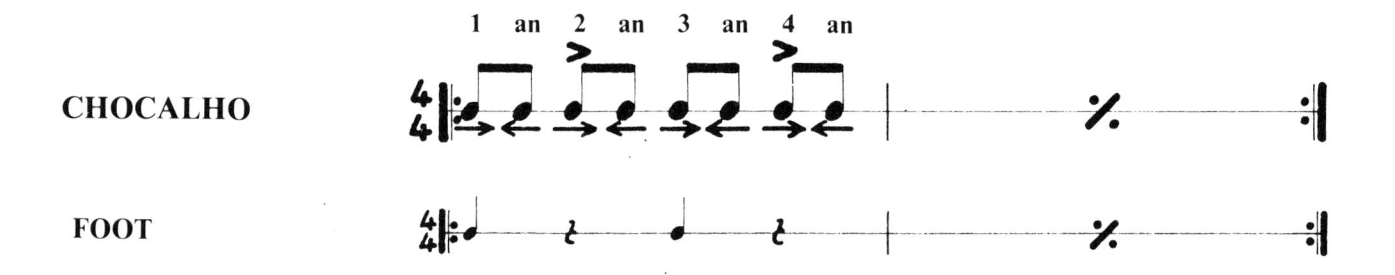

Reco-Reco

The *reco-reco* is a scraper made of bamboo. It is cylinder-shaped with grooves running horizontally across the instrument.
The *reco-reco* can also be made of metal, with springs mounted on the top side of the instrument. This instrument is called a *spring reco-reco* and will produce a larger sound than the *bamboo* variety. The *spring reco-reco* is primarily used in larger bands, for instance in the carnivals.

The *reco-reco* is held horizontaly in the left hand. The right hand plays the instrument by scraping it with a small stick, usually made of metal.

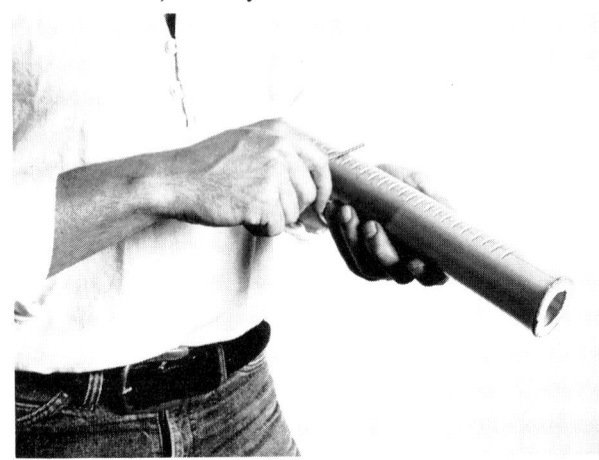

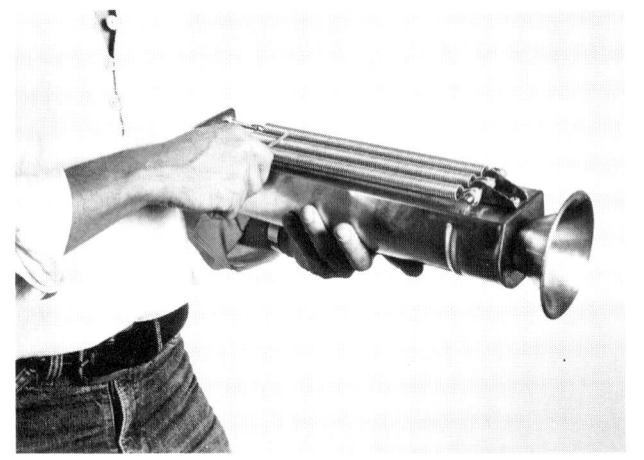

Bamboo reco-reco   *Spring reco-reco*

The rhythm of the right hand is played as eighth notes and should be practiced until it can be played steadily.

1: away from the body. **and:** towards the body. **2:** away from the body etc. etc.
The hand should not be removed from *the reco-reco* while playing.

Samba

1

The basic rhythm for *Samba* is played by using accentuated strokes on the counts **2** and **4** while executing the steady eighth note movement with the right hand (*»balance« rhythm* see page 61).

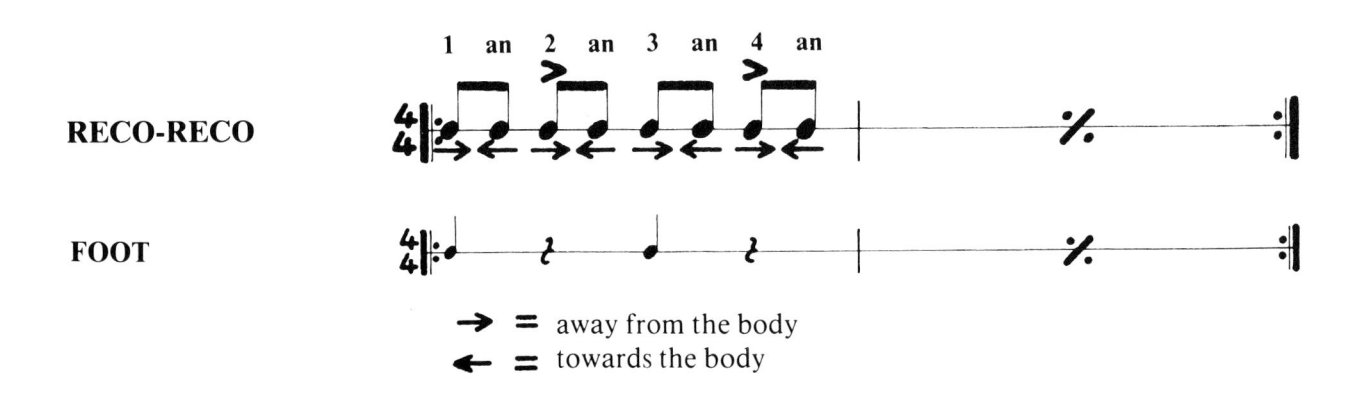

→ = away from the body
← = towards the body

If other rhythms are played on *the reco-reco*, it is necessary for another instrument to play the accentuated strokes on **2** and **4**, in order to balance out the rhythm.

2

The steady eighth note movement is also the foundation for this next rhythm, which is played over a two bar period. Notice that the accentuated beats on the counts of **and** (upbeats) are played towards the body and vice versa on the counts **1-2-3-** or **4**. The arrows are used to depict this.

RECO-RECO

FOOT

3

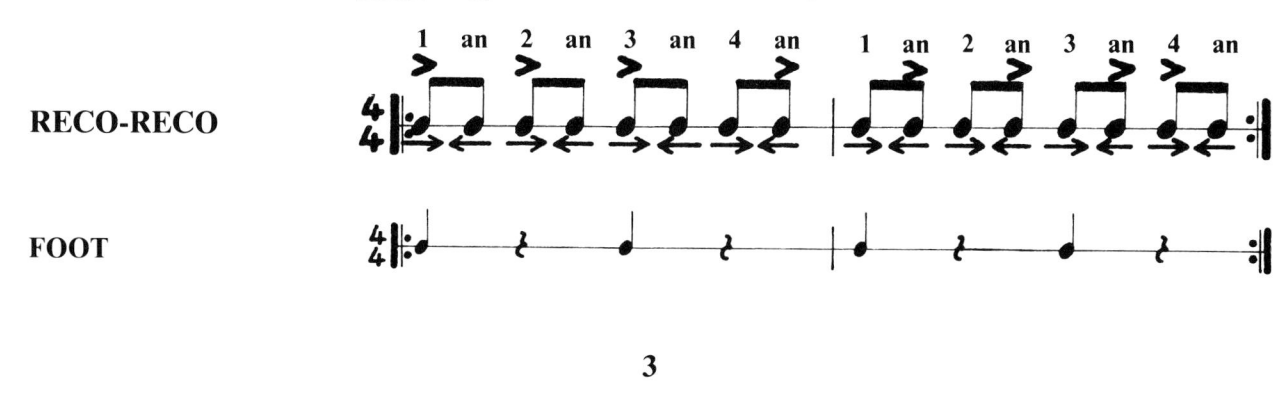

Note that the movement of the right hand is opposite in every other two-bar period (see the arrows).

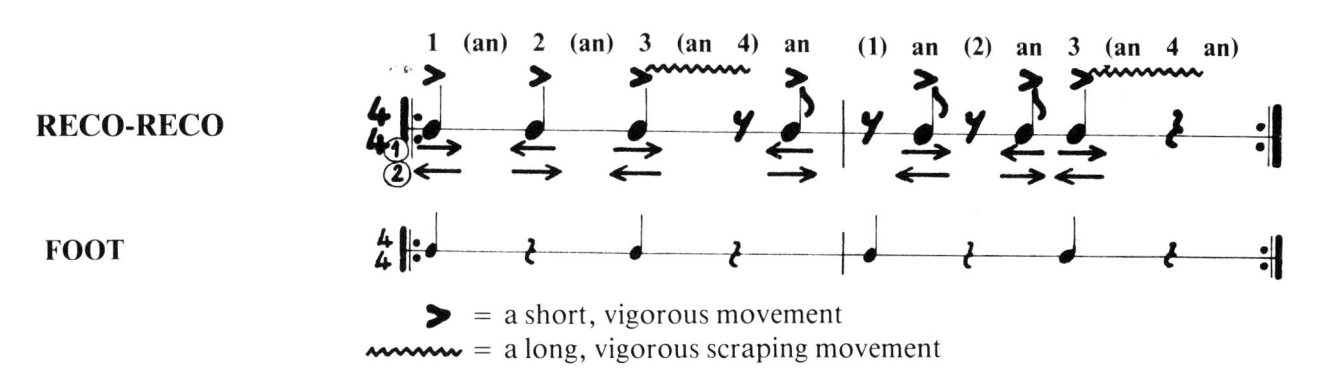

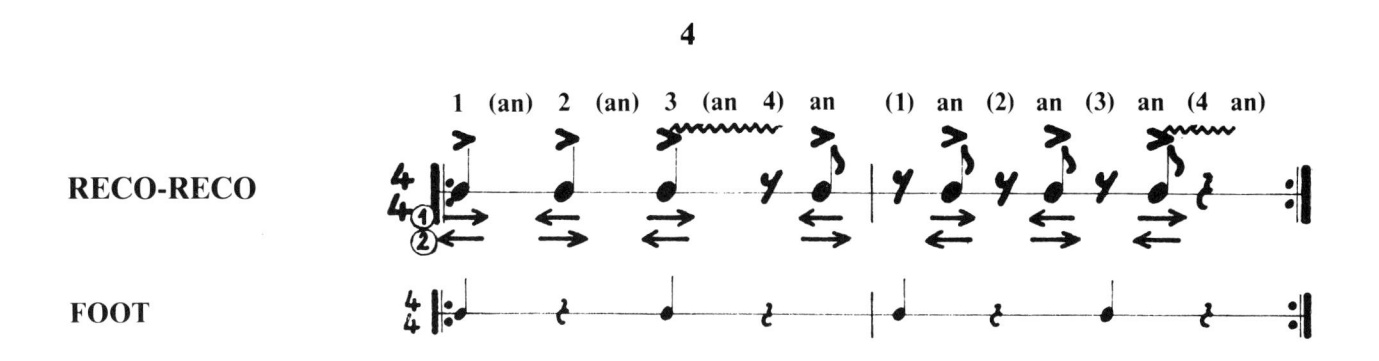

RECO-RECO

FOOT

> = a short, vigorous movement
~~~~ = a long, vigorous scraping movement

4

RECO-RECO

FOOT

Remember that the rhythms can also start with the second bar first. Refer to page 61.

Number »2«, »3« and »4« rhythms are often played on the edge of a metal plate using a knife as a scraping stick. The knife is drawn along the edge of the plate. This is called »**Prato e faca**«.

Other *reco-reco rhythms* are shown in part two.

Pandeiro

The *pandeiro* is the national instrument of Brazil and is used in a multitude of rhythms. The *pandeiro* is a single-headed *tambourine* fitted with jingles. The jingles are small tin discs, put together in groups of two. Tin gives the jingles a dry sound which is characteristic of the *pandeiro*.
Tambourines made outside of Brazil often have clean-sounding jingles **not** of tin. You can obtain the dry sound by replacing them with flattened-out beer bottle caps.

The pandeiro is usually about 28 cm (11'') in diameter but some are as large as 40 cm (16'').

Apart from being used as a rhythm instrument, *the pandeiro* is also used as a prop for juggling. There is a contest each year at the carnival in Brazil in order to find the best *pandeiro player* — and *juggler.*

Closed stroke (+)

Open stroke (o)

The *pandeiro* is held in the left hand (see photo).
The middle- and ring finger (possibly also the pinky) muffle the head when playing the muffled strokes (+) (see photo) .....
..... and are removed from the head when playing the open (o) strokes. This allows the head to sustain.

Pandeiro strokes:

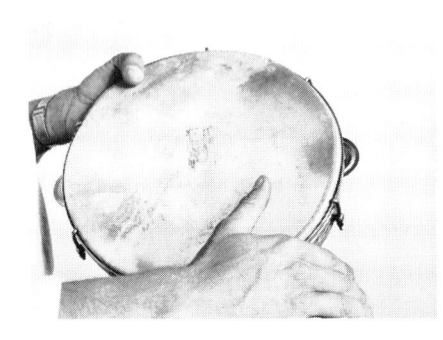

»A«
The side of the thumb — rotate the wrist.

»B«
The finger tips — wrist movement.

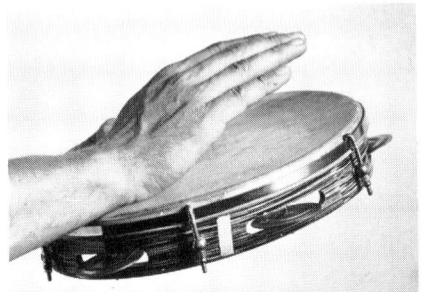

»C«
The heel of the hand — downwards movement of the heel of the hand.

Samba and Baion

1

The pandeiro plays eighth notes with accentuated strokes on the counts **and 1** and **and 3** as the basic rhythm. This is *the basic Samba rhythm* (see page 61).
On the counts **and 3**, the strokes are played open (o) all the rest are muffled (+).

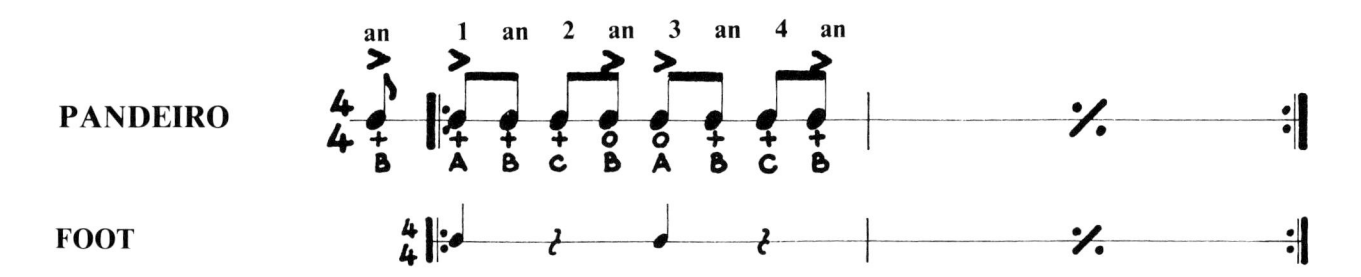

	LEFT HAND	**RIGHT HAND**
1:	muffles the head (+)	accentuated stroke with the thumb near the edge of the head (A-stroke), rotate the wrist
and:	muffles the head (+)	stroke with the fingertips, wrist movement (B-stroke)
2:	muffles the head (+)	stroke with the heel of the hand, wrist down (C-stroke)
and:	open tone (o)	accentuated B-stroke
3:	open tone (o)	accentuated A-stroke
and:	muffles the head (+)	B-stroke
4:	muffles the head (+)	C-stroke
and:	muffles the head (+)	accentuated B-stroke

2

This is the same rhythm but now there are also accentuated strokes on **2** and **4**.
The strokes on **2** and **4** are now more heavily accentuated than the strokes on **and 1** and **and 3**.

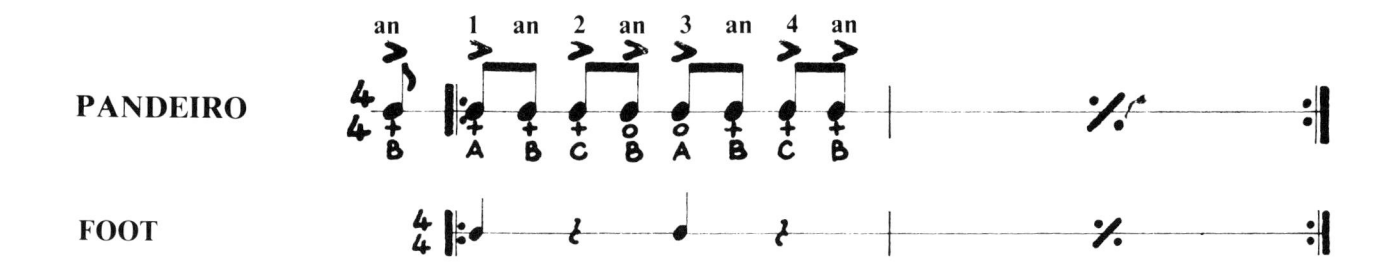

Tamborim with an »M«!

The *tamborim* is a small hand-held drum with a single head. The shell of the drum is usually made of metal. The drum is held in the left hand by the thumb and index finger (see photo).
The middle- and ring finger are used to muffle the head when playing muffled (+) strokes and are removed from the head when playing »open« strokes (o) (see photo).

The right hand strikes the head with a small stick, such as a *timbale* or *drum stick*.

The *tamborim* is used in almost all the *Samba rhythms*, playing over a two-bar period.

The thumb rests on the side of the head without muffling.

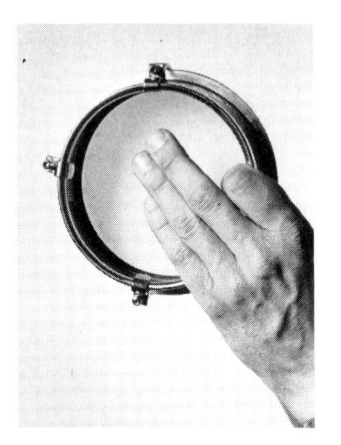

»Open« stroke (o) — the fingers are removed from the head to let the tone sustain.

»Muffled« stroke (+) – middle- and ring fingers muffle the head.

Samba

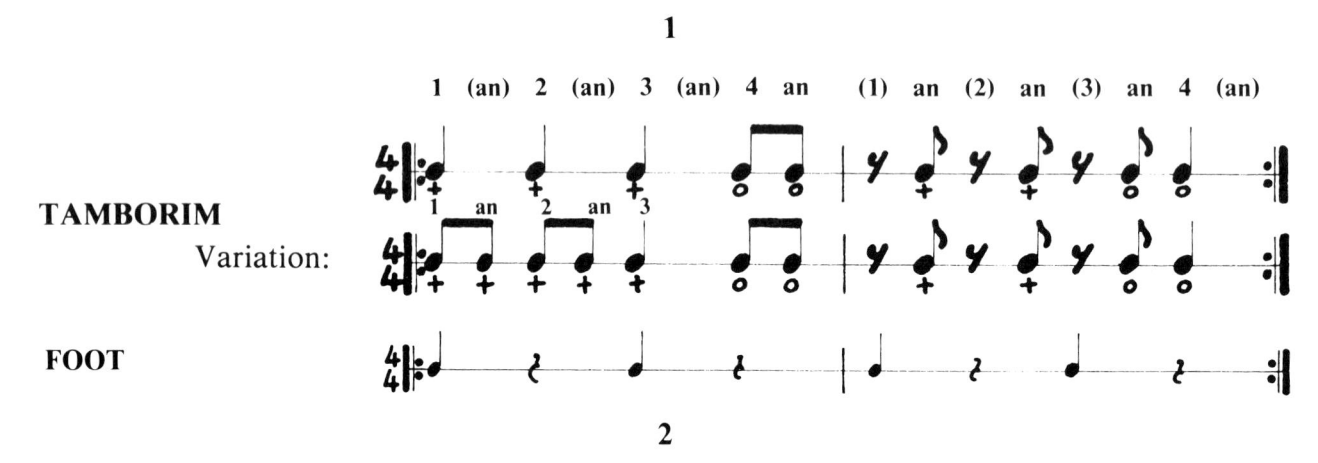

1

TAMBORIM
Variation:

FOOT

2

This is almost the same rhythm as before, but the one muffled stroke (+) in each bar gives the rhythm a different character.

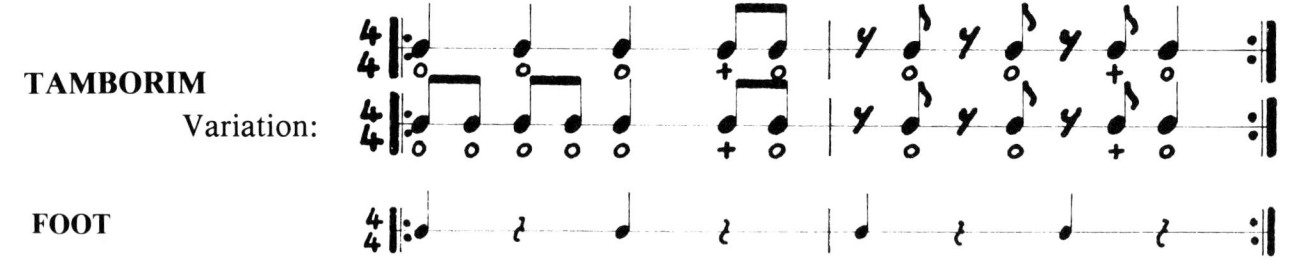

TAMBORIM
Variation:

FOOT

Remember that the rhythms can also start with the second bar first. Refer to page 61.

Ago-go

Ago-go are two small, usually cone shaped *cowbells* with two different tones.
They are held in the left hand with the right hand playing the rhythm with a *drum* or *timbale stick*.

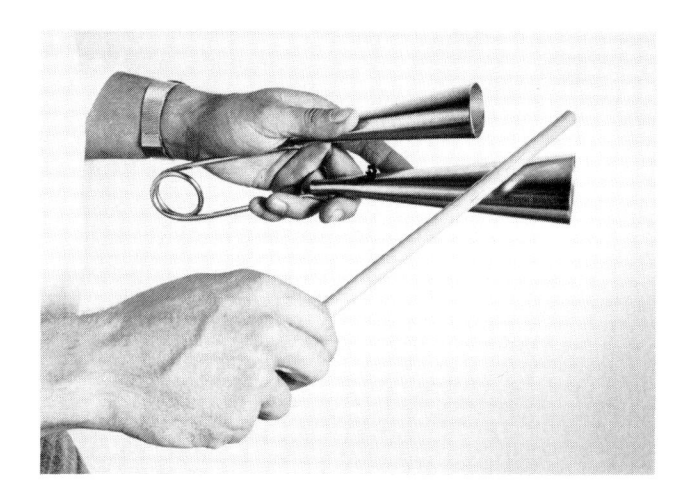

The ago-go bells are used for *Samba, Baion* and *Maracatú*.

Samba

1

2

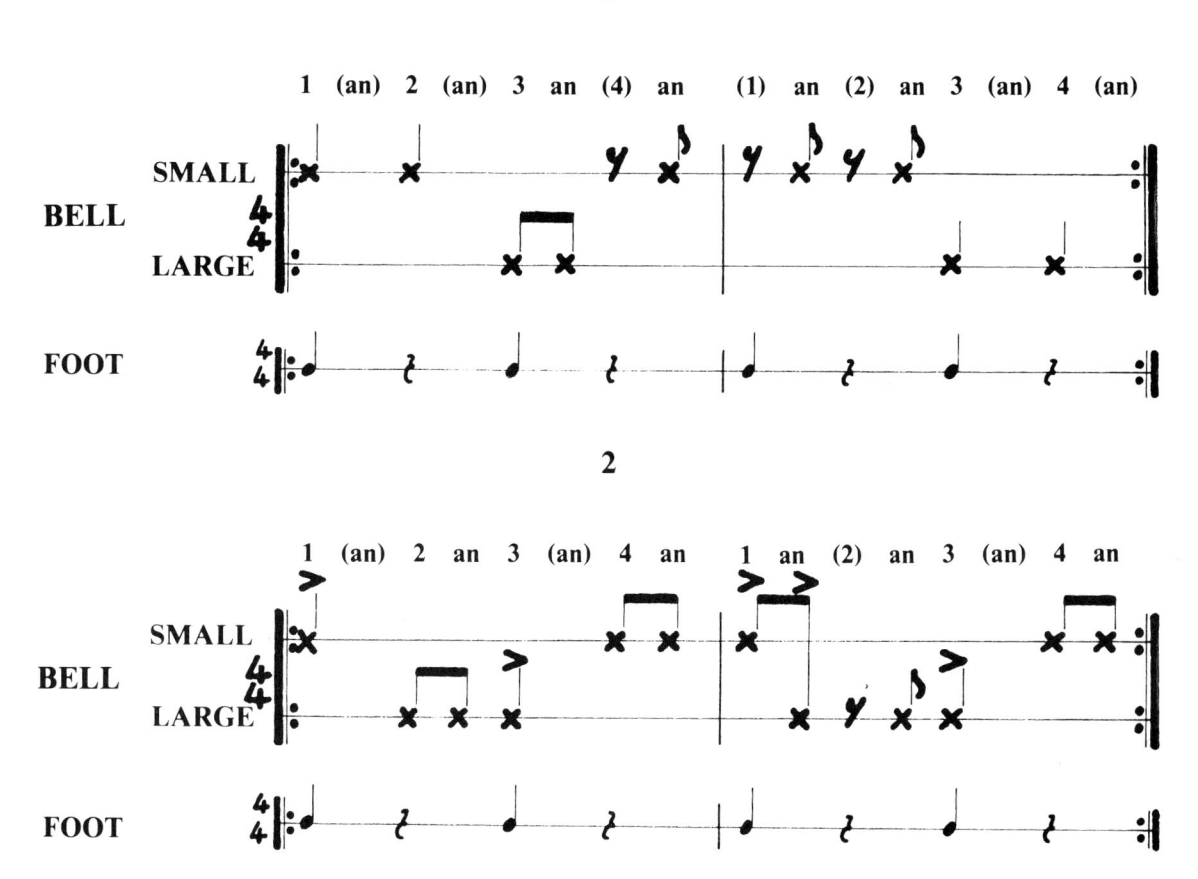

Remember that the rhythms can also start with the second bar first. Refer to page 61.

After practicing the rhythms for a while, you can press the two bells together with the left hand when there is an »empty« eighth note (eighth note rest) between the right hand strokes (refer to the notes).
The clicking sound of the left hand will fill out the rhythm.

$\mathbf{x}$ = right hand stroke $(\mathbf{x})$ = left hand presses the bells together

When buying *ago-go bells*, make sure that the rod between the two bells is flexible enough to allow you to press the bells together easily.

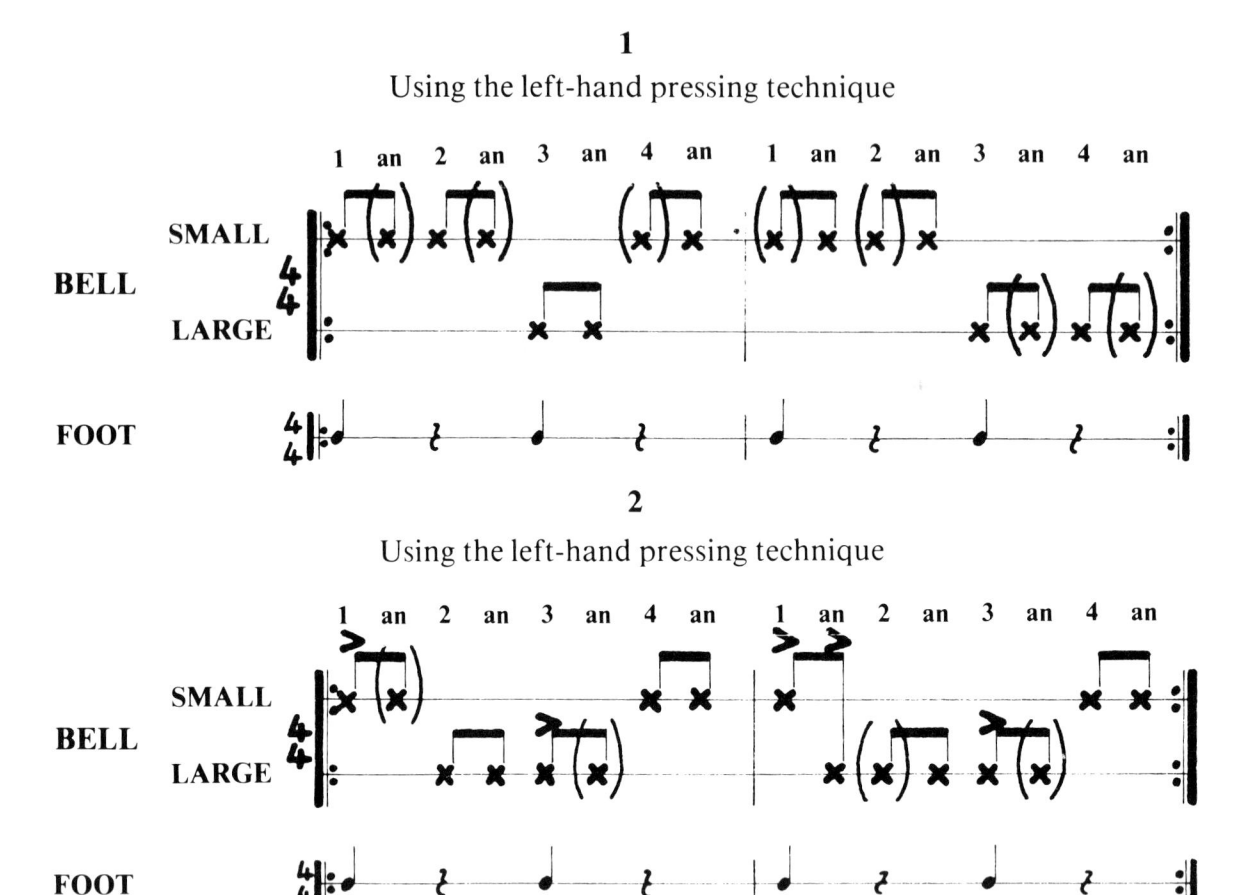

1
Using the left-hand pressing technique

2
Using the left-hand pressing technique

There are certain rhythms such as *Baion* and *Maracatú* in which the bells are not pressed together.

Other ago-go rhythms for Samba

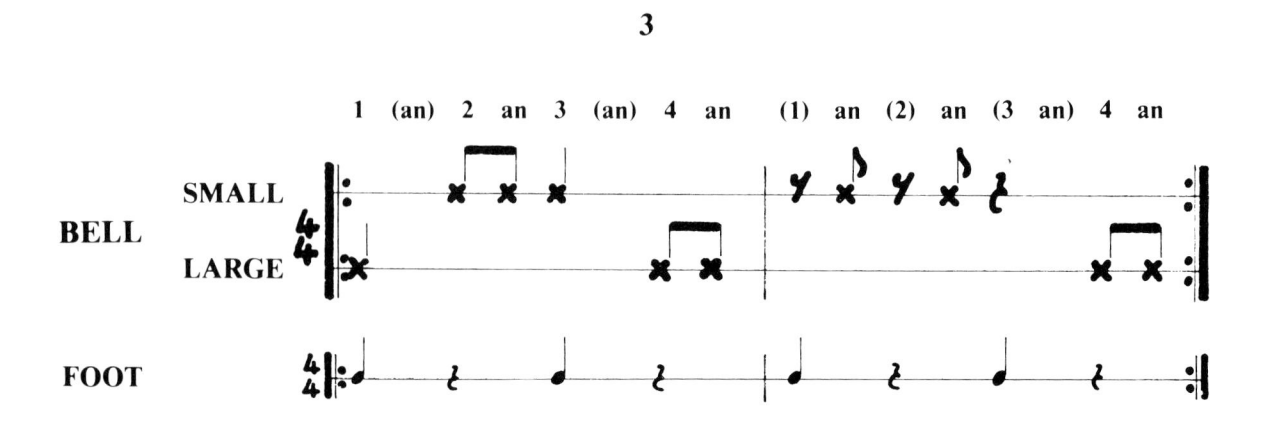

3

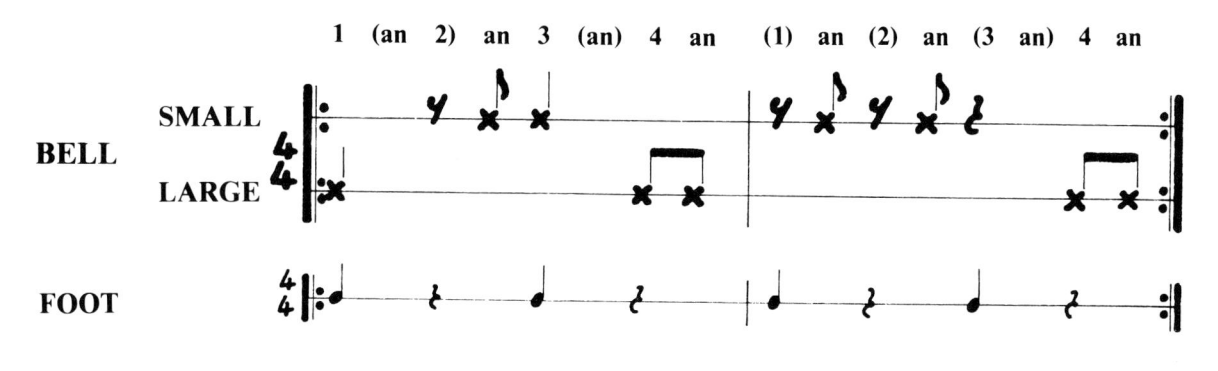

Baion

The bells are *not* pressed together between strokes.

There are other examples of *ago-go rhythms* in part two.

Cuica

The Cuica is a funny yet indispensable rhythm instrument used in the *Samba Batucada*. It sounds like the bark or growl of a dog.

The *cuica* is a single-headed drum. Inside the drum there is a small bamboo stick fastened to the inside of the head. The stick is tied to the skin while still wet, before the head is mounted onto the drum.

The shell of the drum is normally made of metal, but wood and fiberglass are also used.

The drum has tension lugs so that the head can be tuned – the head must be taut in order to produce the correct sounds.

The *cuica* is carried by a strap, e.g. a saxophone strap, around the neck.

The sounds of the *cuica* are produced by rubbing a small damp piece of cloth along the stick inside the drum, using the right hand.
When using short, abrupt movements along the stick, the drum will produce high-pitched sounds like the barking of a dog.
If the movements are lengthened and not applied so abruptly, the sound will become deeper and more drawn out. This effect is used as a variation in rhythms and solos.

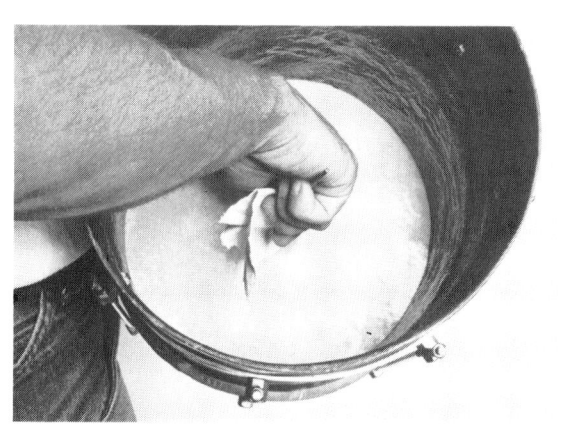

The stick is held between the pinky and the palm to keep it from breaking.

The pitch of the drum is altered by applying pressure to the head with the fingertips of the left hand on top of the head. The fingertips are applied close to the center of the head near the tip of the stick but do not use the fingernails, this will harm the head (see photo).

Release — deep tone

Press — high tone

The tone is deepest when the head is not under pressure.
The harder the pressure on the head, the higher the tone.
To begin with, we will only work with two tones, high and low, but later on you will find a great assortment of tones on the instrument to work with.
The right hand can also change the pitch of the drum and the volume of sound it produces by altering the amount of pressure applied to the stick while rubbing.

Practicing

As with the first exercise, try playing steady eighth notes alternately towards and away from the head. The stick must be held quite loosely, so that the pitch of the drum remains constant, and the rhythm steady and even. The sound should not be forced.
The left hand is not on the head, so the deep tone, which is used as the starting point, is practiced first.

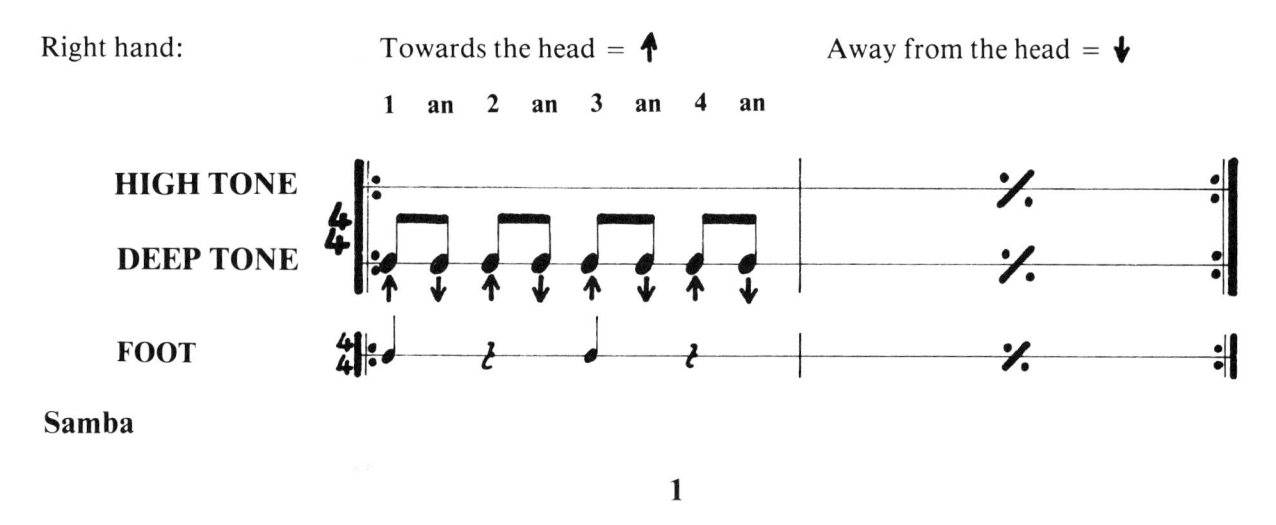

Right hand: Towards the head = ↑   Away from the head = ↓

Samba

1

In this rhythm the first four eighth notes are played with a high tone (left hand presses) and the next four are played with a deep tone (left hand is removed from the head).

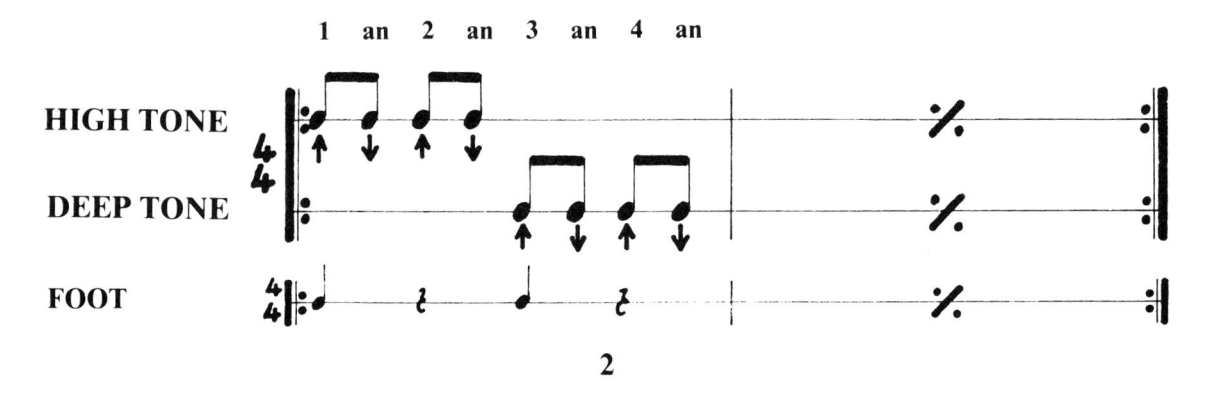

2

In this rhythm the tone is changed one eighth note <u>before</u> **1** and **3**.

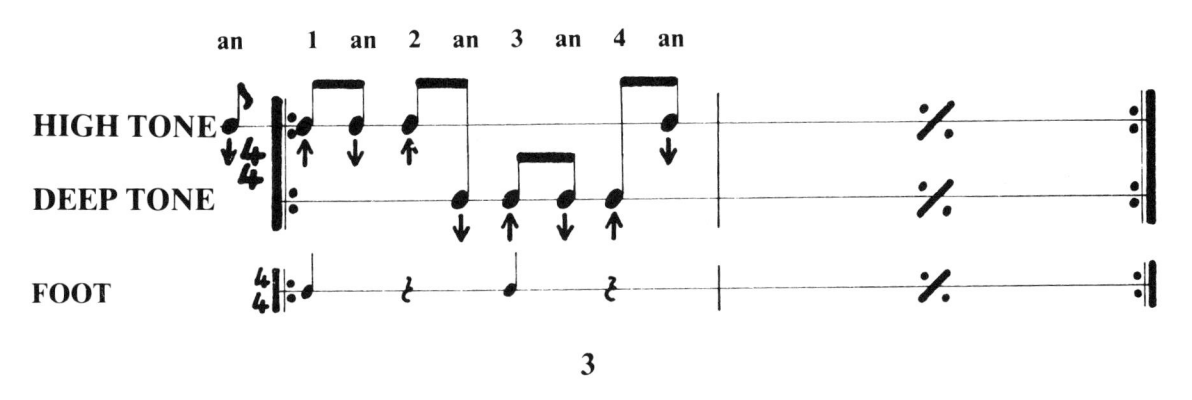

3

The starting point here is the same as in the first exercise, with all the eighth notes played as deep tones. On the count of **1 <u>and</u>** in the second bar the high tone is produced by a short and abrupt movement. The rhythm is continued on the count of **2 <u>and</u>** (deep sound) away from the head. Refer to the arrows for correct movement of the right hand.

(See following page)

(Rhythm example »3« continued)

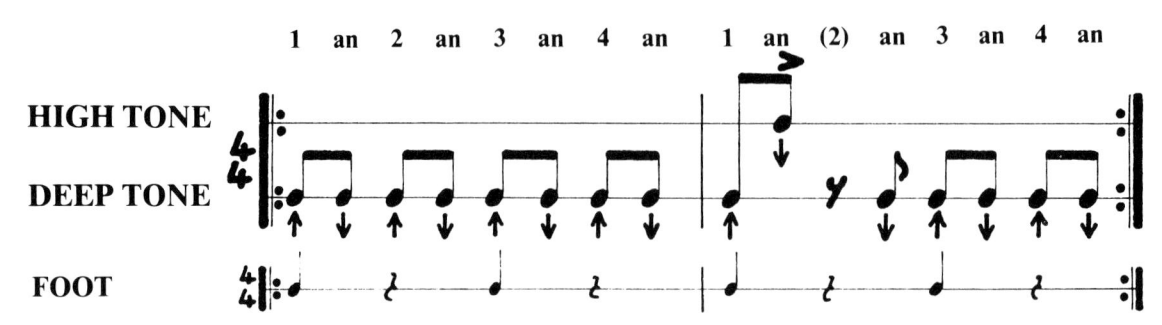

A high tone on the count of **1 and** in both bars can be used as a variation.

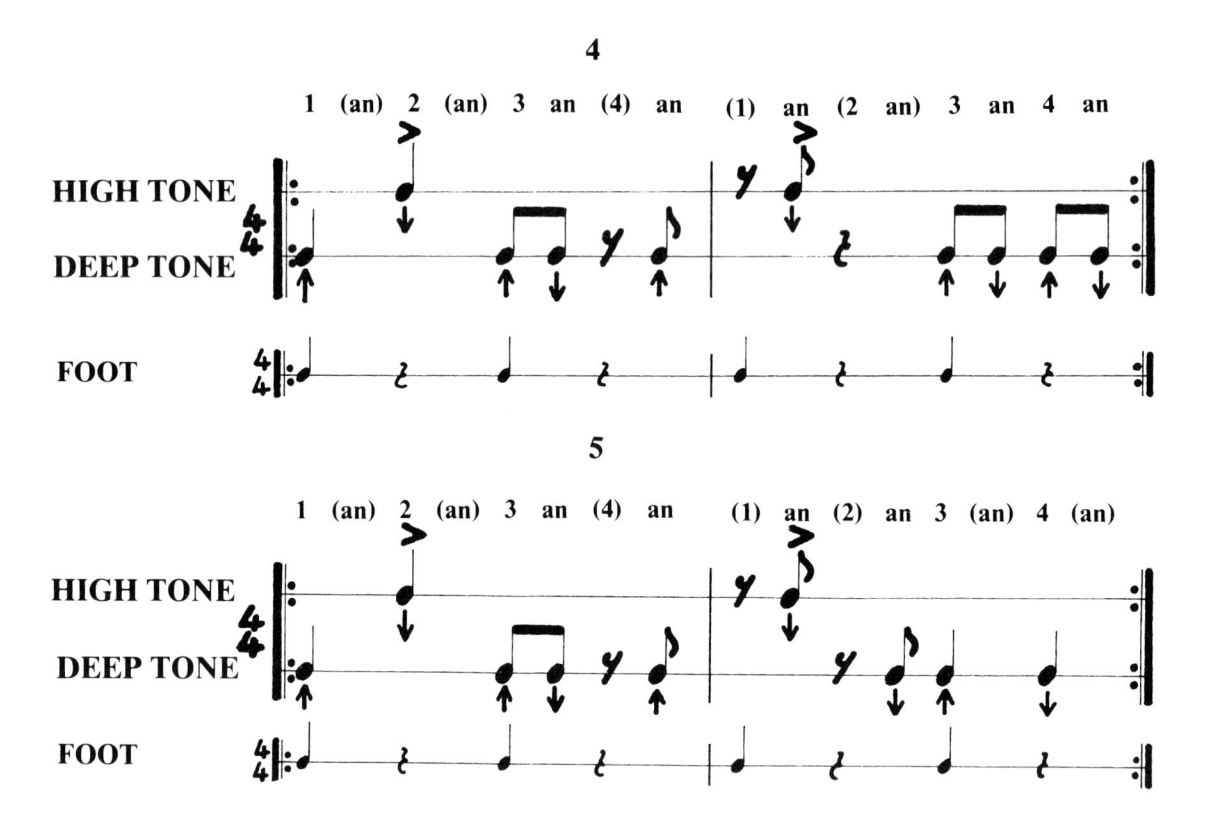

4

5

Pratos (Marching cymbals)

Pratos are one of the many instruments that marching bands have introduced to the Brazilian carnival music.

The cymbals are used as an effect only, and not as a basic rhythm instrument, but the effect is very useful when the music is to be intensified.

One of the typical ways of using *the cymbals* is:
A loud stroke on the count of **1** in the first bar (let the cymbals sustain) and a loud stroke on the count of **3 and** in the second bar, after which *the cymbals* are muffled immediately.

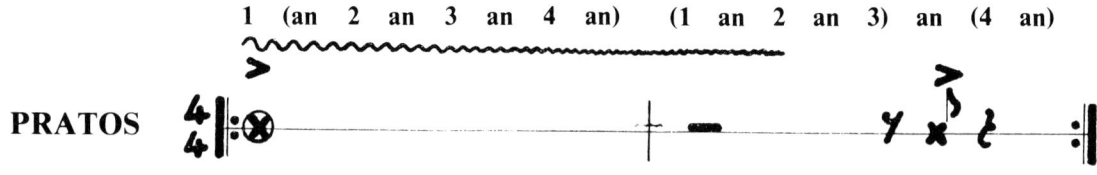

Cabasa

The *cabasa*, also called »**Afoxé**« is a pear-shaped gourd with grooves running down the length of it. The thin end is used as a handle.
Beads are strung on a net around the gourd.

When the net is rotated on the gourd the beads rub against the grooves, producing a high-pitched scraping sound.

The handle of *the cabasa* is held in the right hand and the large part is laid in the left hand as shown in the photo.

Original cabasa

There is also a modern version of the *cabasa*. This consists of a serrated metal plate folded around a wooden wheel with a handle. Instead of beads, small chains with metal balls are used.

This model is more solidly built than *the original cabasa* and will last longer. The sound is sharper and more distinct.

Modern cabasa

Both models are played in the same manner.

The right hand turns *the cabasa* from side to side in a relaxed, easy manner, the turns being played as eighth notes.

1: turn right (clockwise) written in the music as:
and: turn left (counter clockwise) written in the music as:
2: turn right
and: turn left   etc.

From this steady basic rhythm which is played with the right hand only, you produce the accentuated sounds by turning the left hand contra the right with a quick movement (the bead net is rotated in the opposite direction to *the cabasa*, see photo).

The cabasa is NOT lifted from the left hand while playing.

1

Samba and Bossa Nova

Accentuate the counts of <u>**2**</u> and <u>**4**</u> on *the cabasa* in this rhythm (*balance rhythm*).

CABASA

FOOT

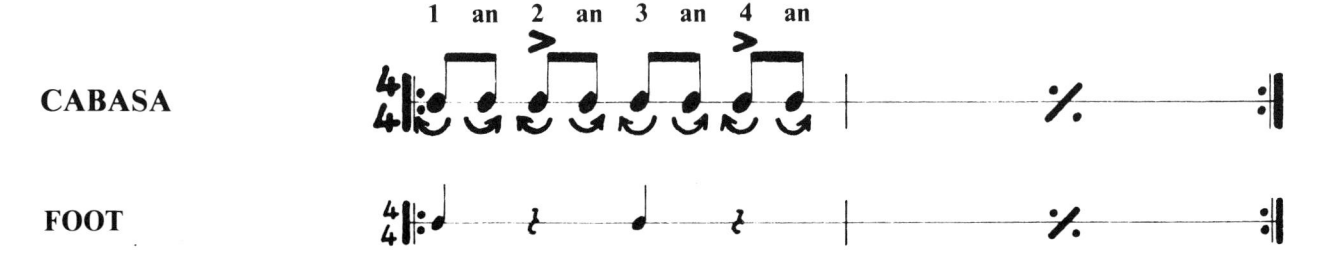

Baion, Samba and Bossa Nova

2

CABASA

FOOT

Note that the movement of the right hand is to the left on **2 and** (vigorous movement).

Samba and Bossa Nova

3

The rhythm will gain a more fluid feeling when the counts **and 1** and **and 3** are played with more accentuation. This means two vigorous movements followed by two lighter movements *(Samba »basic« rhythm)*.

The right hand turns here are opposite to the two preceding rhythms shown:

1:	LEFT turn (counter clockwise)
and:	right turn (clockwise)
2:	left turn
and:	right turn

etc.

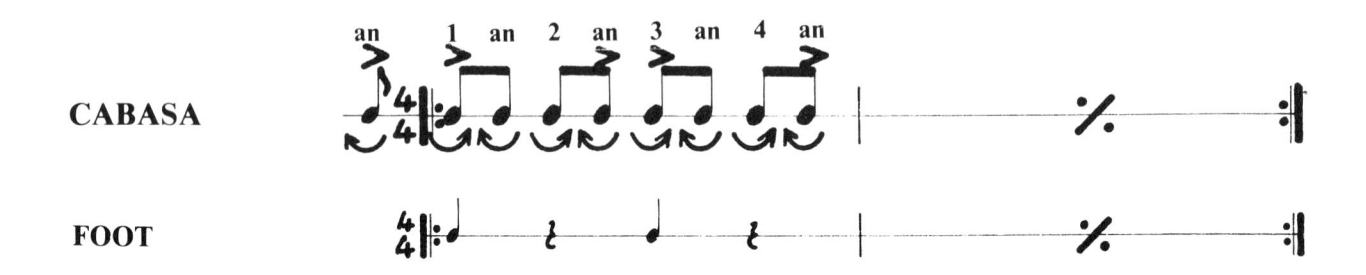

CABASA

FOOT

It will help the movements of the hands to move *the cabasa* towards the body on the **and** beat before **1** and **3** and to move *the cabasa* away from the body on **1** and **3**.

This rhythm requires another instrument to play on the counts **2** and **4**.

Triangle (Triangulo)

The great popularity of the *triangle* started with the *Baion*, in which the instrument has an indispensable function.
Later on the *triangle* also became popular in rhythm sections when playing the *Samba* and *Bossa Nova*.

All sizes of *triangle* can be used, but I would personally recommend the large model (as shown) which is the easiest to handle. It will also produce more sound than the smaller model.

The *triangle* is held in the left hand, and the right hand plays the rhythm with a small beater. The thumb presses the beater against the first joint of the index finger, this finger being bent. The strokes are played using these two fingers only — and the wrist.

The rhythms consist of open and muffled strokes.

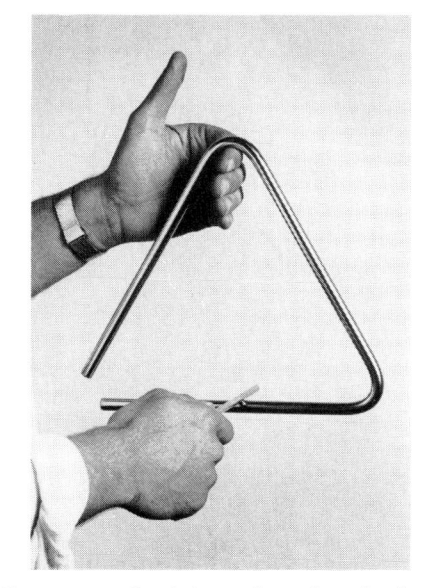

»Open« stroke (o) — the *triangle* rings   Muffled stroke (+)

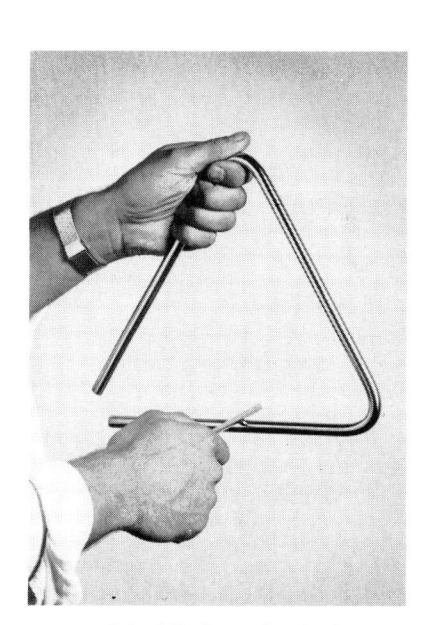

»Open« stroke (o): when the *triangle* is to ring, it should hang on the first joint of the index finger. The fingers should be held together and bent at right angles to the hand (see photo).
The *triangle* must not come to rest on the other fingers — this will muffle the tone.

»Muffled« stroke (+): when muffling the *triangle* the fingers are clenched, so that they all muffle.
It is not sufficient to muffle with the thumb only.

Samba
Slow and medium tempo

1

All the strokes are played on the bottom bar of the *triangle*.
The »open« strokes (o) should be played louder than the »muffled« ones (+).

The basic *triangle* rhythm is played with loud open strokes (o) on **and 1** and **and 3** (refer to »basic« *Samba* rhythm, page 61).

Basic Samba rhythm

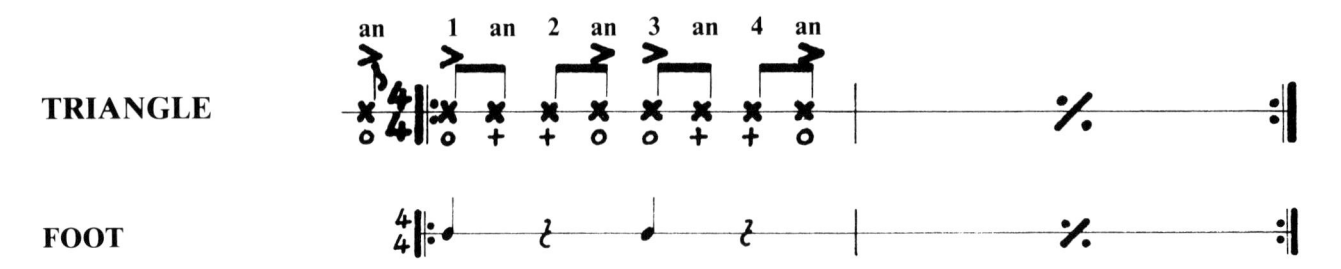

TRIANGLE

FOOT

Fast tempo

When playing in fast tempi, it is impossible to play all the strokes on the bottom bar of the *triangle*. You now have to use two sides of the *triangle:*

The bottom bar and the right hand side (see photo).

It is now a question of getting the beater to play from the bottom bar to the side (up and to the right).

1:	bottom bar
and:	up and to the right
2:	down
and:	up and to the right
etc.	

Practice this rhythm using muffled strokes only.

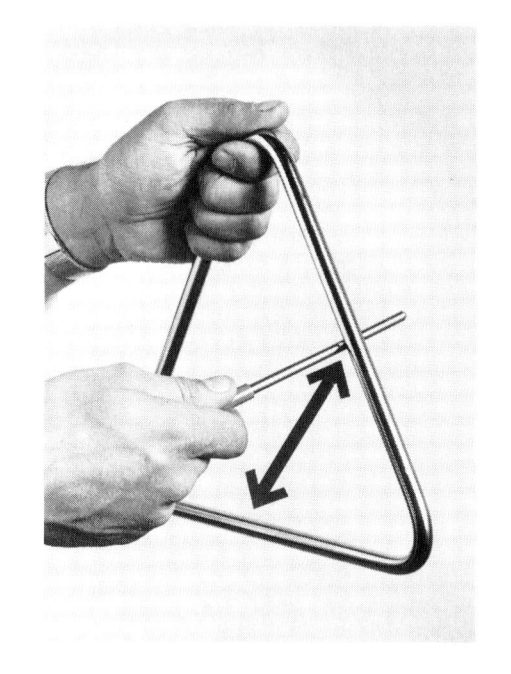

Beater movements (right hand) ↓ = down ↗ = up and to the right

1

This is the same rhythm as in slow tempo but using the other playing technique.

Basic Samba rhythm

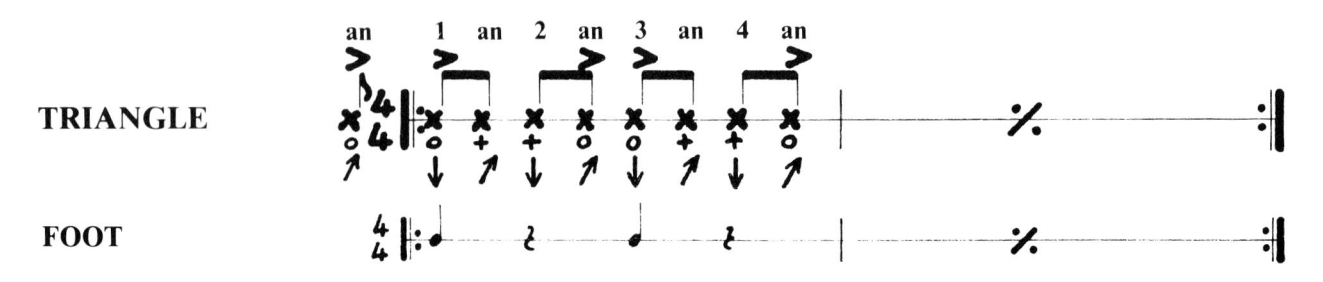

TRIANGLE

FOOT

Rhythm in fast tempo shown in pictures:

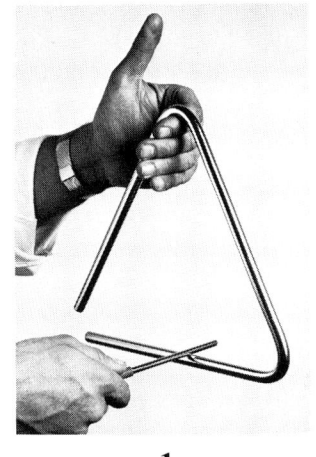

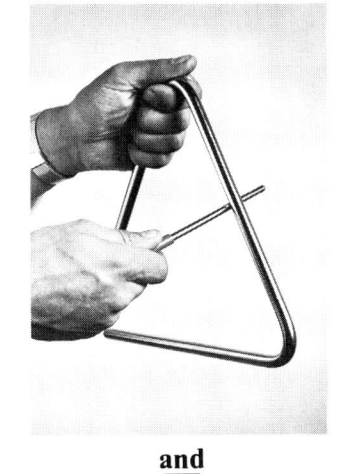

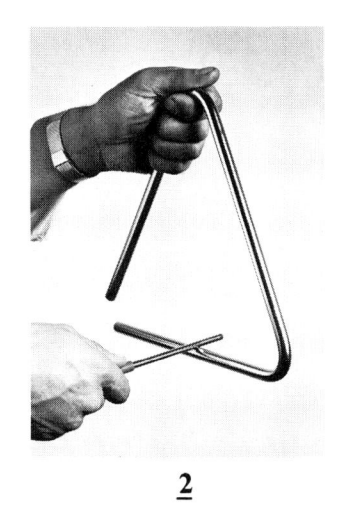

<u>1</u>

<u>and</u>

<u>2</u>

<u>and</u>

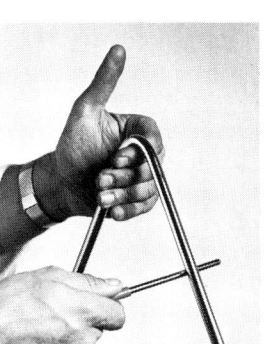

$$\underline{3} = \underline{1}$$
$$3\,\underline{and} = 1\,\underline{and}$$
$$\underline{4} = \underline{2}$$
$$4\,\underline{and} = 2\,\underline{and}$$

Baion, Samba and Bossa Nova

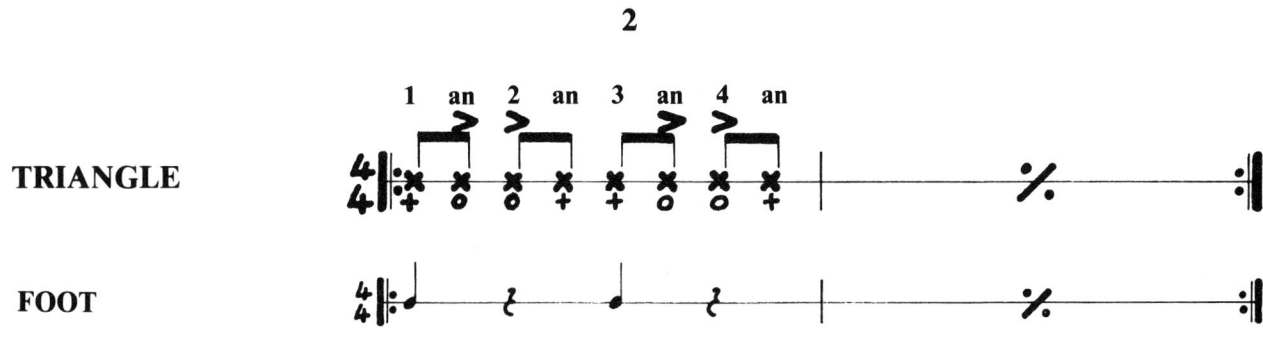

Baion, Maracatú, Samba and Bossa Nova

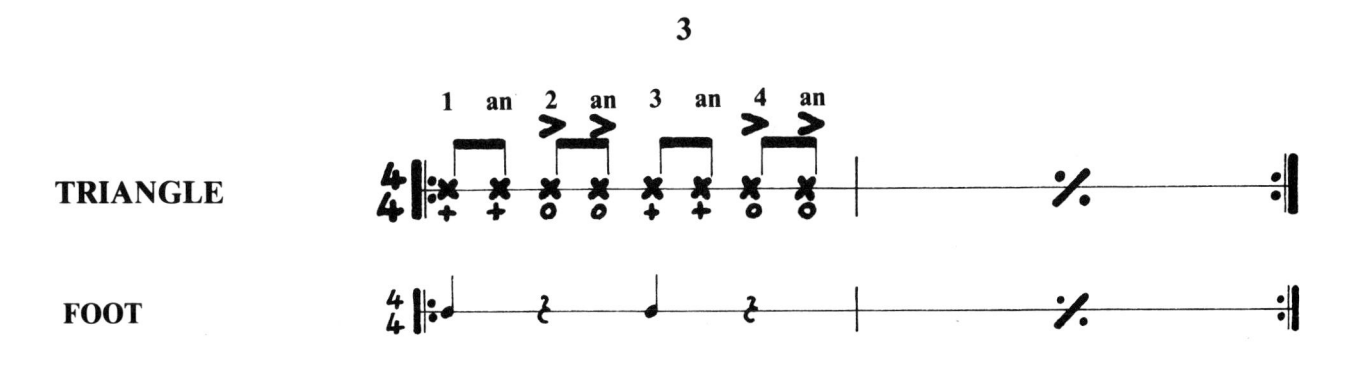

Caixa (snare or marching drum)

The Caixa is a *marching drum* or *snare drum*. The drums can be approximately 10-50 cm (4-20 in) deep and are used with or without *snares*.
The snare is a row of small strings made out of metal or cat-gut, which is strung across the bottom head.

The *caixa* which is now used in almost all the *Samba* and *marching bands* originated from military bands. The drummers in these bands had learned the European playing techniques and transferred them to the Brazilian rhythms.

The rhythms are played with two hands and the normal stick technique is applied.
Concerning stick technique and reading, refer to the recommended drum guide books on page 181.
In order to make the rhythms sound correct, due attention must be paid to the differences in accentuation (>). Playing rim-shots on the accentuated strokes will produce a nice effect but do not play them to excess. Refer to the explanation and photo on page 55.

Samba

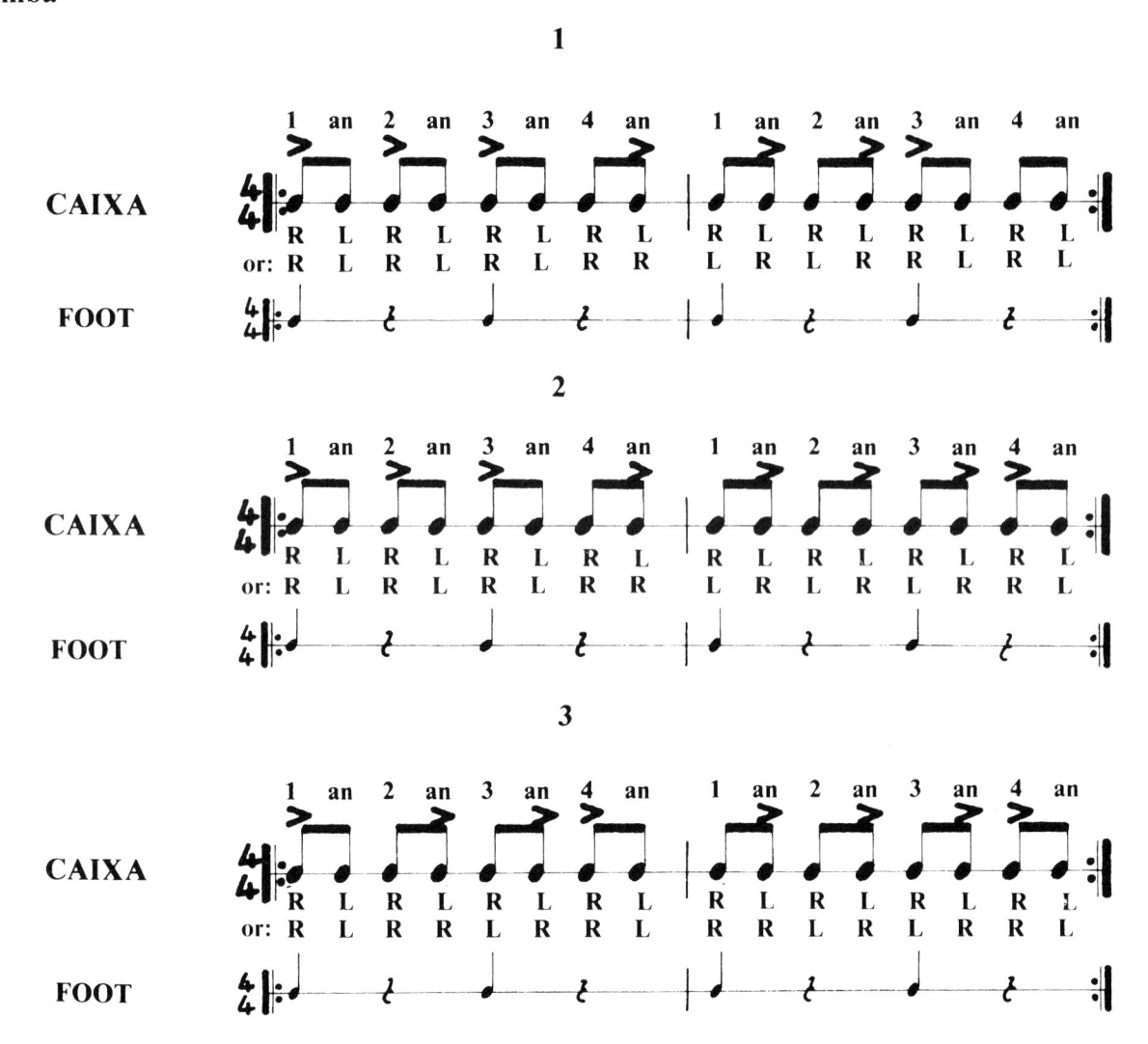

1

CAIXA
R L R L R L R L | R L R L R L R L
or: R L R L R L R R | L R L R L R R L

FOOT

2

CAIXA
R L R L R L R L | R L R L R L R L
or: R L R L R L R R | L R L R L R R L

FOOT

3

CAIXA
R L R L R L R L | R L R L R L R L
or: R L R R L R R L | R R L R L R R L

FOOT

The rhythms can also be played starting with the second bar. Refer to the explanation on page 61. Refer also to the rhythms on page 152.

Caixeta (wood block)

The caixeta is a hollowed block of wood which is used in many of the Brazilian rhythms.
It is held in the left hand and the right hand plays the rhythms with a regular drumstick.

The Cuban claves or a *Chinese temple block* (see photo) can also be used.

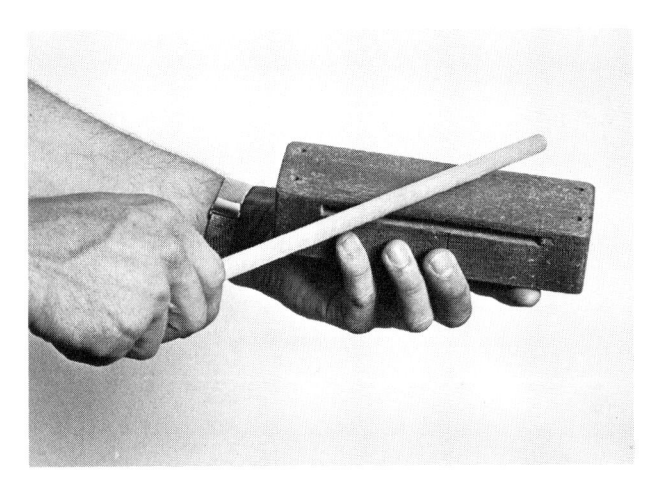

Wood-block   *Chinese temple block*

Samba

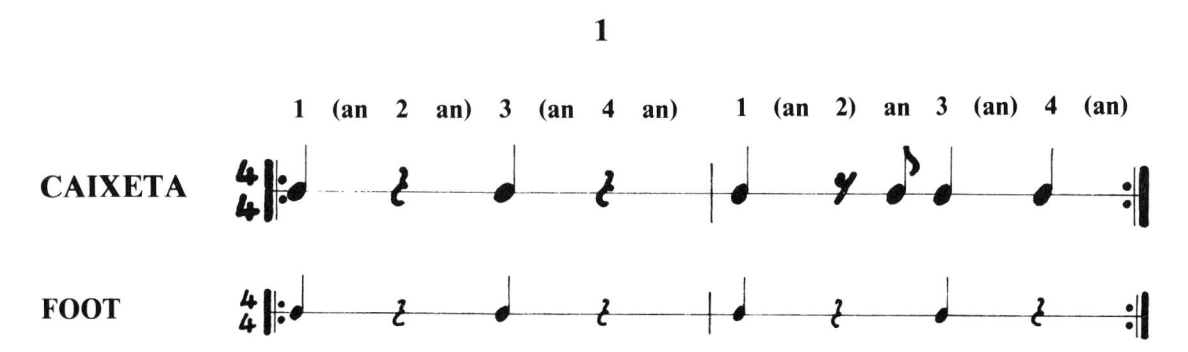

Baion

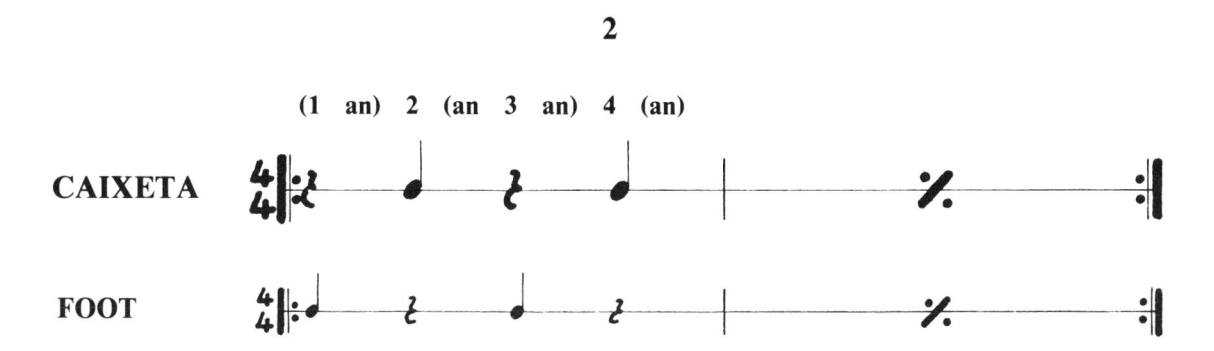

Refer to the rhythms in part two.

Apito (whistle)

The whistle is used for signaling and directing the entire percussion group in *the Samba Batucada*.
This can be a regular *police whistle* or *train whistle*.
There is also an *original Samba whistle* made of wood.
This *whistle* has three tones and has a small hole on each side to alter the pitch of the tone (see photo).
The three-toned whistle can also be made of metal, and is used in the same manner as the wooden model, but the tone is more shrill and distinct.

The whistle is used as a rhythm instrument and as a signal for *breaks* and such.
When *the whistle* is used as a signal, a pre-arranged figure is played on *the whistle* which can, for instance, be a long tone lasting two bars.

There are a great many *whistle-figures*. I have shown one example here but it should only be used as an idea in order to have something to start with.

The figure is changed all the time and is not used constantly throughout the number.

Wood and metal Samba whistle

Samba

APITO

Atabaque (Brazilian conga drum)

Atabaque is the name of *the Brazilian conga drum* that is used in Afro-Brazilian folk music (*»Batuque«*). This drum has been introduced into the popular music of Brazil, and it is in this context that we shall study it.

The playing technique for the Brazilian rhythms is completely different from *the Cuban conga technique*, but the strokes – »open«, »closed« and »slap« – are the same as the strokes shown under »congas« in the Cuban section (page 37-40).
Make sure that you understand the strokes and play them correctly.

Atabaques and congas have in this day and age the same sound and appearance.

Basic Atabaque rhythm for Samba

Samba is played from hand to hand (R-L-R-L...)
The rhythm is based on the »*basic*« *Samba rhythm* which means eighth notes accentuated on the counts **and 1** and **and 3** (**1** and **3** with the upbeats).
On the counts **and 1** with »open« strokes (o) and on the counts **and 3** with closed strokes (+).

The strokes on the counts **and 2** and **and 4** should be very light closed strokes (+).

In order to produce the correct *Samba sound* there should be a considerable difference in the accentuation of the stroke. **This is done by playing the light closed strokes with only a light touch of the finger tips on the head** — without putting pressure on the head (wrist movement). Refer to the photos and explanation on the following page.

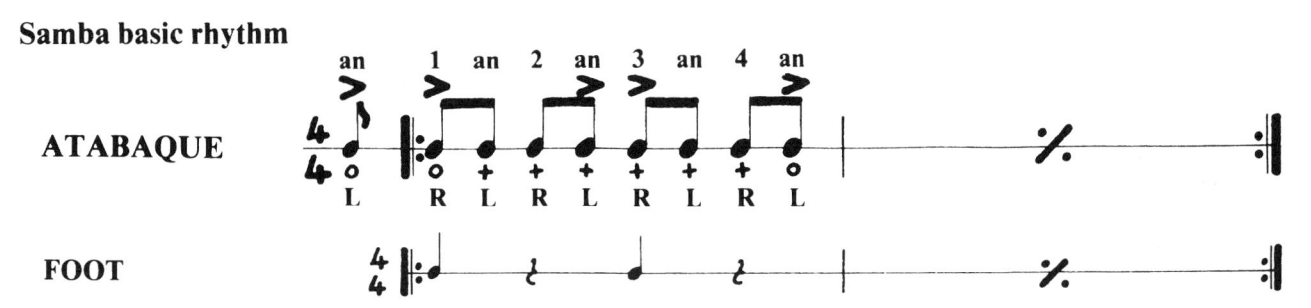

Samba basic rhythm

Remember: The left hand plays the **upbeat** to (the beat before) the counts of **1** and **3**.

	LEFT HAND	RIGHT HAND
and	accentuated »open« stroke (o)	
1:		accentuated »open« stroke (o)
and:	light stroke — »closed« stroke (+)	
2:		light stroke — »closed« stroke (+)
and:	accentuated »closed« stroke (+)	
3:		accentuated »closed« stroke (+)
and:	light stroke — »closed« stroke (+)	
4:		light stroke — »closed« stroke (+)
and:	accentuated »open« stroke (o)	

See photos on the following page.

LEFT HAND

Atabaque rhythm

and 1 (upbeat to 1)
Accentuated »open« stroke (o).

AND

and 2
Soft »closed« stroke (+).
Light stroke using the fingertips only.
Remember to relax the wrist.

AND

and 3
Accentuated »closed« stroke (+).
Using the flat of the hand.

AND

and 4
Soft »closed« stroke (+).
Light stroke using the fingertips only.
Remember to relax the wrist.

AND

or Samba

RIGHT HAND

1

$\underline{1}$
Accentuated »open« stroke (o).

2

$\underline{2}$
Soft »closed« stroke (+).
Light stroke using the fingertips only.
Remember to relax the wrist.

3

$\underline{3}$
Accentuated »closed« stroke (+).
Using the flat of the hand.

4

$\underline{4}$
Soft »closed« stroke (+).
Light stroke using the fingertips only.

4 <u>and</u> = <u>and</u> 1

Atabaque basic Samba rhythm (Continued)

The Samba rhythm should have a wave-like quality. Down on the accentuated strokes and up on the lighter strokes.
Try to use your arms to illustrate this when playing, though not overly exaggerated.

When playing variations it is advisable to refer back to *the »basic« rhythm* once in a while to make sure that the basic *Samba feeling* is there.

2

The »closed« stroke on the count of **3** in the basic rhythm is now changed to a »slap« stroke (s). The preceding stroke is still an accentuated »closed« stroke (+) with the left hand.

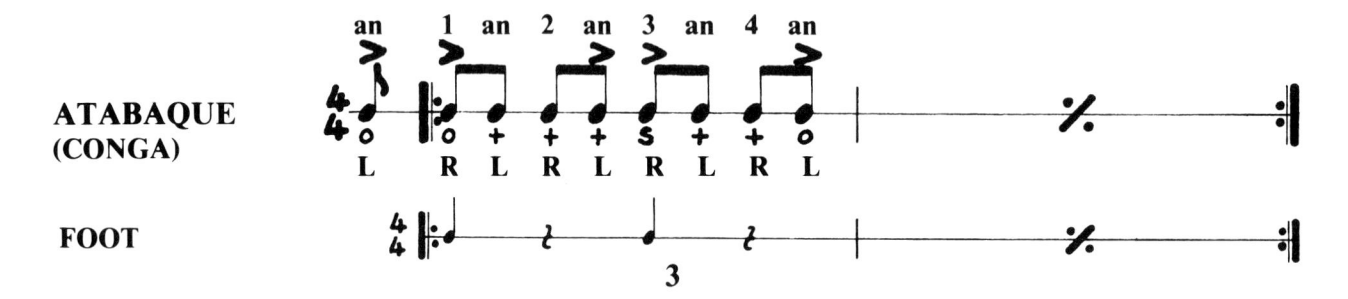

3

This rhythm covers a two bar period.
The first bar is the same as in the basic rhythm. The second bar has a light »closed« stroke (+) on the count of **1** and an accentuated »open« stroke (o) on the count of **1 and** the remainder of the bar is identical to *the »basic« rhythm*.
Be sure to play the two »open« strokes with the left hand **4 and** and **1 and** as precisely as possible.

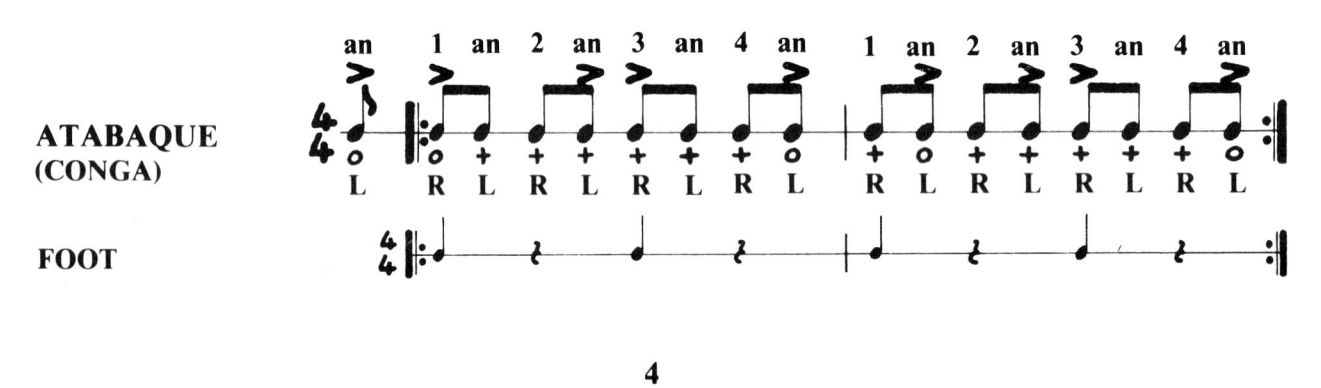

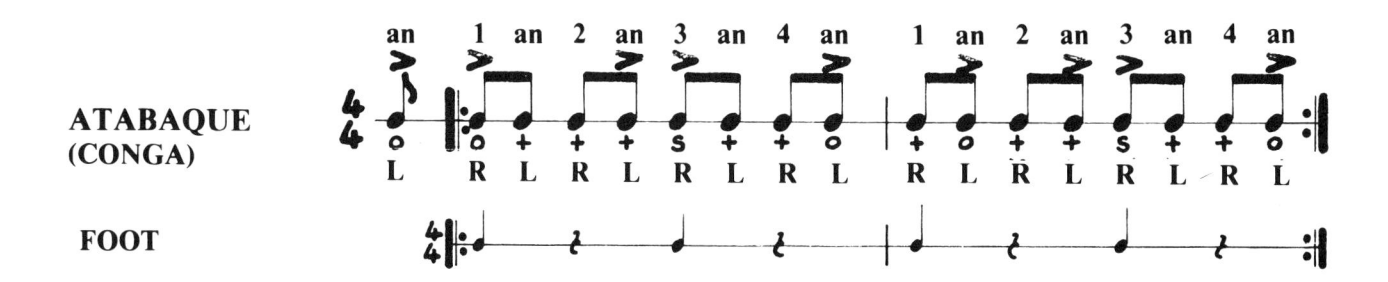

4

The same rhythm, but now with »slap« strokes (s) on the count of **3** in each bar.

The following rhythms use the »slap« stroke (s) played with either hand (refer to the explanation on page 40). When the rhythms are played in fast tempo the »slap« strokes should be played open (refer to page 40) in order not to impede the flowing feeling of the rhythms.

Remember that the soft strokes should only be played as a soft tap using the underside of the fingertips (wrist movement).

Practice the rhythms alternately with the »basic« rhythm so as not to lose the basic *Samba feeling*.

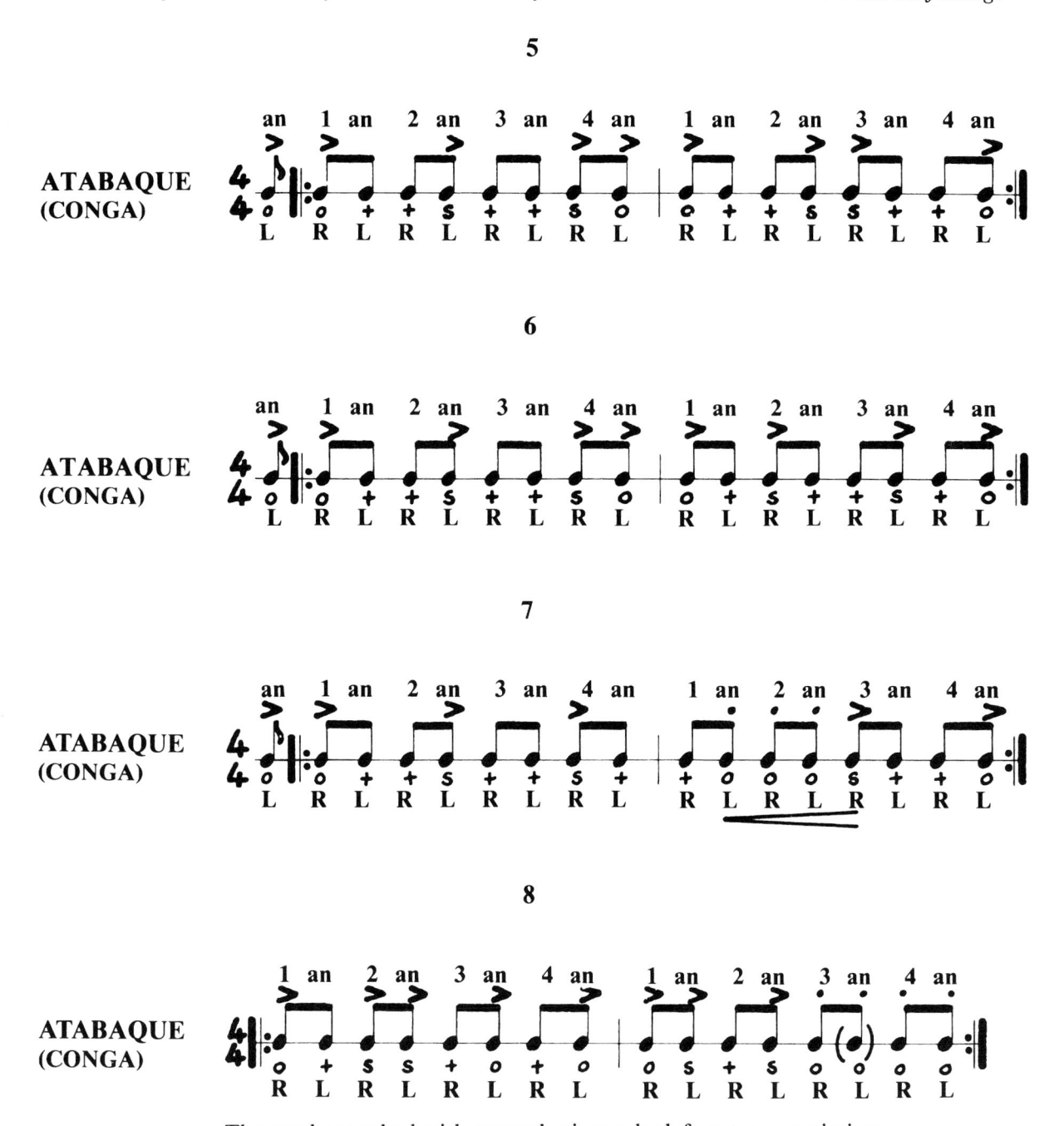

5

ATABAQUE (CONGA)

6

ATABAQUE (CONGA)

7

ATABAQUE (CONGA)

8

ATABAQUE (CONGA)

The stroke marked with parenthesis can be left out as a variation.

Rhythm »4« and other rhythms in which the »slap« strokes are used can also be used when playing *Rock* rhythms with a *Samba feeling*.

The rhythms can also be played starting with the second bar first. Refer to the explanation on page 61.

Bongos for Samba

The Cuban *bongo drums* are often used in the more modern variety of Brazilian music. One example of how *bongos* are used together with other rhythm instruments is shown in the *Samba Moderno* in the second part of the book.

Refer to the Cuban section on page 29 for *bongo strokes*.

The *basic bongo rhythm* for *Samba* is based on the *basic Samba rhythm*, meaning accentuated strokes on the counts **and 1** and **and 3**.

In order to acquire the correct feeling in the rhythm, the lighter strokes should be played with a very light stroke of the finger tips on the head.

The rhythm is played from hand to hand starting with the right hand on the count of **1** or with the left hand on the **and** before **1**.

The counts **4 and 1** are to be played on the large drum (to the right).
All the other strokes are played on the small drum (to the left).

Samba

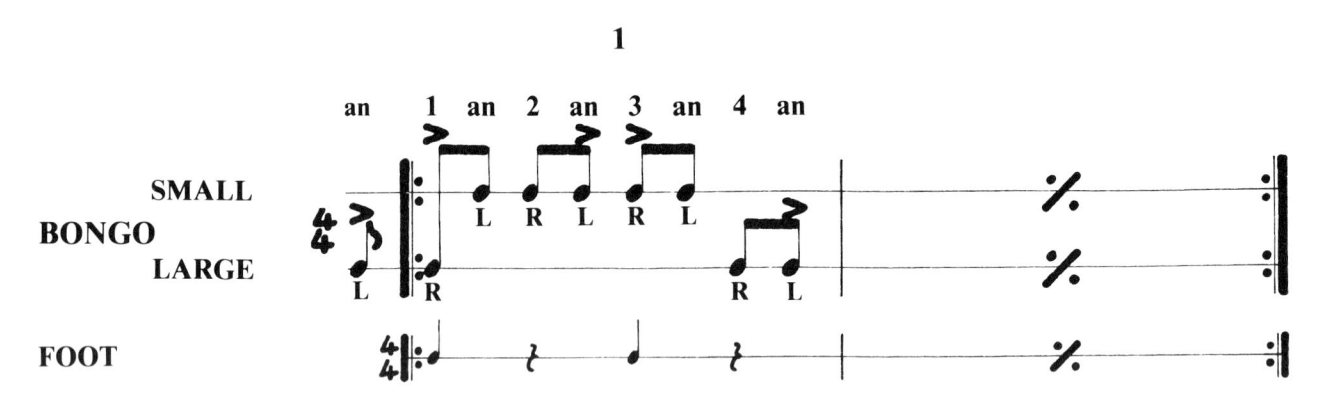

In order to obtain the correct feeling in the rhythm, the light strokes should be played with a very light stroke of the fingertips on the head.

	Small drum LEFT HAND	RIGHT HAND	Large drum LEFT HAND	RIGHT HAND
and:	(upbeat)		accentuated stroke	
1:				accentuated stroke
and:	light stroke			
2:		light stroke		
and:	accentuated stroke			
3:		accentuated stroke		
and:	light stroke			
4:				light stroke
and:			accentuated stroke	

91

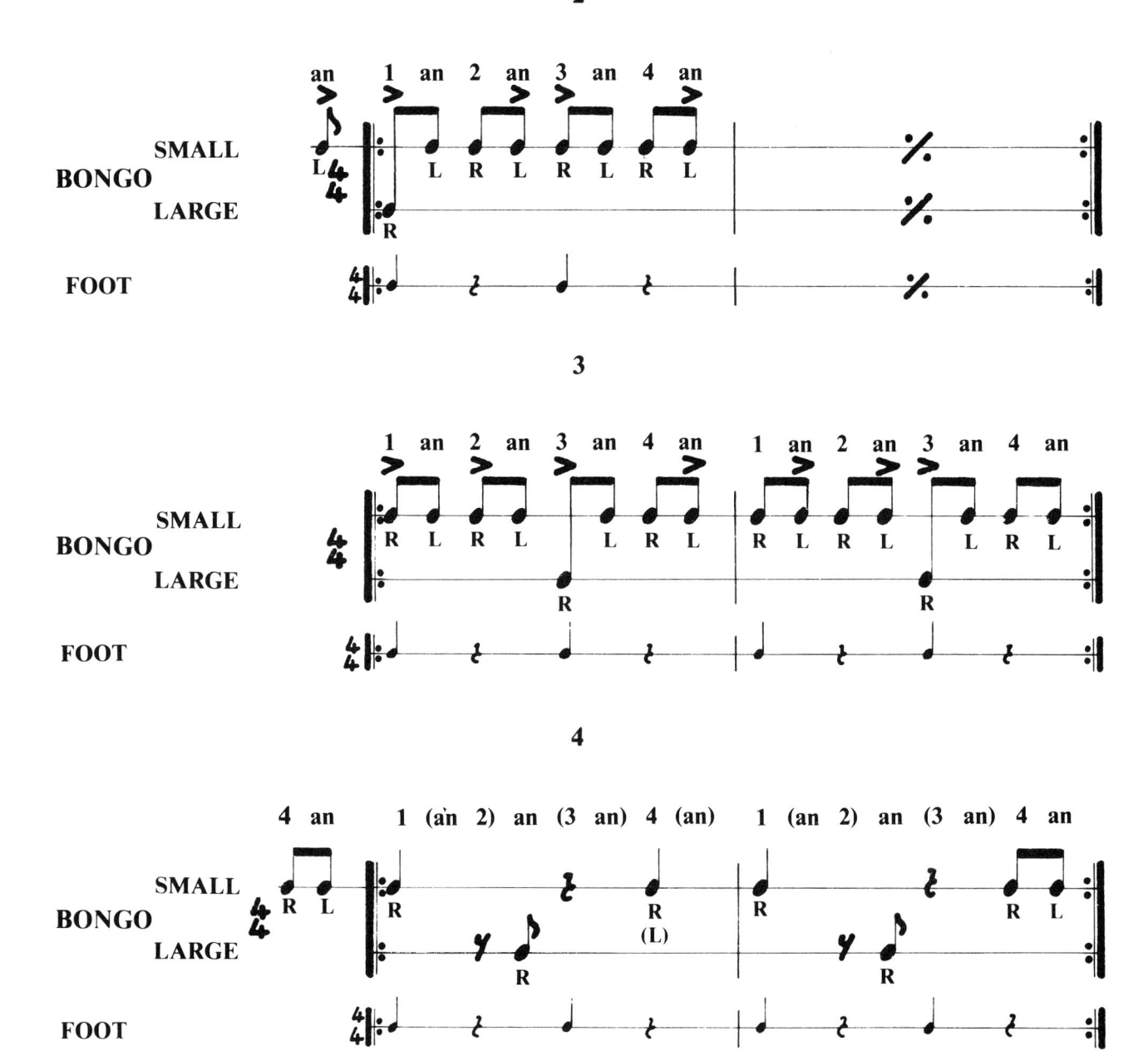

Caixa de Fósforos

The proper rhythm instruments are not always at hand, but if you have seen Brazilians at parties or other social gatherings you can rest assured that the lack of actual instruments is of no great importance. *Caixa de Fósforos* is one of the solutions, along with other such impromptu instruments as *plates, knives, tables, bottles* etc.

Caixa de Fósforos is quite simply a *box of matches* with just the right amount of matches in it to enable them to move back and forth in the box.

The left hand holds the box using the thumb and index finger on the ends with the picture side facing upwards.
Play two strokes **and 1** with the thumb of the right hand on the flat side of the box.
The left hand then moves the box to the left (**1 and**) and to the right (**2**) so the matches hit the sides of the box.
Two more strokes with the thumb (**and 3**) and the box is moved from side to side (**and 4**).

When playing with larger groups and for electric music I would recommend an *economy-size matchbox!*
Remember, never go to town without your *Caixa de Fósforos*.

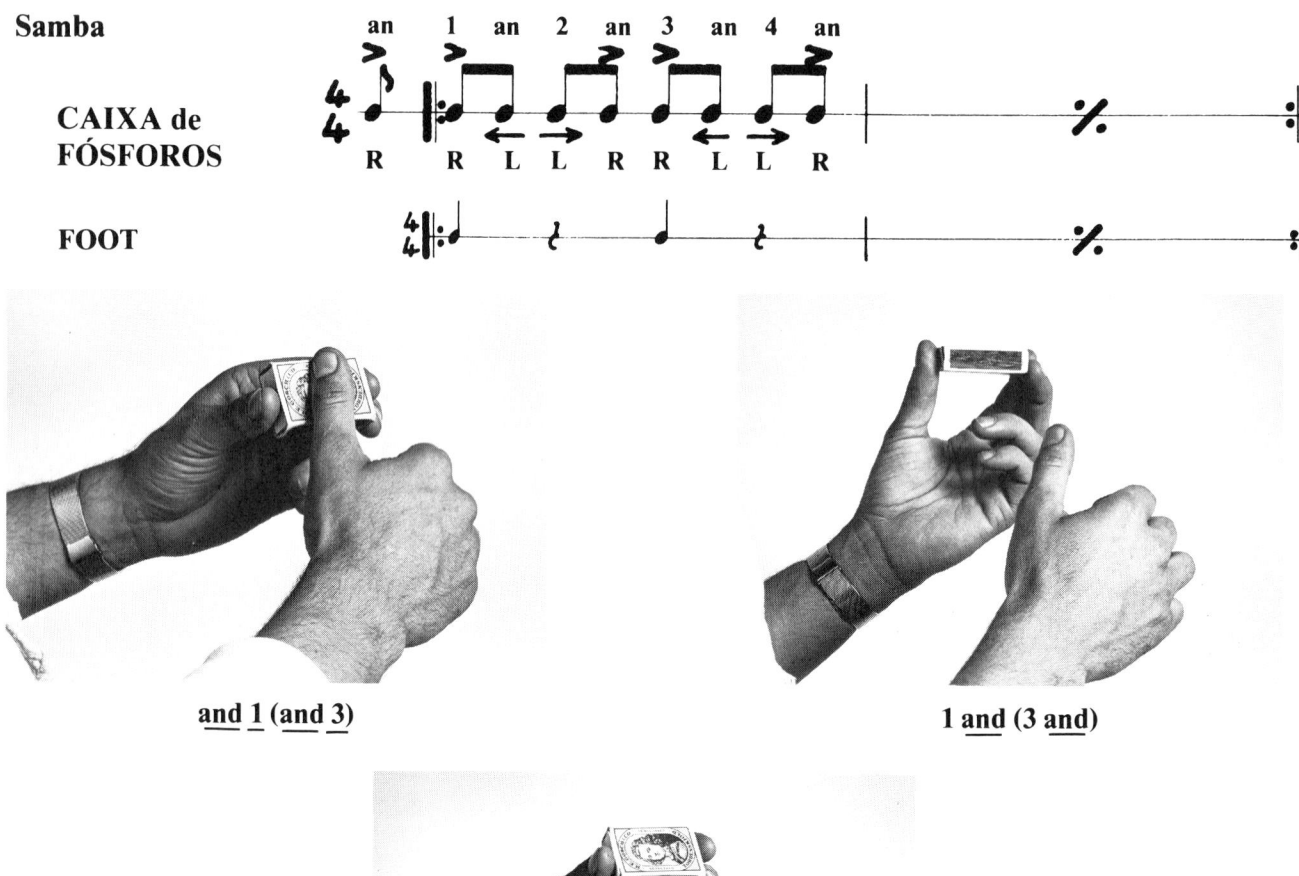

Samba

and 1 (and 3)

1 and (3 and)

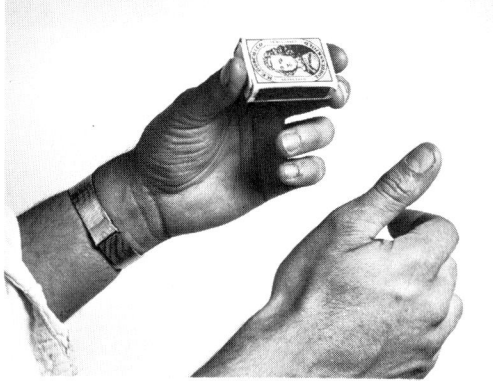

2 (4)

Other Brazilian rhythm instruments

Berimbau

The *Berimbau* was originally an African instrument which later became part of the Afro-Brazilian ritual »*Capoeira*« (see page 145).

The Berimbau consists of a bow with a metal wire and a gourd which is used as a resonator.

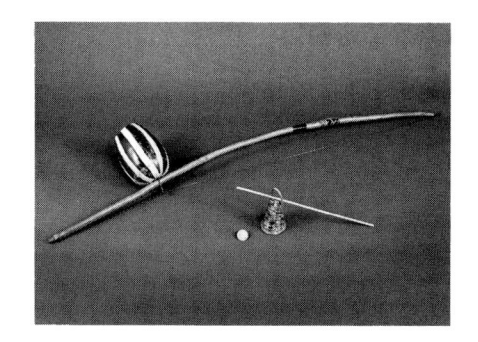

The pitch is altered by pressing a coin against the wire. The bow and coin are held as shown in the picture.

The right hand holds a thin stick and a small »*caxixi*« (see below).

The stick plays the rhythm on the wire and *the caxixi* produces a shaker-like effect at the same time.

By moving the gourd back and forth with the open end placed against the stomach, you can produce a »wah-wah« type sound.

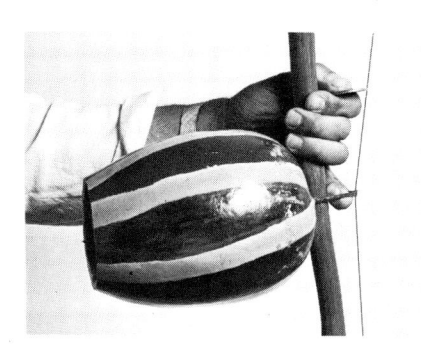

Caxixi

The Caxixi is, like *the Berimbau*, an instrument from the music of *the »Capoeira«*.

It consists of a straw basket which is woven up from a base made from a piece of gourd. The contents are small shells or pebbles.

The larger model is used as a type of *maracas* (see picture).

The small model is used together with *the berimbau* (refer to top of page).

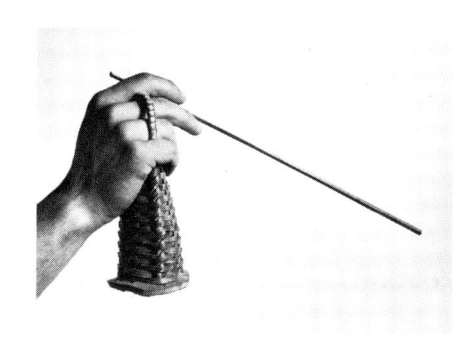

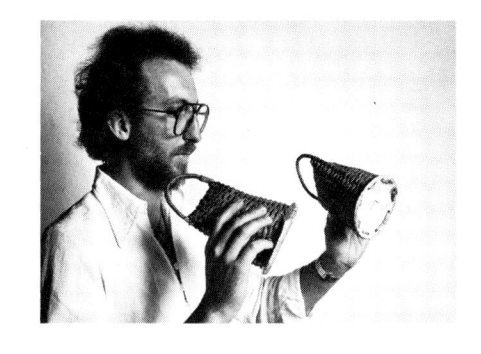

Listen to the examples on cassette number 2.

PART TWO

Cuban and Brazilian rhythms

Calypso from Trinidad

Cuban rhythms

Introduction

Cuban music is a mixture of African and Spanish culture with strong roots in the rhythms that were brought to Cuba by African slaves.
The music is performed with a perfect combination of discipline and freedom, and the emphasis is on rhythms and feelings and not on intricate melodic and harmonic structures.

Over the years Cuban music has become divided up into two different styles: »*Folklorico*« and »*Popular*«.

Folklorico: 1) The folk music from the rural areas of Cuba, a style which was originally based on Spanish traditions. 2) The music from the religious customs which the African slaves had brought with them to Cuba.

Popular: Popular music of an urban nature, developed in the larger towns and cities with Havana as the core. This style is often a further development (or rather a simplification) of the folk music.

It is hard to differentiate between these two groups or styles because many of the older types of music are still popular, and also because many of the new types of music have strong ties to the old folk music styles. Further explanation is thus required, as the type of music played is also determined by which type of orchestra is playing the music.

The Rumba groups and the carnivals
The essential ingredients of parties and carnivals held in Cuba are the rhythms, the songs and the dances. A »*Rumbon*« is a gathering where *Rumba* is played on a variety of *tumbadoras* (*congas* and *tumbas*) and *quinto*. In the past, wooden boxes (»*cajones*«) were used instead of drums and the rhythm was called »*Rumba de Cajón*« – »Box Rumba« (refer to *Rumba* page 122).
To accompany the rhythms there are one or more vocal soloists and a chorus (*coro*). When the rhythm begins, the theme (*el canto*) is sung, after which the »*call and answer*« section of the song begins, which is a section that alternates between the *coro* and an improvised part from the solo vocalist. This type of *coro-solo* is an indispensable part of Afro-Cuban music and is still an important part of the modern arrangements.

Comparsa
La Comparsa is the name of the communal street dance of the Cuban carnival. *La Comparsa* was originally the slave's ritual march which, in Colonial times, was only allowed on special occasions.
The rhythm played is *La Conga* and the instruments used are: *congas, cowbells, frying pans, bass drums, brake drums, trumpets, cornets* and much more.

Musica Guajira – refer to page 116.

Son
The one Cuban style of music which has had the most influence on Latin music as we know it today is called *Son*. *Son* is a style based on a combination of the Spanish guitar/vocal tradition and African rhythms. In the older *Son groups* the vocals were accompanied by guitar and »*tres*«, which is a guitar fitted with three double strings. The bass was often played by two instruments: a »*marimbula*« which is a large type of the African thumb piano called »*kalimba*«, and the »*botija*«, which is an oil-jug with a small opening on top. A small hole is drilled in the side of the jug and by blowing over one of the holes, a deep bass sound is produced. The pitch of the tone is changed by moving the hand over the opposite hole.

The rhythm instruments used were *bongos, maracas, guiro* and *claves.*
The Son groups are the link between Cubas rural folk music and the urban popular music – the style that is most familiar to us.
During the 1920s *the Son* grew in popularity in the urban areas. The music started to change structure slightly and the groups playing it were expanded, with more percussion. The trumpet, which was evidently an inspiration from the playing style of the Spanish military bands was also introduced.
There are many well-known and important groups from this period, among others: *Septeto Nacional* and *Septeto Habanero*, and the term »*Septeto*« is often used to describe the urban *Son style.*

The above mentioned types of orchestras are still very much in function at present in Cuba and the term *Son* is now often used as a general term for the traditional Cuban music.

Montuno
The Son groups started using a »*B-section*«, called *Montuno*, in their arrangements. In this section the melody stops and the rhythm becomes more predominant and pulsating. *The piano* or *the »tres«* plays rhythmic patterns called »*guajeos*« which are repeated consistently over a two or four bar period. *The bass* plays a steady pattern (»*tumbao*«) and *the bongo player* changes from *bongos* to *the hand cowbell.*
In this section the rhythm section forms a foundation for solos for both melody instruments and percussion. Behind these solos there is oftentimes a chorus (*coro*), or an alternating chorus and vocal- or instrumental soloist (*coro-solo*).
This »*Montuno*« section is still an important part of the modern arrangements and is used now by all the different types of orchestras.
The term *Montuno* was already used in the old *Son style - Son Montuno. Monte* means mountain and this style comes from the mountain areas in the Oriente district in eastern Cuba.

Conjunto
Conjunto is the successor of the *Son group* and is probably the most well-known of the *Afro-Cuban* orchestra and music styles.
The personnel of the group consists of three or four *trumpets, piano* or *tres, bass, congas, bongos, guiro* and possibly *maracas* and *claves.*
The most well-known *Conjuntos* were lead by Arsenio Rodriguez, Miguel Matamoros and Felix Chapottin.

Charanga
Charanga is another more European influenced style that arose in the Oriente province of Cuba.
Instead of the trumpets of *the Conjuntos, the Charanga orchestras* used *violins*, and the melody line was played by the Cuban *flute* which is made of ebony.
The rhythm section consisted of *bass, piano, timbales, guiro* and *congas* but **without** *bongos.*
Orquesta Tipica is another term for these orchestras that introduced such rhythms as: *Cha-cha-cha, Danzon* and *Pachanga.*
The term »*Orquesta Tipica*« does however have a double meaning, in that it was originally the name of an old type of orchestra which used strings and brass/woodwinds.

Apart from the traditional orchestra types, there are also a variety of combinations that, on account of instrument combinations and the influence of other types of music, deviate from the aforementioned styles.
Already at this time the trumpet players in *the Son groups* had started to play with a slight jazz feeling due to the influence from North America.

The Big Bands/Jazzband Cubana/Banda
Jazz also introduced *saxophones* to the Cuban orchestras. Large dance bands arose in which *the saxophone section* was used to play the steady pattern »*guajéo*« that the *piano* or *tres* had played until then. This figure is also known as »*montuno*« and »*tumbao*«.

The modern rhythm section
There are still orchestras that use the traditional rhythm sections from the *Son, Conjunto* and *Charanga orchestras* but as mentioned before, there are a great number of combinations that are not easily defined. The instrument combination that is most typical now is: *piano, bass, conga/tumba, timbales, bongos, guiro* and possibly *maracas* and *claves*. Remember that *the bongo player* changes to *hand cowbell* in *the Montuno sections*.

Descarga
Descarga is a piece of music of improvised nature in which the rhythm section plays alone, leaving room for different rhythm instruments to play soli.
In contrast to *Montuno*, which is mentioned earlier, *Descarga* is a self-sufficient arrangement. *The Descharge* and *the Montuno* section can be played in any rhythm and can change between different rhythms and tempi.
This section of rhythm can be played with a background of *bass* and *piano (or tres)* these also being part of the rhythm section.

Descarga can also mean a *jam session* in which a steady horn riff is played. The major function is still for soloing, but in this case both rhythm and melody instruments are able to play solo.

Cierre (break)
Collective rhythmic figures are sometimes played by parts of the rhythm section, the entire rhythm section, or the whole group.
These figures are known as »*cierre*« or »*breaks*«, and are used when changing from one section of an arrangement to another.
Because of the vast number of tonal possibilities of each rhythm instrument, each player should decide how to play *the breaks*.
Whether the player in question wants to play the rhythmic figure from hand to hand or with both hands at the same time (on two drums) is a matter of individual choice, depending on the tempo and the sound desired.

Salsa
Salsa is a Spanish word meaning *sauce*. The term is used in and about Cuban music and should be elucidated in two ways:

1: The expression *Salsa* has been used in Cuba for many years as an exclamation shouted when, for instance a musician plays a solo. I have heard the expression on old recordings with, for instance Septeto Nacional.

2: *Salsa* has recently acquired yet another meaning.
The popularity of Cuban music in the United States and especially in New York was triggered off by the *Rumba craze* in the thirties. The large Latin American population in New York has kept the music thriving since then. Even though the population is a combination of immigrants from Puerto Rico, Cuba, Panama, Columbia and many other countries, Cuban music has always been the most popular style.
The term *Salsa* came about in New York in the late sixties and early seventies, now being used as a special name for this city's version of Cuban music — obviously jazz-inspired and influenced by the tempo of the big city.
Record companies and other branches of the music industry quickly picked up the term, using *Salsa* as a catchy way of marketing Latin American music.

But new or old — the word *Salsa* is a term for, in and about Cuban music.

Rehearsing the rhythms and the rhythm section

Rehearsing the rhythm section

Begin by playing the rhythms with the rhythm section only — without bass and piano (refer to *Descarga* on the preceding page).
By rehearsing in this manner you will learn to think of the rhythms as music in themselves — as an independent element.

I have shown an example of a rhythm section arrangement under »*Cha-cha-cha*« (refer to page 107).

When each person has learned the figures to be played on his/her respective instrument, begin to build up the rhythm one instrument (one person) at a time, so that you can hear what each person is playing.
This will make you concentrate on what is going on and will make the rhythm steadier.
When everybody is concentrated, and relaxed, the rhythm can start to swing.
Remember to play as simply as possible; it is the rhythm as a whole and the correct combination of instruments (the sound) that is important – not each persons individual solo performance.
Just one ego-tripper can ruin everything.

Structuring and rehearsing the rhythms

1: Build up the rhythm one instrument at a time.
   Begin with the *clave rhythm*, and each time a new instrument starts, it should start on the count of **1** in the first bar.
   It is important that everybody perceives the two-bar period of *the clave*.
2: Once the rhythm starts working, practice periods and rests.
   Agree on a certain number of bars to be played, and then stop. Or give *a cue* for a stop while the rhythm is still being played — remember to give the cue correctly so that the stop fits to *the clave rhythm*. Take a two- or four bar rest and then come in on the rhythm again all at once, and remember to hit the count of **1** on the first bar of *the clave rhythm (3/2 clave rhythm)*. The rhythm should be tight immediately after commencing again — this is how you can tell whether you have practiced enough or not!
3: Instead of rests, practice some simple breaks which everybody should play. (There are examples of different breaks shown with the various rhythms.)
   Use this type of structure for the rhythm section when rehearsing all *the 4/4 rhythms. Afro-Cuban 6/8* starts with *the cowbell* or *the conga/tumba*.
4: The rhythm section should now be ready to rehearse together with the melody instruments.
   If you wish to work more with the rhythm section alone, then you can arrange the rhythm with a beginning, possible breaks along the way and an ending.

Apart from this structuring and rehearsal of the rhythms, which is the same for all the rhythms, you will find that they differ from each other in many ways. These differences are explained in conjunction with the individual rhythms.

Cha-cha-cha

Cha-cha-cha is, from a rhythmic standpoint, one of the most simple of the Cuban rhythms and one of the most well-known and popular.
Cha-cha-cha is a typical dance rhythm with an even accentuation of all four beats in the bar.
Cha-cha-cha was made popular by *the Charanga orchestras*, which incorporated the use of *violins* and *flute*. The first *Cha-cha-cha* was composed by the violinist Enrique Jorrín (about 1950), using ideas from the *Danzón* rhythm. The *Cha-cha-cha* would later become a part of the repertoire of *the Conjunto groups* and the large *dance bands*. (Refer to orchestra types page 97.)

The simple rhythm and the 4/4 feeling makes *Cha-cha-cha* very compatible with other types of music such as *Rock*.
The Latin Rock group »Santana« is well known for its combination of these rhythms.

Cha-cha-cha is played in medium tempi with the foot tapped to the count of **1-2-3-4**.

Explanation of the rhythm chart on the opposite page:
(All the rhythms are explained in detail in part one.)

* *Clave:* 3/2.
  Guiro: Basic rhythm in medium tempo. Alternative playing technique refer to page 20.
* *Maracas:* Played hand to hand. All the strokes are evenly accentuated.
  Conga and tumba played by two persons:
      Conga plays basic rhythm, (v) stands for variation of stroke.
      Tumba plays »open« (o) strokes in each bar.
      If there is only one drum, no matter which, it should play *the basic conga rhythm*.
  Conga and tumba played by one person:
      All the strokes are played on *the conga* except for the »open« strokes on *the tumba* — on the count of **and 3** in each bar.
* *Bongo:* Martillo.
* *Cowbell:* Is played if there are no *timbales*. All the strokes should be accentuated evenly (A-strokes).
  Timbales: Right hand on small *cowbell*.
  Left hand on the large *timbale* on the counts **2** and **4**, with or without stick.
  Vibra-slap or *Quijada:* The rhythm can be used throughout the whole number or parts of it, but do not overdo it. Breaks are not to be played on this instrument.

* *Clave:* 2/3 (refer to *clave rhythm* page 17).

* *Maracas, bongó, hand cowbell*, and *claves* are not used by the *Charanga orchestras*, but are often used when other types of orchestras play *Cha-cha-cha*.
Even though the *clave rhythm* is not played the feeling is still inherent.

Rehearsal of the rhythm section and the rhythms refer to page 99.

Notice that the instruments are presented here in another order than on the accompanying cassette tape. The order on the tape is made with regard to the music, while the rhythm chart is written for easier understanding of the pattern combinations.

Cha-cha-cha

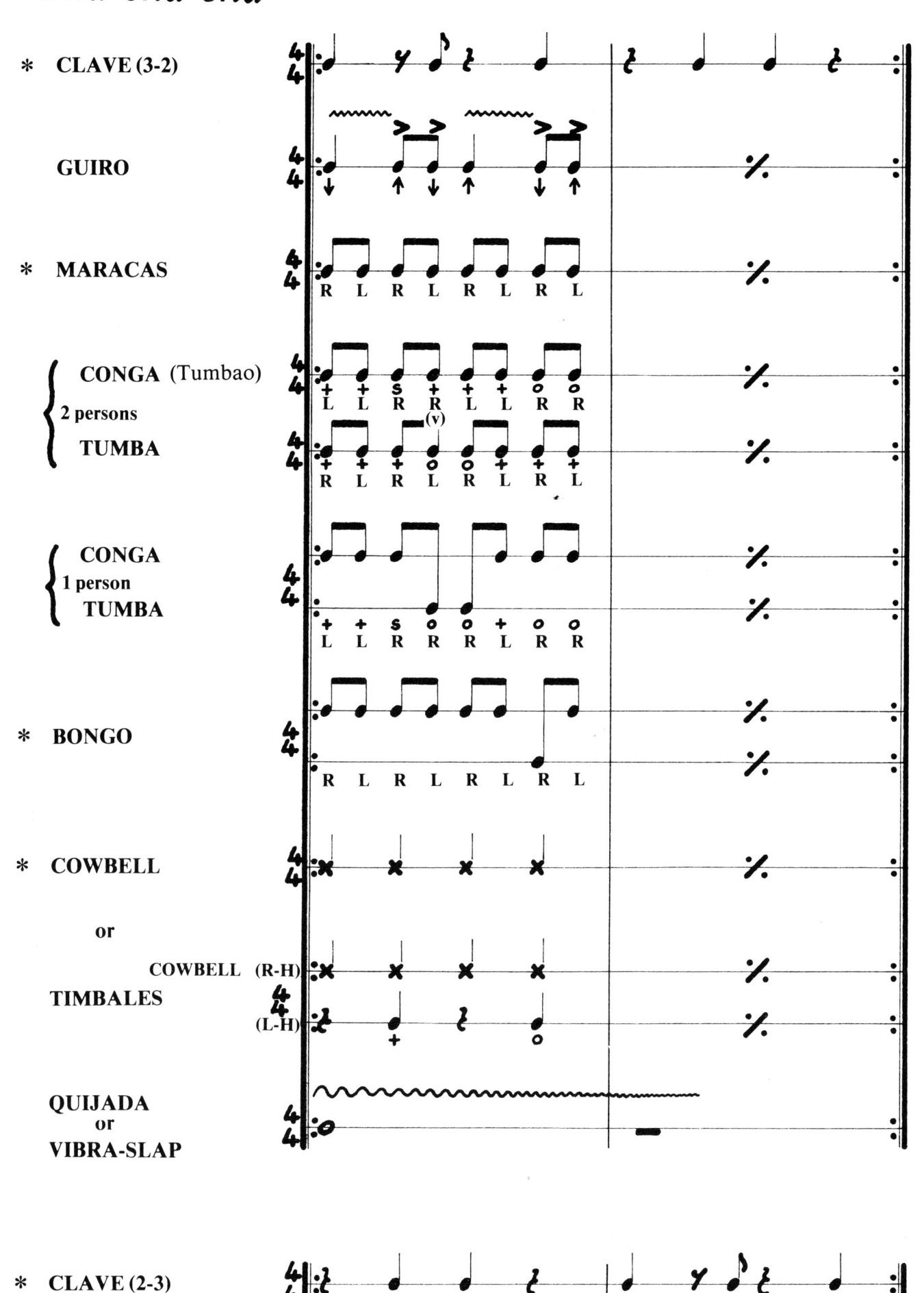

Alternative rhythms for Cha-cha-cha

Conga/tumba

Playing »open« strokes on *the tumba* in each bar in some rhythms may tend to sound cluttered. This is the same rhythm as for *Mambo*, with the »open« strokes on *the tumba* in every other bar.

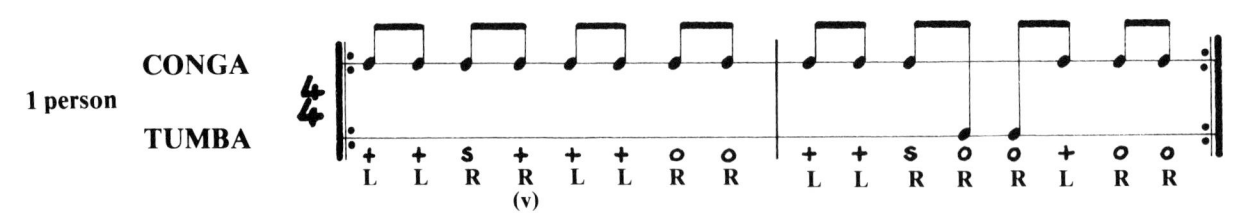

Notice: This rhythm can indicate the direction of the *clave* by always playing the two strokes on the *tumba* in the bar which has three *clave beats*. The rhythm shown in the example would then be in *2-3 clave*.

Timbales (or hand cowbell)

This rhythm can be played throughout the whole number or in parts of the arrangement.
The rhythm can be played on the small or the large *cowbell*.

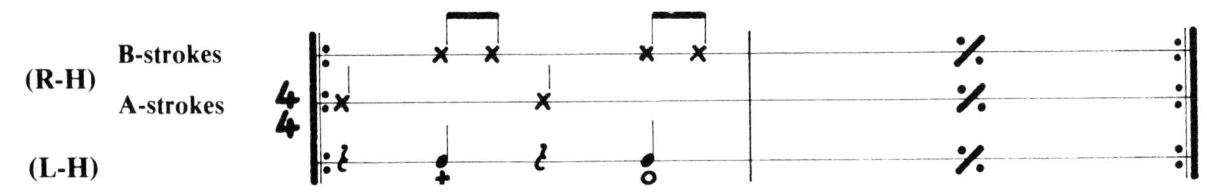

Use the same strokes when playing *the hand cowbell*.

Timbales

The next rhythms are played on the small *cowbell* using A- and B-strokes.

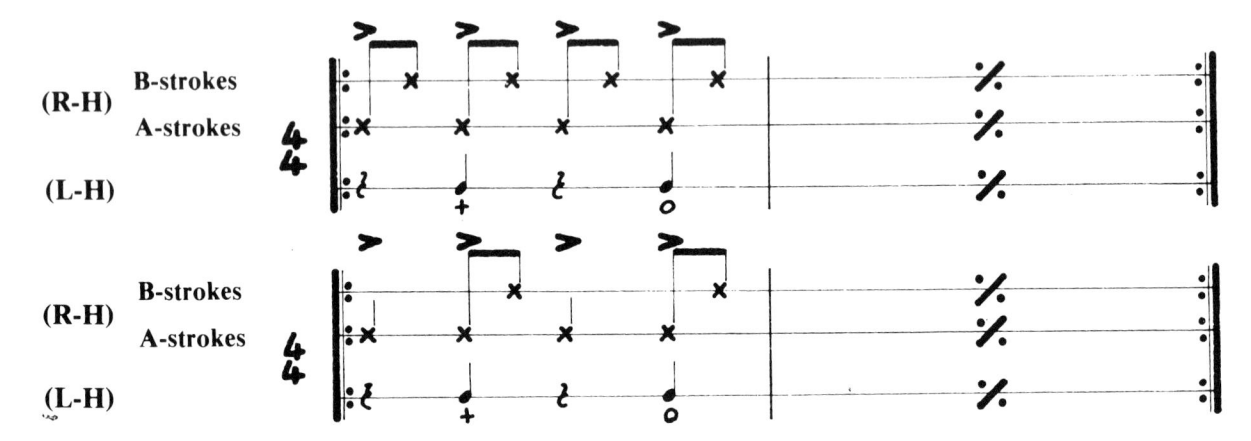

Quijada or Vibra-slap

Shown here is a variation on the count of **2 <u>and</u>** which should only be used occasionaly.

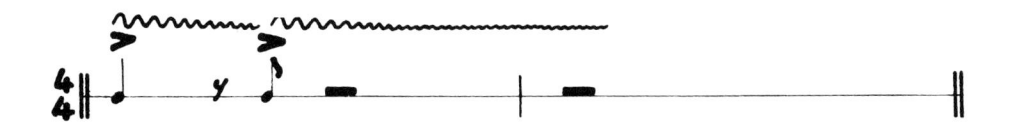

Breaks (»cierre«) for Cha-cha-cha

The breaks shown here can be played in the following ways:
1: The whole rhythm section (except for *the quijada*) plays the break.
2: A part of the rhythm section (*timbales* and *congas*, for instance) plays the break, while the rest of the section continues playing rhythm.
3: The whole group plays the break.

Practice the figures well so that you can play them with confidence.

The breaks shown here can be played for either *2/3* or *3/2 clave*, unless *the clave direction* is stated.

Start by playing *the clave rhythm* as a break.

1:

or 2-3 clave

If the break spans over a four-bar period (*the clave rhythm* played two times) then *the bongo, conga/tumba* and *timbales* should play the first two bars on one drum and the last two bars on both drums at once.

2: one drum   two drums

or 2-3 clave

3:

4:

5:

or 2-3 clave

6:

Last stroke can be omitted.

[Examples 7–16: musical notation exercises in 4/4 time, with annotations]

- 7: (Timb. »Abanico«) Refer to page 55.
- 8: (Timb. small cowbell)
- 9: Abanico
- 10: Abanico
- 12: Or three bars of eighth notes are played before the triplets, so the break will consist of four bars altogether.

There are certain arrangements in which different rhythms are played. This requires a certain amount of routine and is recommendable only when you feel at ease with the rhythms.

The rhythms you can change to from *Cha-cha-cha* are:
Mambo, which is then played in double tempo. This is called *»Ritmo doble«*.
Rumba can also be played in double tempo *(Ritmo doble)*.
6/8. On page 143 there is an example of how to play *6/8* in conjunction with *4/4*.

When changing between *Bolero* and *Cha-cha-cha* in an arrangement, it is called *»Bolero Ritmico«* or *»Bolero Cha«*. Refer to *Bolero*.

The change-over from one rhythm (tempo) to another can either be done directly or by playing a break.

Variations for the basic conga rhythm

The variations can be played using both playing-techniques (refer to pages 44 and 45).

The examples are shown here with the left hand playing all the »closed« strokes (+) in the basic rhythm.

1:

2:

3:

4:

When the rhythm is played with an »open« stroke on the count of <u>1</u>, the rhythm should continue with one »closed« stroke on the count of **1 and**. From then on the rhythm is the same as before.

5:

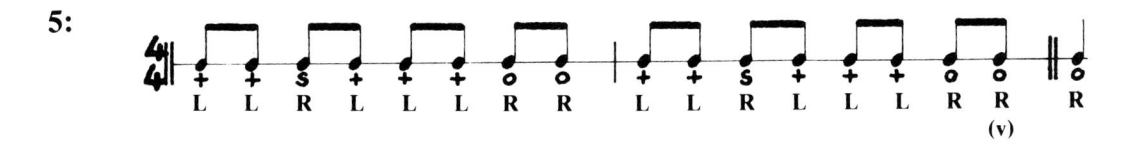

106

Variations for the conga and tumba

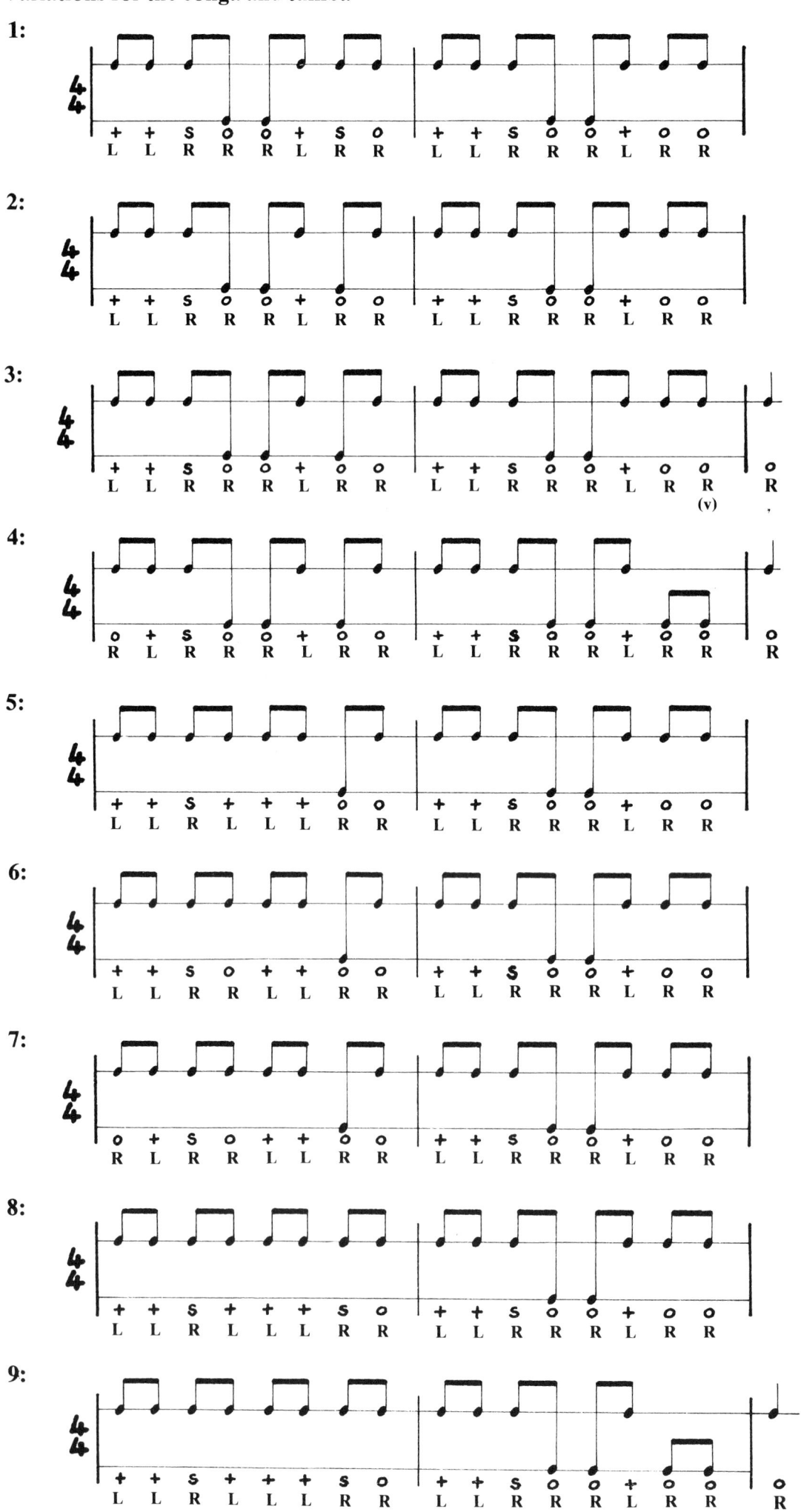

Suggestion for an arrangement with the rhythm section only — »Descarga«

Start: Rhythm build-up. The instruments may play longer than the two bars as shown. The rhythm is built up one instrument at a time.

Rhythm: In this case, shown with eight bars played, but this is only a suggestion. Cues for breaks can also be given as an alternative. Remember to count correctly along with *the clave rhythm*.

Break 1:   Everybody plays the break. Start with *the clave rhythm* and then two bars of eighth notes, starting lightly and increasing in volume through the two bars.

Rhythm: Everybody then plays the rhythm again as shown. Eight bars as shown.

Break 2:   *The congas* and *timbales* should play this break alone while the rest of the section continues the rhythm.

Rhythm: Everybody plays rhythm for 32 bars or »ad libitum«.

Ending: Everybody plays the ending. Be careful not to play on the count of **1** in the fourth bar!

Cha-cha-cha

Mambo

Mambo is, just like *Cha-cha-cha*, a typical dance rhythm (*Popular*) but played mostly in faster tempo. There are different theories as to the origin of the *Mambo*.
Some think that the *tres*-player Arsenio Rodriguez was the first person to introduce the style and rhythm with his *Conjunto*. Others think it was the *Charanga orchestra* »Arcaño y sus Maravillas« who created the style from a section of the rhythm *Danzón*. This section is called »*the third Danzón*« or »*montuno*«. The orchestra's cellist Orestes Lopez composed a *Danzón* entitled »Mambo« and the ideas from this new style are said to have been the origin of the *Mambo* rhythm.
The great popularity of the rhythm, however, was caused by the Cuban piano player Perez Prado and his large orchestra.
The style as we know it today was founded by the great *Masters of Mambo:* »Machito«, Tito Puente and Tito Rodriguez. Refer to orchestra-types on page 97 and the discography on pages 178 and 179.

The Mambo-section
Any arrangement, no matter which rhythm, can incorporate a *Mambo-section*. This section does not have to be played in a *Mambo* rhythm, but is a section in which the trumpets play their characteristic riffs, acting as a contrast to the piano and bass figures. In the larger orchestras the same effect is produced using the saxophones riffs and the trumpet's contra-riffs.

Mambo is played in medium and fast tempi.

Explanation of the rhythm chart on following page:
(All the rhythms are explained in detail in the first part of the book.)

Mambo 1 Medium and medium-fast tempo

Clave: *3/2.*
Guiro: Basic rhythm.
Maracas: Evenly accentuated strokes.
Conga and *tumba* played by two persons:
    Conga plays basic rhythm, (v) stands for variation of stroke.
    Tumba plays only »open« strokes in every other bar **(and 3)**.
    If there is only one drum, no matter which, the drum plays *the basic conga rhythm.*
Conga and *tumba* played by one person:
    Basic conga rhythm in first bar. In the second bar the basic rhythm is interrupted by two »open« strokes on *the tumba* **(and 3)**.
    If there is only one drum, no matter which, the drum plays *the basic conga rhythm.*
Bongo: Martillo. (Cowbell rhythms for the bongo-player, refer to page 113.)
Cowbell: A-strokes.
    The hand cowbell is used if there are no *timbales*. Remember to reverse the *cowbell rhythm* when playing *reverse clave (2-3)* — refer to bottom of page.
Timbales: The right hand plays *cowbell* (C-strokes) or *Paila*, and the left hand plays the counts of **2** (+) and **4** (o) on the large drum, with or without a stick.

Clave: *2/3.*
    Cowbell and *paila* rhythm are reversed.

The necessary instruments for playing *Mambo* are: *conga/tumba, cowbell* or *timbales*.

Alternative rhythms, refer to page 112.

Rehearsal of rhythm section and rhythms refer to page 99.

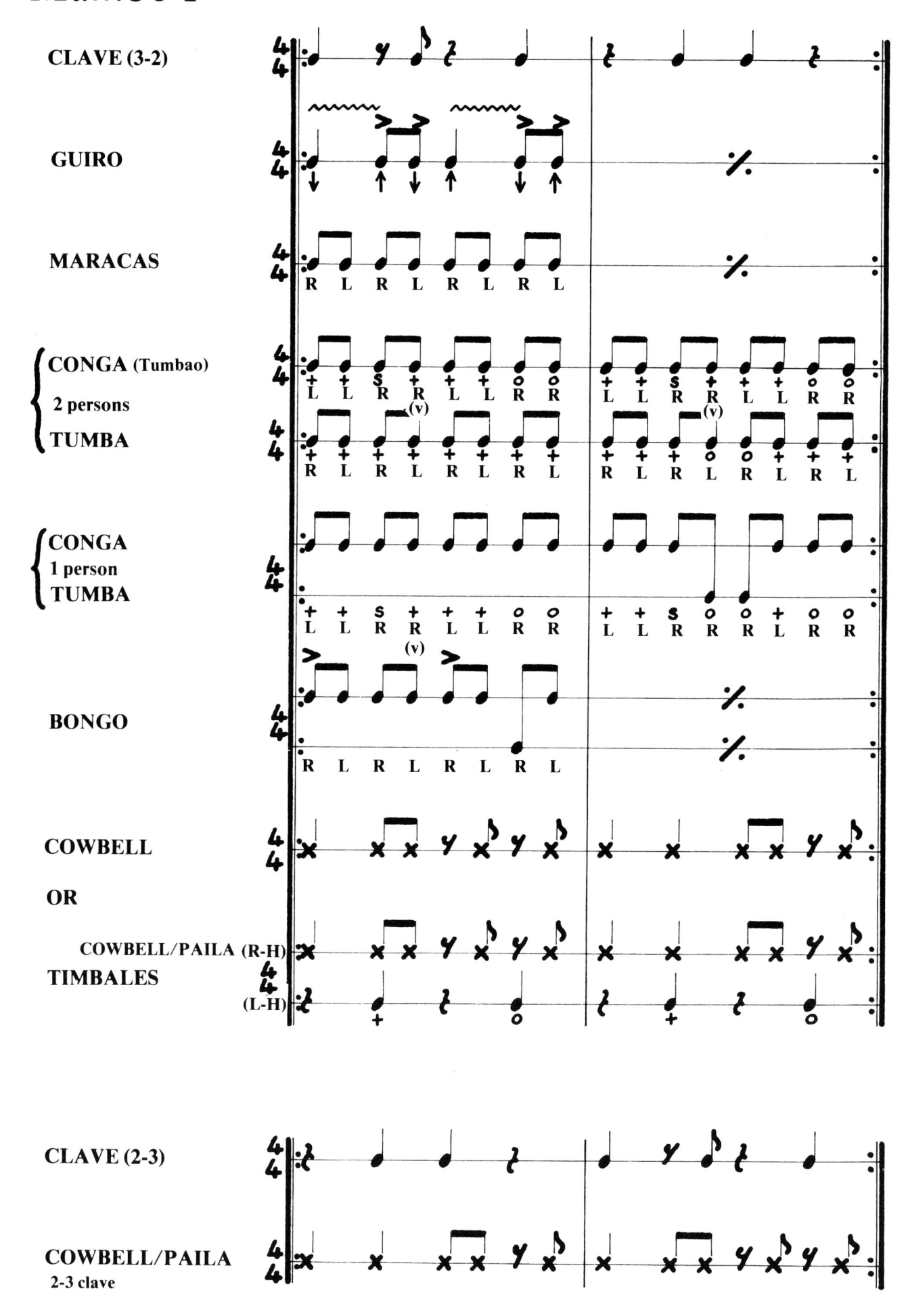

Mambo 1

Mambo 2 Fast tempo

This form is often used in many *modern Rumba* arrangements, which are played in the same way as *Mambo*.

Explanation of rhythm chart on opposite page:
(All the rhythms are explained in the first part of the book.)

Clave: 3/2.
Guiro: Accentuated counts of **and 1** and **and 3**.
Maracas: Played hand to hand (R-L-R-L-.....). Can also be played with accentuations on **and 1** and **and 3**.

Conga and *tumba* played by two persons:
     Conga plays the basic rhythm, (v) stands for variation of stroke.
     Tumba plays »open« strokes **(and 3)** in the second bar only.

* Notice: This rhythm can indicate the direction of the *clave* by always playing the two strokes on the *tumba* in the bar which has three *clave beats*. In this example (*3-2 clave*) the strokes on the *tumba* should be played in the first bar.

Conga and *tumba* played by one person:
     The basic rhythm is played in the first bar, and in the second bar the rhythm is interrupted by the two »open« strokes on *the tumba* **(and 3)**.

Bongo: *Martillo*, accentuated on counts **1** and **3**.
Cowbell: A-strokes. *The hand cowbell* is used if there are no *timbales*. Remember that *the cowbell* rhythm is reversed if *the clave rhythm* is reversed *(2/3)*. Refer to bottom of page.
Timbales: The right hand plays C-strokes on the *large cowbell* or *Paila*. The left hand plays the counts of **2** (+) and **4** (o) on the large drum, with or without a stick.
Cowbell: This rhythm is played on *the hand cowbell* together with *the timbales* in places where the rhythm should be more intense.
     In the traditional group it is *the bongo player* that changes to *hand cowbell*.

Clave: 2/3.
     The cowbell and *Paila* rhythm is played together with *the clave rhythm*.

The necessary instruments for *Mambo* are: *Conga/tumba, cowbell* or *timbales*.

Alternative rhythms refer to page 112.

Rehearsal of the rhythm section and rhythms refer to page 99.

Mambo 2

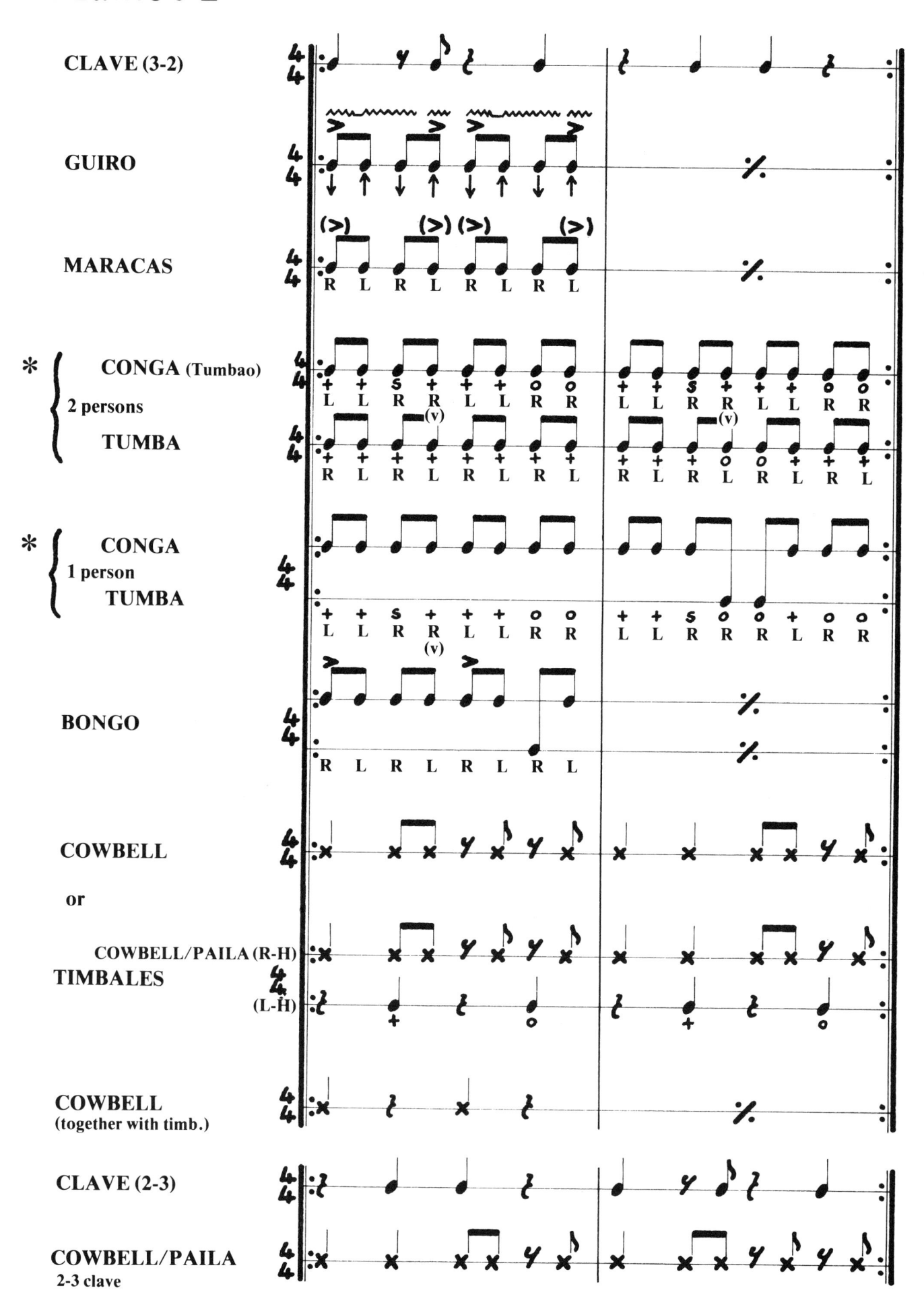

Alternative rhythms for Mambo

Guiro: Refer to page 20.

Conga/tumba

1

The tumba plays »open« strokes in each bar. The same rhythm as in *Cha-cha-cha*.

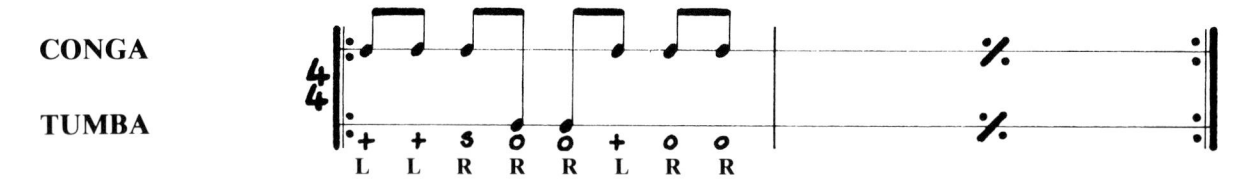

Played by two persons: Refer to *Cha-cha-cha*.

2

When playing in fast tempi there is often only one »open« stroke (o) on *the tumba* in the second bar. (**2 and**).

Timbales

1

The rhythm is played on *the large cowbell*.
The rhythms can be played on *hand cowbell* if there are no *timbales*.

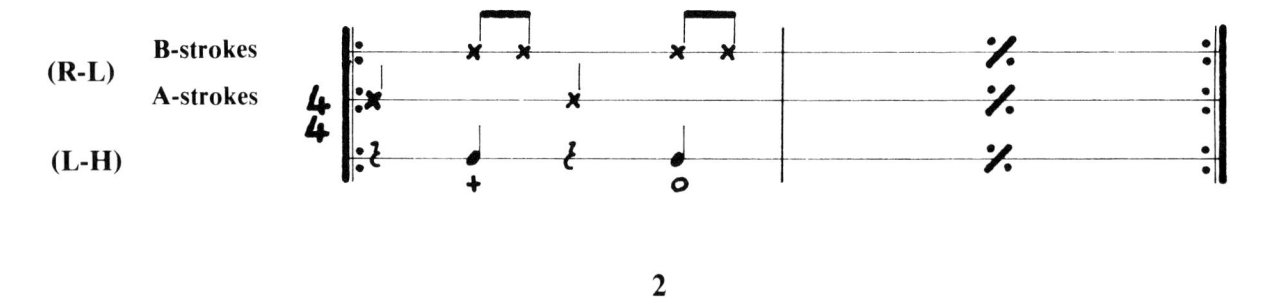

2

This rhythm is often used as a *Paila rhythm* in the beginning of an arrangement. Change to *the large cowbell* when the rhythm should be intensified, either playing the same rhythm or the rhythm shown in the chart.

All the strokes on *the cowbell* are played as C-strokes, or the regularly accentuated strokes as C-strokes and the heavily accentuated ($>$) as A-strokes. (See opposite page.)

3-2 clave

2-3 clave

3-2 clave

2-3 clave

Hand cowbell

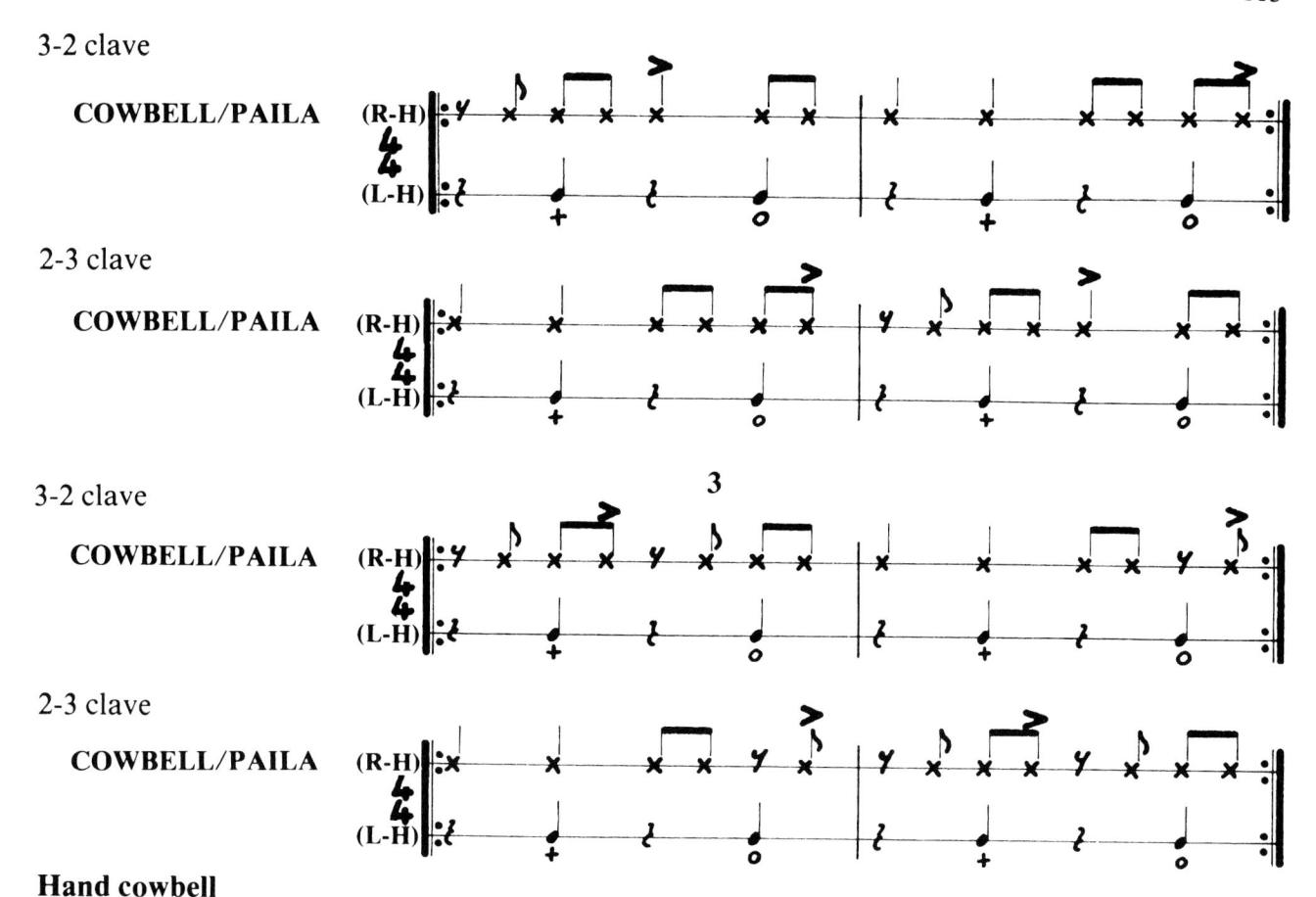

These rhythms are played together with *the timbales* when the rhythm is to be intensified. *The timbales* now play two-bar rhythms.

In the traditional groups *the bongo player* changes to *hand cowbell*.

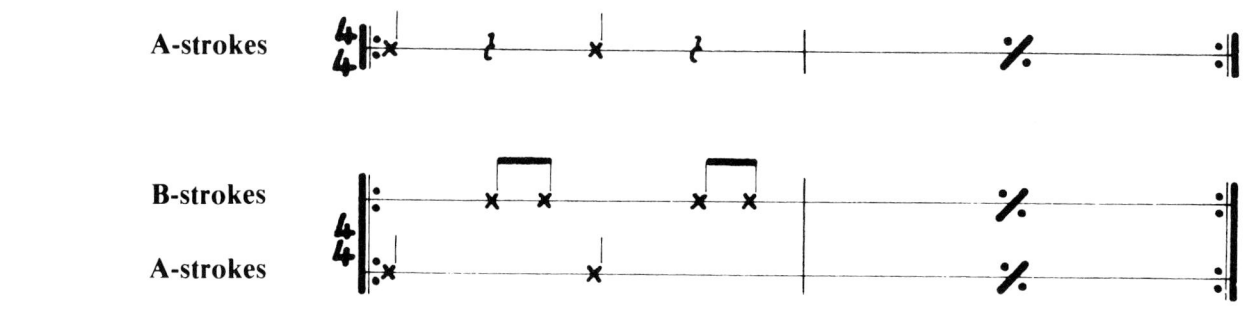

A-strokes

B-strokes
A-strokes

This rhythm indicates the direction of *the clave* in the bar with two *clave strokes*.

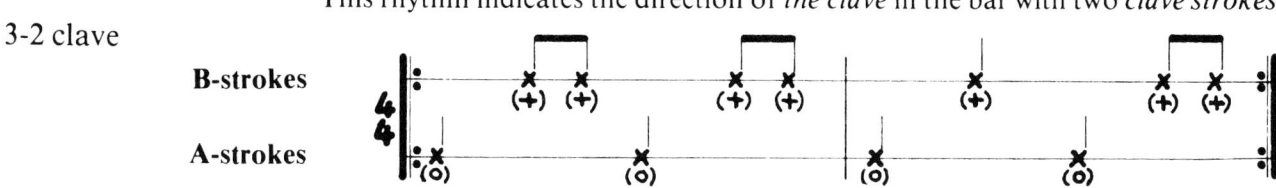

3-2 clave

B-strokes
A-strokes

2-3 clave starts with the second bar first.

There are certain arrangements in which there are changes of rhythms, but it is necessary to feel at ease with the rhythms before attempting this.

The following rhythms can be used in changing to and from *Mambo*:
6/8. There is an explanation as to how to go to or from *6/8* in conjunction with *4/4* on page 143.
Cha-cha-cha is played in half tempo in conjunction with *Mambo*.
The change-overs between the various rhythms can either be done directly, or by playing a break.

See following page.

Breaks (»cierre«) for Mambo

The breaks shown here can be played in the following ways:
1: The whole rhythm section plays the break.
2: A part of the rhythm section (*the congas* and *timbales*, for instance) plays the break while the rest of the section continues to play rhythm.
3: The whole group plays the break.

Rehearse the figures well in order to feel at ease with them.

Notice the direction of *the clave*. When not stated, the break can be used for *2/3* or *3/2* clave.

Example 1 and 2 are often played twice (4 bars).

115

Son Montuno

Son Montuno is one of the old, traditional rhythms that were originated in the *Son groups*. This is explained in more detail in the introduction to the Cuban rhythms on page 96.

Rhythmically speaking, *the Son Montuno* can be compared to the *cha-cha-cha* but is often played with a looser type of feeling.

The rhythm chart for *Cha-cha-cha* (page 101) can be used for *Son Montuno*.

Son Montuno can either be played with an »alla breve« feeling or with a *4/4* feeling. (The foot can be tapped on the counts of **1** and **3** or **1-2-3-4**.)

The tempo is medium to medium fast.

Guajira

Musica Guajira and *Musica Campesina* are both terms for music of the rural population. »*Guajiro*« and »*campesino*« are words meaning peasant or farmer. This style of music comes from the Spanish guitar- and vocal tradition and the groups often consisted of *guitar, tres, clave* and sometimes *guiro* and *maracas*. The old style, *Punto Guajiro*, was played in 6/8 or 3/4 time or alternating between one bar 6/8 and one bar 3/4 time.
Guajira as we know it today is the younger, citified version which is now played in 2/4 or 4/4 time. The lyrics still consist of oftentimes satirical episodes from the farmer's everyday life. The *Guajira* rhythm is now played by most of the different types of orchestras.
It is quite usual that *Guajira* arrangements contain elements from the *Son* style: *Montuno*/»coro-solo« for instance. This combination is called *Guajira Son*.
Rhytmically *Guajira* is played just like *Son Montuno*, but usually in a slower tempo.

Explanation of rhythm chart on opposite page:

Clave: *3/2*.
Maracas: The basic rhythm is shown here, but the other rhythms shown on page 23 can also be used for *Son Montuno*.
Conga and *tumba* played by one person:
    The conga plays *the basic rhythm* but the second bar is interrupted by the two »open« strokes on *the tumba*.
Conga and *tumba* played by two persons — refer to *Mambo*, page 109.
Bongo: *Martillo* with accentuated strokes on the counts of **1** and **3**.
Timbales: The rhythm is either played as *Paila* on the side of the small drum or with C-strokes on *the small* or *large cowbell*.

           The left hand plays closed strokes (+) on the count of **2** and »open« strokes (o) on the count of **4** in each bar.

           Timbales and *hand cowbell* can either be used together or separately.
           There were no *timbales* in the traditional *Son groups* — only the *hand cowbell*.
Cowbell: A stroke on the counts **1** and **3**. B-strokes on the counts **2 and** and **4 and**.

Clave: *2/3*.
           Timbales rhythm for *2/3 clave*.

The necessary instruments for *Son Montuno* are: *Bongos* and *maracas*, after which *conga* and *cowbell*.

Rehearsal of the rhythm section and rhythm refer to page 99.

Son Montuno

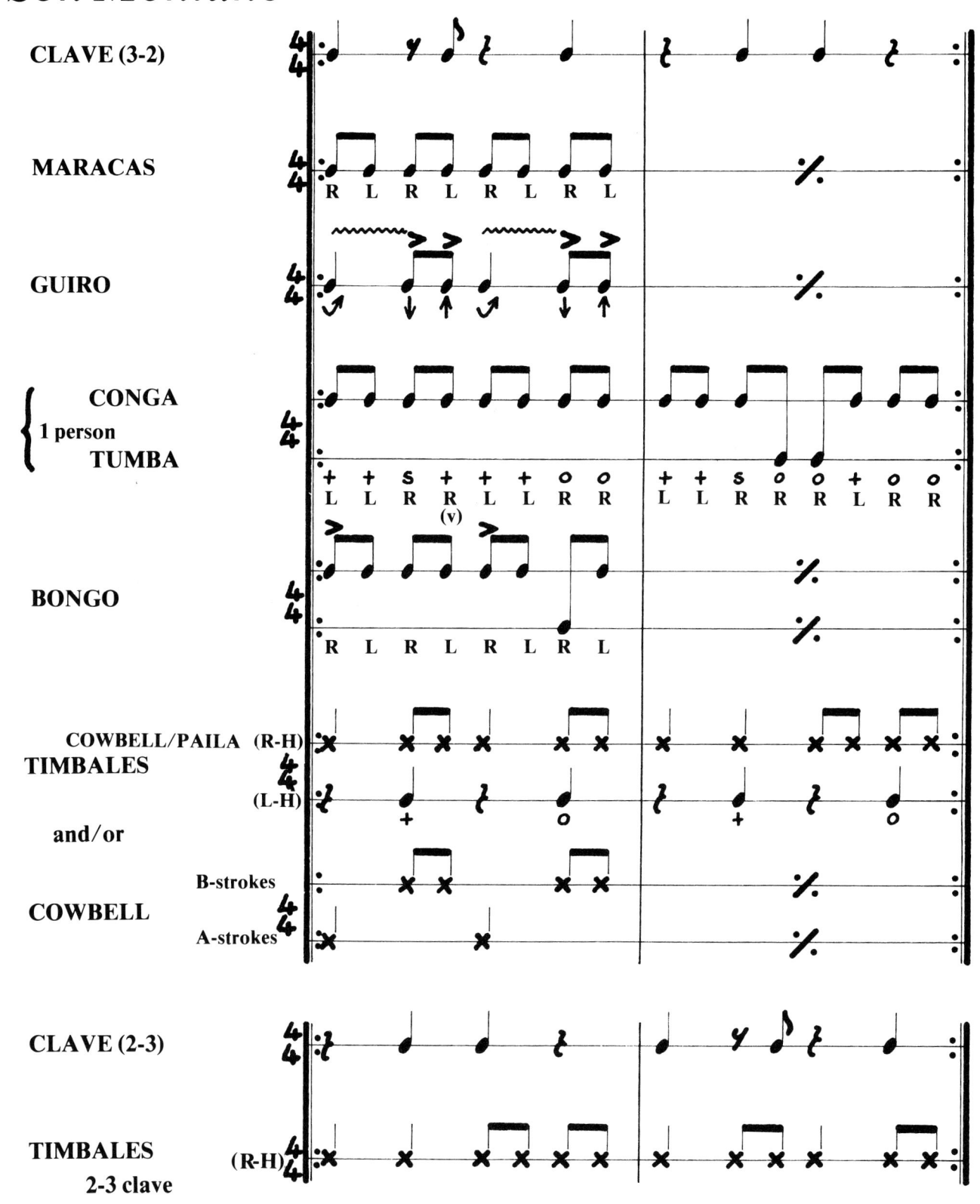

Alternative rhythms

The rhythm is played either on the *large* or *small cowbell* (A- and B-strokes).

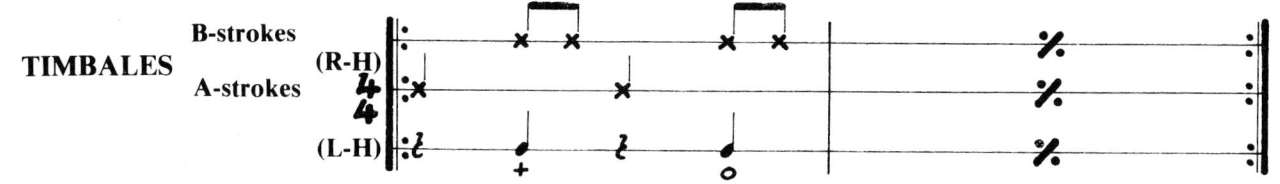

The timbales often play *the Paila rhythms* as shown under *Bolero* page 119.

Bolero

The Bolero is a type of *ballad* — a piece of music which is usually played with a vocal soloist.
The tempo is either slow or medium slow, and the lyrics are almost always of the romantic and sentimental variety.

The Bolero rhythm sounds good when played in conjunction with other styles of music in slower tempi.

The foot should be tapped to the count of **1-2-3-4** when playing the rhythm.

Explanation of rhythm chart on opposite page:
(All the rhythms are explained in detail in the first part of the book.)

Clave: *3/2.*
Maracas: The maracas always play the same rhythm as *the timbales (Paila)* when playing *Bolero*. Evenly accentuated strokes.
Conga/tumba played by two persons:
> *The conga* plays the *basic rhythm* with ONE »open« stroke. The stroke written in parenthesis can be omitted. (v) stands for variation of stroke.
> The »open« stroke of *the conga* is played together with the stroke on *the larger bongo* (**4**).
> *Tumba* plays *the basic Bolero pattern* for one drum.

Conga/tumba played by one person:
> Refer to page 50.

Bongo: *Martillo* — evenly accentuated strokes.
Variations are shown on page 120.
Timbales: *Paila* throughout the entire number. The same rhythm as *the maracas*.

Clave: *2/3.*

Rehearsal of the rhythm and rhythm section — refer to page 99.

Alternative rhythms and combinations of instruments
(Explanation of the opposite page.)

Two persons play *bongo* and *conga* without *the tumba:* refer to page 49.
When *the bongo* plays the rhythm together with *the conga, the Martillo* is played without too many variations.

Maracas and *timbales* are shown together because the rhythms are identical.

The necessary instruments for playing *Bolero* are: *Maracas* and/or *timbales (Paila), bongo/conga* or *conga/tumba.*

Bolero Ritmico

There are many arrangements in which the rhythm is changed from *Bolero* to *Cha-cha-cha* in order to intensify the rhythmic feeling of the number.
When both rhythms are used in an arrangement it is called »*Bolero Ritmico*« or »*Bolero Cha*«.
Both rhythms are played in the same tempo.

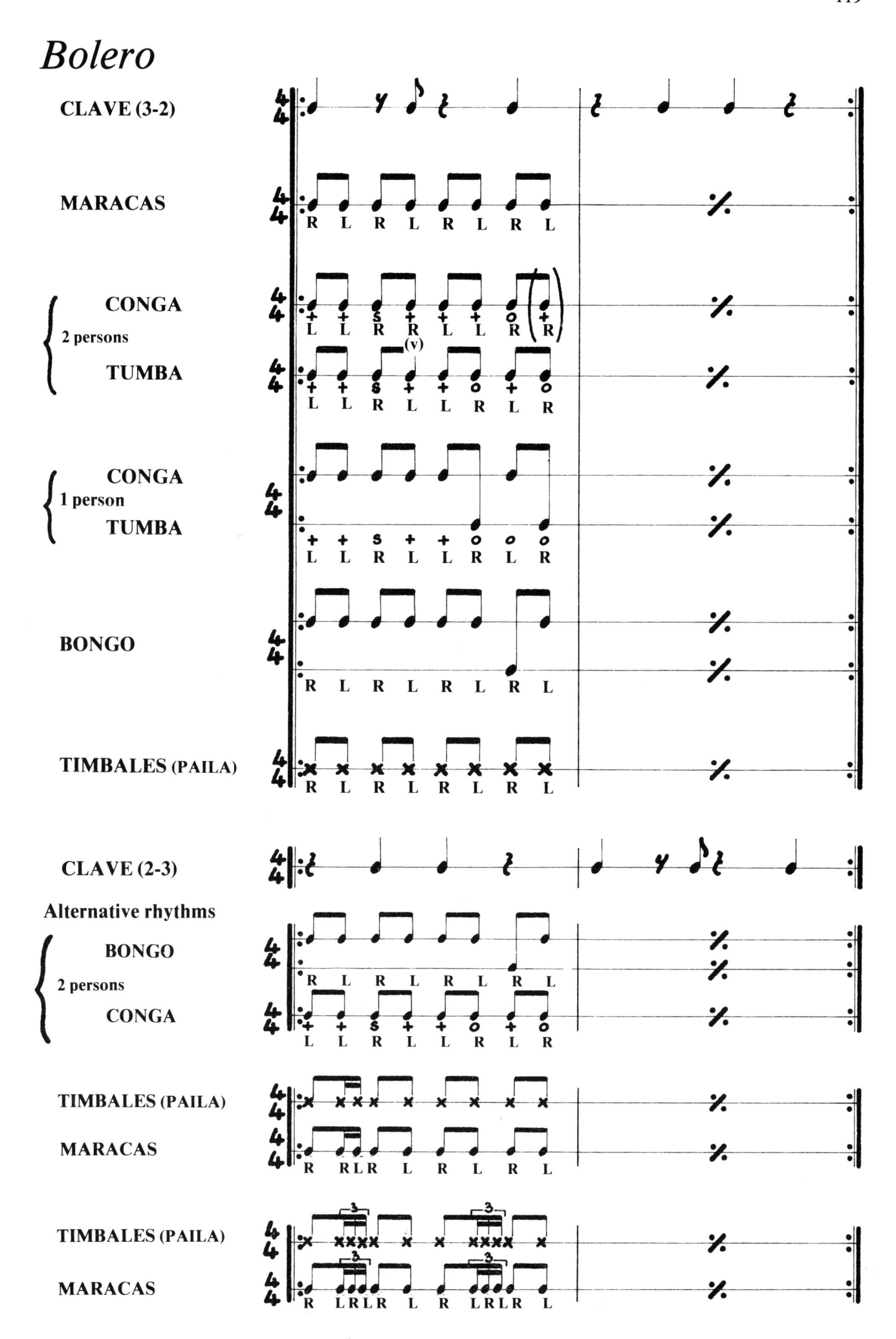

Bolero

Alternative rhythms or variations for congas and bongos

Conga/tumba

This figure is used as a basic rhythm or as a variation of the basic *conga/tumba rhythm for Bolero*.

The rhythm is explained on page 51.

Bongo

This rhythm is used as a basic pattern or as a variation of *the Martillo*.

The first two strokes are played with the index finger of the right hand while the side of the thumb of the left hand is used to muffle the head. (**1 and**).
The count of **1 and ah** is played with the fingertips of the left hand (bottom side).
From here on the rhythm is played as in *Martillo*.

It is very common to play an accentuated stroke on the count of **4 and** in the first bar when playing *Bolero*. This stroke is played with the fingertip (index finger) of the left hand (the right hand is up off the head). The second bar can be continued in various ways but always as *The Martillo* as the fundamental rhythm.

Shown here are three examples of how to continue in the second bar:

1: As *Martillo* except that the thumb does not muffle the count of **1** in the second bar.
The stroke should be played lightly.

2: The stroke on the count of **1** in the second bar is played on the large drum. Remember the stroke on the count of **4** on the large drum.

3: The counts of **1, 2,** and **4** in the second bar are all played on the large drum, and the rest are played on the small drum. The stroke on the count of **1 and** should be either omitted or played lightly.

Bongo fills for Bolero

The examples are played in the second bar of *the clave rhythm* and function as pickups to the next two-bar period.

The bar before (first bar) is often ended as shown on the preceding page with an accentuated stroke on the count of **4 and**.

The clave rhythm is shown to indicate the two-bar period.

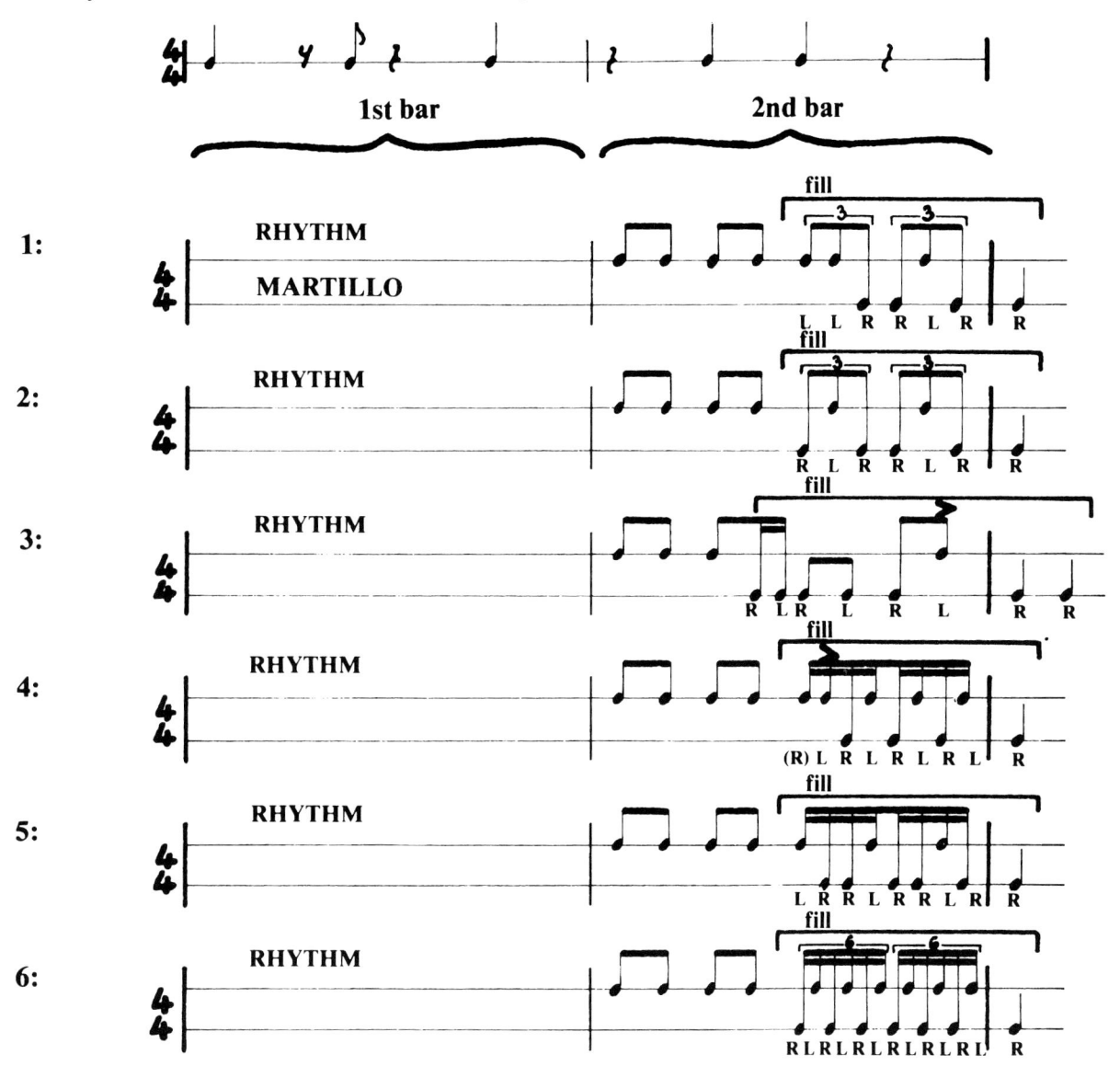

Single-stroke rolls are often used when playing fills. These are played either with both hands on the same drum or with one hand on each.

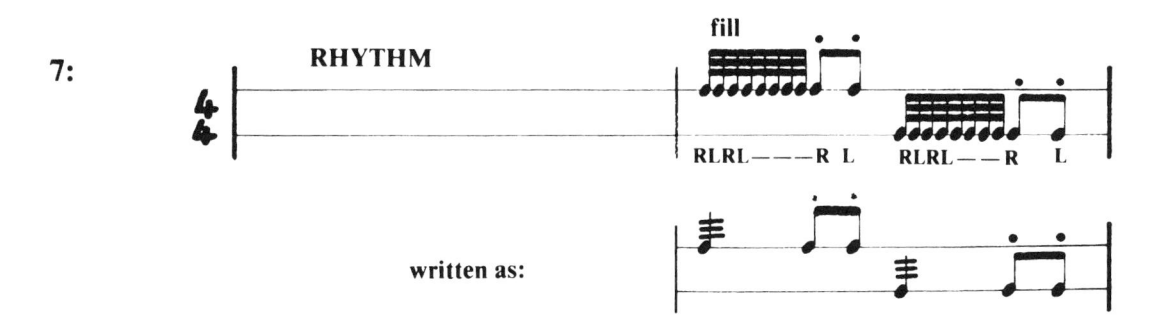

Rumba

Rumba is not only a rhythm but a term for a combination of rhythms, dancing and singing. This Afro-Cuban style came into being, contrary to the religious rituals, through informal gatherings where the contents were a mixture of the old African traditions given a shot of new ideas.
La Rumba can happen anywhere: on the street or in a cozy backyard, but it can also be a large – scale *Rumba party:* a *Rumbón*.

The most well-known types of *Rumba* are:
Yambú – slow to medium tempo.
Guaguancó – medium to fast tempo.
Rumba Columbia – fast tempo, often played in 6/8 time.
Rumba Abierta – fast tempo, often used as a general term for *Rumba* played in fast tempo.
Yambú and *Guaguancó* both originated in the cities. The songs are sung in Spanish and the dance is performed by a couple.
Rumba Columbia came about, however, in the rural areas and the songs are sung in a mixture of Spanish and the African languages used in religious rituals. The acrobatic type of mime-dance which accompanies this style is always performed by one male dancer.
All the types of Rumba make use of one or more lead singers and a chorus (*coro*). The song begins with a vocal introduction, which varies from style to style, and goes on to the main theme *el canto*. The next part is the »call-answer« section (*Montuno*) in which the chorus alternates with the lead vocalist or *quinto-player* improvising.
This style of *coro-solo* is an indispensable part of the Afro-Cuban music and is still an important part of the modern arrangements.
Yambú, the oldest of the types of *Rumba* mentioned here, was originally played on wood boxes »*cajones*« therefore lending itself the name *Rumba de Cajón* – the *Box Rumba*.

By and by, the different styles have assumed approximately the same instrumention: *Tumba (tumbadora), conga (tres golpes/segunda), quinto, claves* and *cascara (palitos/guagua)*.
Cascara is a rhythm played with two sticks on the side of a *conga* or anything capable of producing a wood-like sound.

Guaguancó is the most well-known of the *Rumba* styles mentioned here, and the most influential.
In a rhythmically simplified and polished version it became a very popular rhythm with the dance orchestras.
We will be working with the traditional »*folklorico*« style and the modern »*popular*« style, starting with the simplified »*popular*« style.

Notice: The types of *Rumba* mentioned here are not identical with the style made popular in America and Europe in the 30's and which is now played at the international dance competitions. This style is often played like a *Bolero* but in a slightly faster tempo and with a looser type of feeling. (Refer to *Bolero* on page 118.)
Many of the *Rumba-hits* from the 30's came from the *Son style* and are now often, both in Cuba and New York, called »*Rhumba with an H*«.

The *Rumba's* characteristic basic rhythm is called *tumbao*, and is played on the *tumba* with accentuated closed strokes (+) on counts **1** and **3** and one open stroke (o) on the count of **4**.
The *Rumba* is played with an alla breve feeling. (The foot is tapped on the counts of **1** and **3**).

even # Rumba 1 *(Popular) older style*

The older, popular style *Rumba* is shown first. There is a nice contrast created between the even eighth notes that are played by *the maracas* (and possibly *the timbales — Paila*) opposed to the rhythms with the accentuated strokes (+) on the counts of **1** and **3** and the »open« stroke on the count of **4** which are played on *the tumba* and *bongo*.

All the instruments are explained in detail in part one.

Clave: 3/2.
Maracas: Played hand to hand with evenly accentuated strokes on all eighth notes.
Tumba: *The tumba* plays the basic *Rumba rhythm (tumbao)*.
Bongo: Martillo or with the fingertips of both hands. The rhythm should be played with accentuated strokes on the counts of **1** and **3**.
Cowbell: The rhythm is played on the *hand cowbell* when the rhythm section is to be more predominant.
Timbales: If *timbales* are used they should play *Paila* — the same rhythm as *the maracas*.

Clave: 2/3.

The necessary instruments for this style are: *Bongos* and *maracas*, then *tumba*.

Rehearsing the rhythm and rhythm section refer to page 99.
Alternative rhythms refer to page 128.

Rumba 2 *(Popular)*

This is a rhythm developed from the »*Rumba 1*«, shown here with all the instruments that can be used.

Explanation of the rhythm chart on the opposite page:

Clave: 3/2.

Maracas: Played hand to hand. Evenly accentuated strokes. The rhythm can also be played with accentuations on **and 1** and **and 3**.

Tumba/congo played by two persons:
> The tumba plays the basic *Rumba rhythm (tumbao)*.
> The conga is played hand to hand with »open« strokes (o) on **and 3** in each bar.
> The muffled stroke on the count of **1** should be accentuated to make the rhythm steady.
> All the muffled strokes (+) without accentuations should be played lightly and in a relaxed manner. (Refer to the explanation on page 38).
> For variations refer to page 128.

Conga/tumba played by one person:
> All the strokes are played on *the conga* except for the stroke on the count of **4** (o) on *the tumba*. If there is only one drum, no matter which, the basic *Rumba rhythm* »*tumbao*« should be played.

Bongo: *Martillo* with accentuated strokes on the counts of **1** and **3**.

Timbales: *Paila* rhythm played with both hands.
> The rhythm for *2/3 clave* is shown at the bottom of the page.
> In some arrangements the rhythm is played with both hands on *the large cowbell* when the rhythm section is to be more predominant.
> *Timbales* can also play the *Mambo cowbell rhythm*.

Cowbell: The rhythm is played on *the hand cowbell* when the rhythm section is to be more predominant.

Clave: 2/3.
> *Paila* and *cowbell* rhythm shown with the *2/3 clave rhythm*.

The most necessary instruments for this style are: *Bongo, conga/tumba* and *maracas* — then *Paila*.

Practicing the rhythm and rehearsing the rhythm section refer to page 99.

Alternative rhythms refer to page 128.

Rumba 2 *(Popular)*

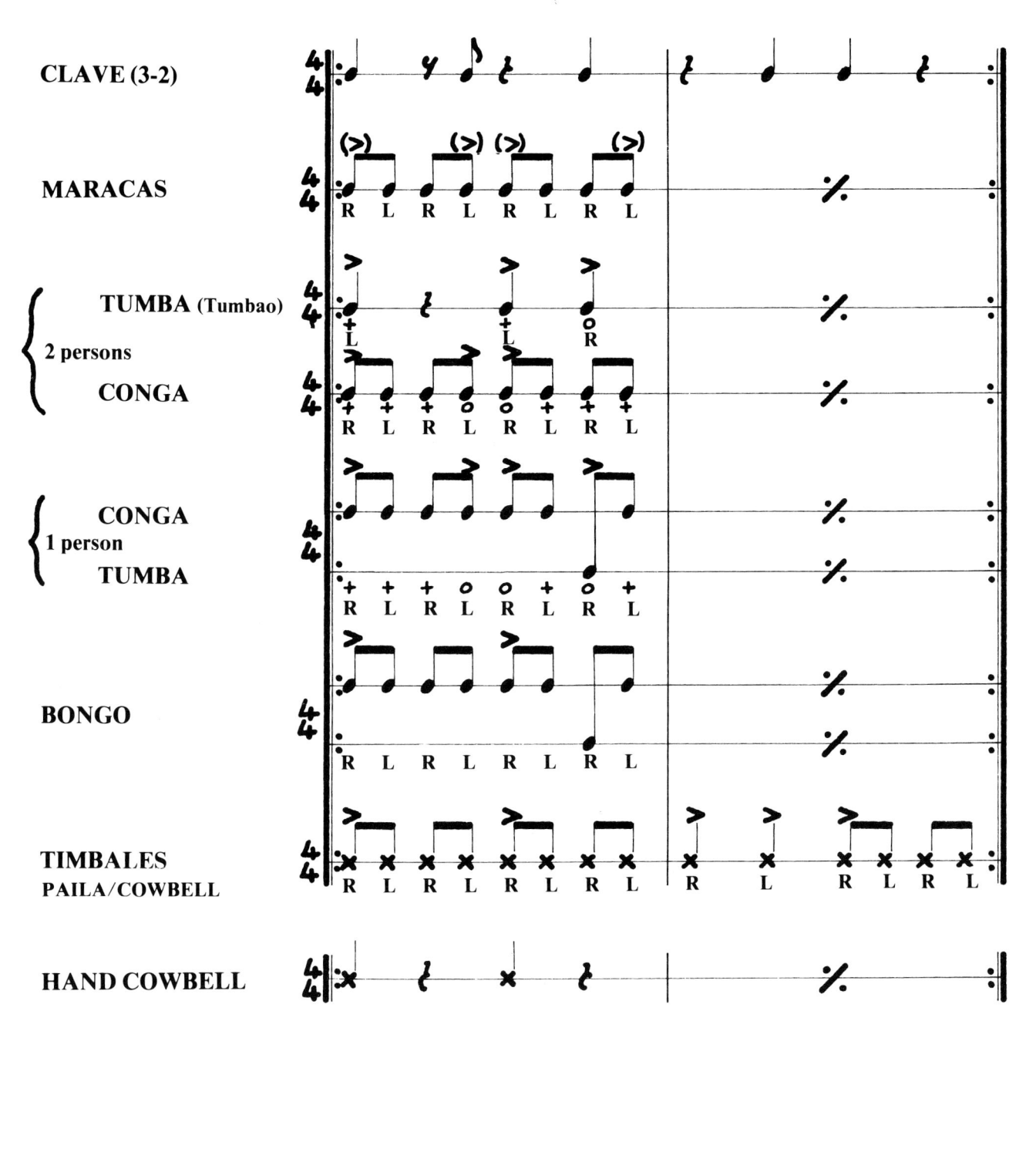

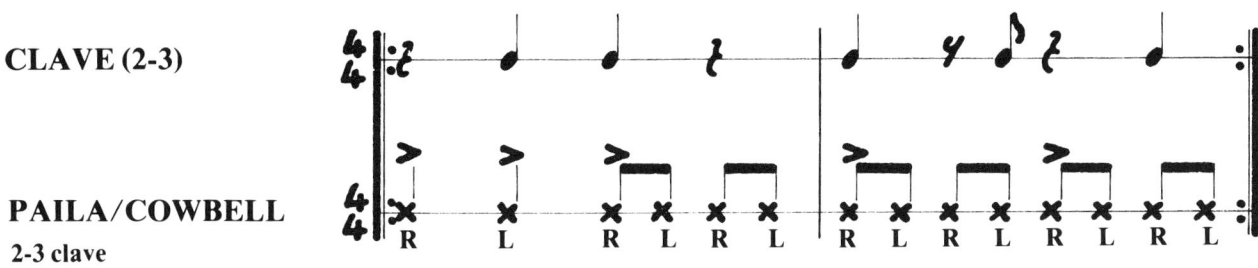

Rumba 3 *(Popular)*

The modern *Rumba* arrangements are akin to *the Mambo* style. The examples shown under »*Mambo*« can be used for this style. The most typical is »*Mambo 2*« on page 111.

In this example *the guiro* and *the cowbell* rhythm are elements taken from *Mambo*.

Explanation of the rhythm chart on the opposite page:

Clave: 3/2.
Maracas: Played hand to hand. Evenly accentuated strokes.
              The rhythm can also be played with accentuations on **and 1** and **and 3**.
Guiro: Guiro rhythm in fast tempi refer to page 19.
Tumba/conga played by two persons:
              The tumba plays the basic *Rumba rhythm (tumbao)*.
              The conga is played hand to hand with two »open« strokes in the first bar on the counts of **1** and **2 and**.
              There are two accentuated »closed« strokes in the second bar on the conts of **and 3**.
              »Closed« strokes without accentuations are played very lightly.
     * This *conga rhythm* can be played in the following ways:
        1:     The two open strokes are played in the first bar – independent of the direction of the *clave*.
        2:     The two open strokes are played together with the *clave beats* on **1** and **2 and**, also in the *reverse clave rhythm (2-3)*. In his case the two open strokes are played in the second bar.
        3:     The two open strokes are played as a balance to the *clave rhythm*. When playing in *3-2 clave* the two open strokes are played in the second bar and in *2-3 clave* the two open strokes are played in the first bar. This is the way in which most Cuban *conga-drummers* play.

Here is the *conga rhythm* shown with a simplified technique. Refer also to the alternative rhythms on page 128.

Conga/tumba played by one person:
              All the strokes are played on *the conga* except for the »open« stroke on *the tumba* on the count of **4** in each bar.
Bongo: Martillo with accentuated strokes on the counts of **1** and **3**.
Cowbell: The rhythm is played on *the hand cowbell* if there are no *timbales*.
Timbales: The right hand plays *the large cowbell* or *Paila* and the left hand plays on the large drum — with or without a stick.
              The rhythm from »*Rumba 2*« can also be used here, either as *Paila* or played on the *large* or *small cowbell*.
Cowbell: This rhythm is played on *the hand cowbell* together with *the timbales* in places where the rhythm section is to be more predominant.

Clave: 2/3.
              Paila and *cowbell rhythm* shown with the *2/3 clave rhythm*.

Alternative rhythms refer to page 128.

Practicing the rhythm and rehearsing the rhythm section refer to page 99.

Rumba 3 *(popular)*

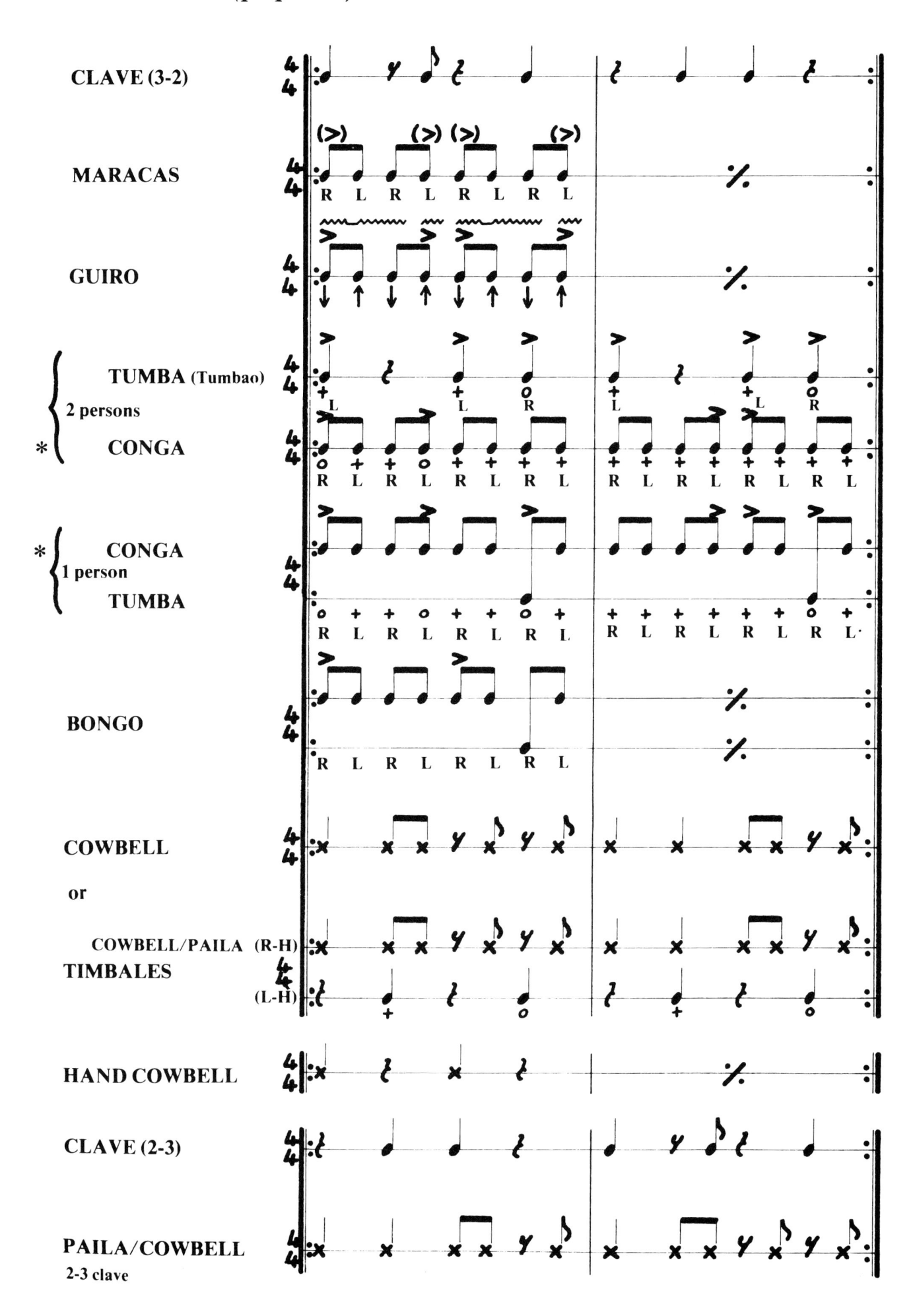

Alternative rhythms for Rumba

There is a note alongside each example showing in which style (»*Rumba 1, 2 or 3*«) the rhythms can be played.

> *The clave rhythm* is sometimes altered slightly when playing *Rumba*. This is the only instance in which *the clave rhythm* is changed. The difference is in the third stroke which is played an eighth note later. This means that the third stroke is played on the count of **4 and** instead on the count of **4**.
> This *clave rhythm* can be used for »*Folklorico*« and »*Popular*«.
>
> *Basic 3-2 clave*
>
> *Rumba-style clave*

Conga/tumba played by one person

Conga/tumba played by two persons refer to page 133 and 134.

The explanation on page 40 shows how the slap strokes can be played with both the left and right hand. To make the rhythms technically easier, in the beginning, you can play the »slap« strokes as accentuated muffled strokes.

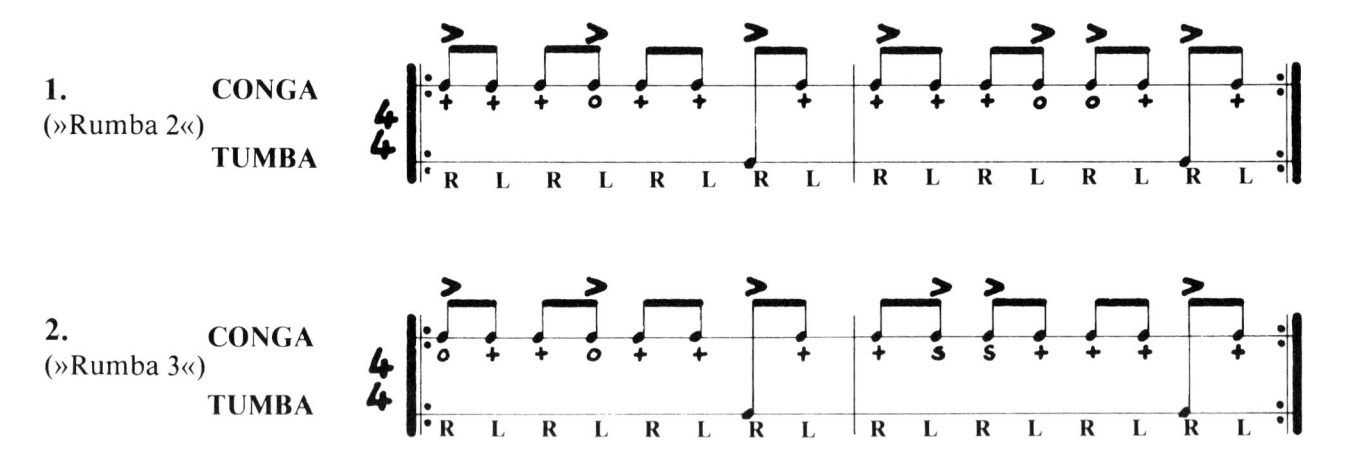

1. CONGA
(»Rumba 2«)
TUMBA

2. CONGA
(»Rumba 3«)
TUMBA

This rhythm can be used for »Rumba 2« and vice versa.
As to *clave direction* refer to page 126 under »*conga*«.

3. (»Rumba 3«)

The same hand-tipping technique on the count of **3 and** is used here, as in the *basic conga rhythm*, in order to even out the open stroke of the right hand on **2 and**.
The rest of the rhythm is played hand to hand (R-L-R-L-...).
It is easier to phrase the rhythm correctly when both open strokes are played with the right hand.

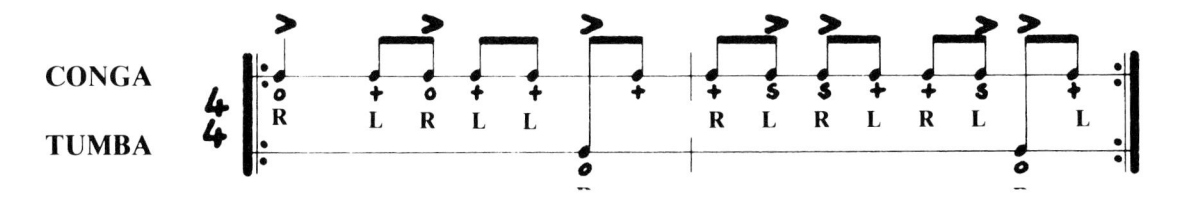

CONGA

TUMBA

4. (»Rumba 3«)

In this example the left hand performs the same tipping motion on the count of **3 and**. In the second bar the hand repeats the motion following the »bass« stroke of the right hand, which is played as an accentuated muffled stroke in the center of the head.

If you are playing seated the drum is lifted up from the floor slightly, simultaneously using the inside of the heels and the thighs – this will give the »bass« stroke resonance.

The many »slap« strokes and this lift make this rhythm quite difficult.

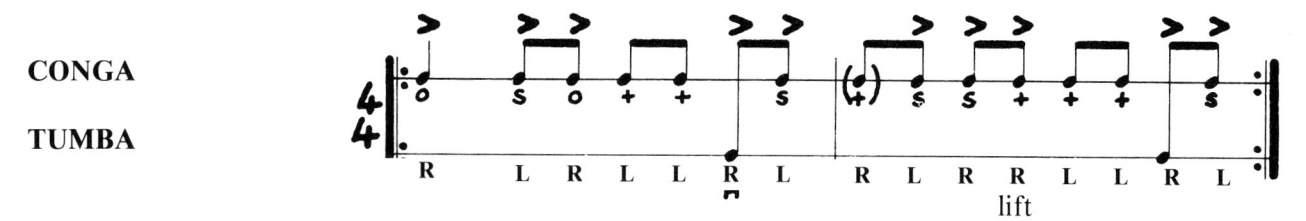

Conga/tumba

Alternative playing-techniques for one person (»*Rumba 2 and 3*«):

The right hand **stays** on *the tumba* and plays the *basic Rumba rhythm*.
The left hand **stays** on *the conga* and plays the rhythms shown here:

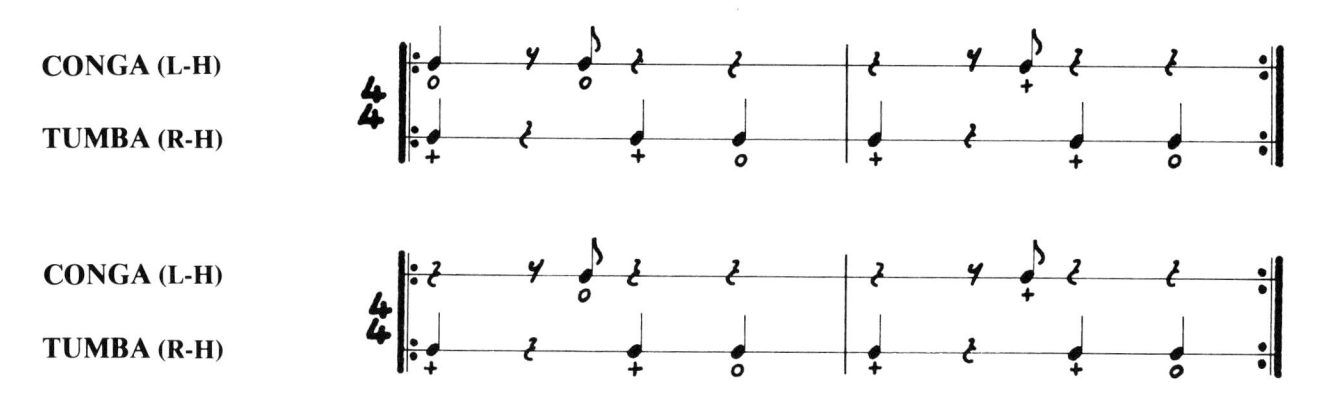

When playing modern *Rumba* arrangements in a *Mambo* style the following rhythms are used: either the regular *Mambo conga/tumba rhythm* or the rhythm shown here with only one stroke on *the tumba* in the second bar.

The rhythm can indicate the direction of the *clave* by playing the stroke on the *tumba* together with the *clave beat* on **2 and** – in either *clave direction*.

The rhythm shown here would then be in *2-3 clave*.

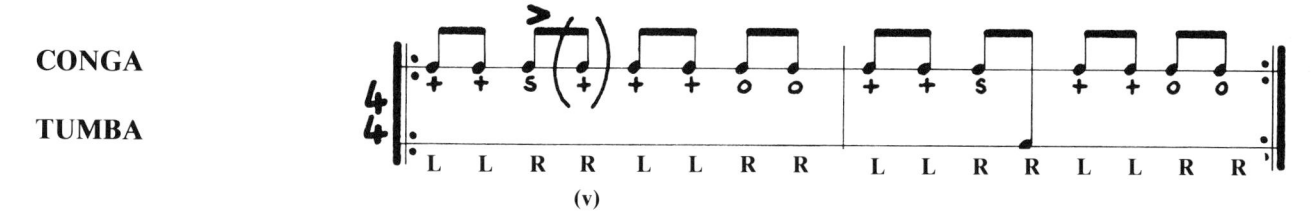

Bongo (»Rumba 1, 2 and 3«)

The rhythm is played with the index fingers of both hands.

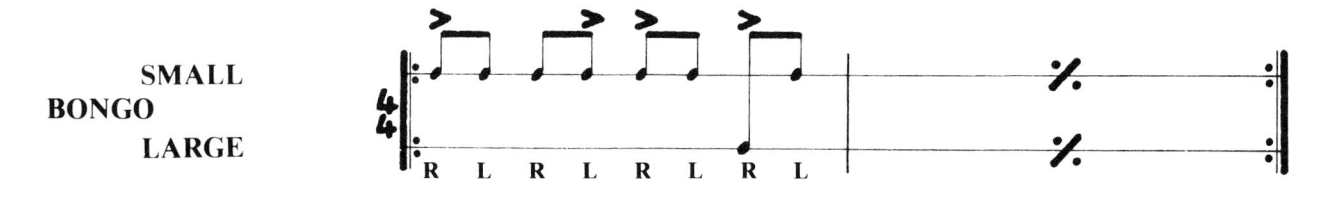

Timbales (Paila) and maracas

When playing *Rumba* the same *Paila* and *maracas* rhythms are used as shown for *Bolero* — refer to page 119.
This style is shown for »*Rumba 1*«, but can also be used in the two other rhythm examples.

Timbales

The various *Mambo cowbell* and *Paila rhythms* are also used for *Rumba* (»*2 and 3*«) — refer to *Mambo* on pages 57-58 in the first part of the book.

The following rhythms are played on one of the two *cowbells* or as *Paila* — using both hands.

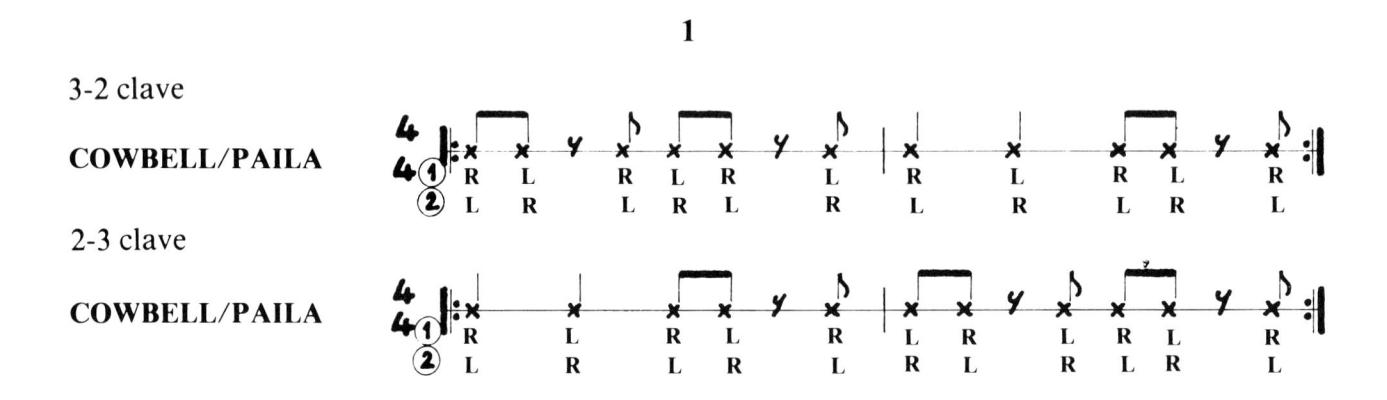

1

3-2 clave

2-3 clave

For Rumba in fast tempi

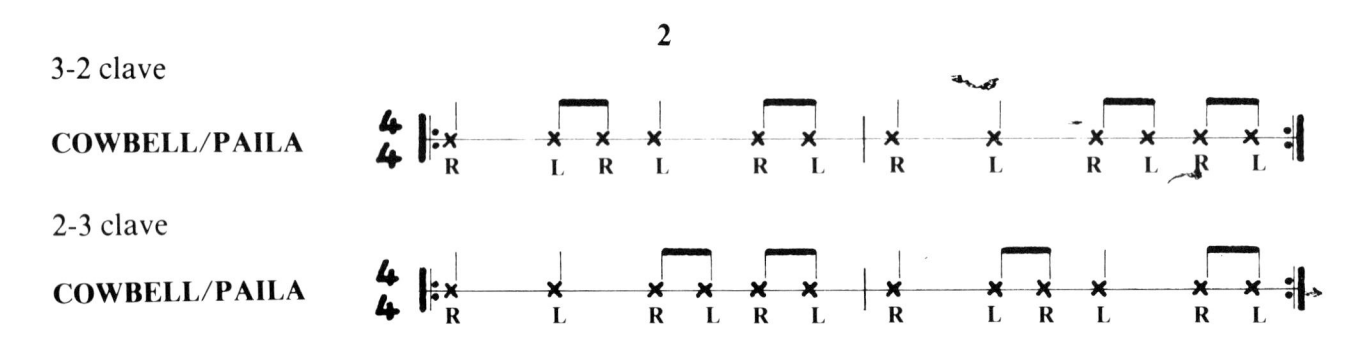

2

3-2 clave

2-3 clave

Once in a while you will find arrangements which alternate between various rhythms. It is important to feel at ease with the different rhythms before attempting such changes in the rhythm.
In *Rumba* arrangements it is possible to change to *6/8 rhythms*.
There are examples of how to play *6/8* in conjunction with *Rumba* (4/4) on page 143).

The change of rhythm can either be played directly or by playing a break before making the change.
Refer to opposite page.

Breaks (»cierre«) for Rumba

The breaks shown here can be played in the following ways:
1:   The whole rhythm section plays *the break*.
2:   Part of the section (*conga* and *timbales* for instance) plays *the break* while the rest of the section continues playing the rhythm.
3:   The whole orchestra plays *the break*.

Rehearse the figures thoroughly so that you feel at ease with them.

The breaks shown here can be played with either the *3/2* or *2/3 clave rhythm* unless otherwise shown.

Mambo breaks are also used in *Rumba* — refer to page 114.

Rumba Folklorico

The old types of *Rumba* are based on the rhythm patterns of the *tumbadoras* (*tumba* and *conga/tres golpes/segunda*). The *quinto* plays a solo to inspire the dancers and the other musicians in the group. The *cowbell* is not usually used, instead *cascara/palitos/guagua* is played with the rhythms (meaning the rhythm is played with two sticks on the side of a *conga* or other wood-sounding instrument). Refer also to the introduction to *Rumba* on page 122.

The rhythms are started either by the *claves* or the *tumba* followed by the secondary rhythm on *conga*. In *Rumba Folklorico* the percussion group always starts in *3-2 clave*. If the first theme or chorus of the song is in *2-3 clave*, it will start in the second bar of the rhythm – reversing the feeling of the song to *2-3 clave*.

The tempo can be from medium-slow to very fast. (Refer to *Rumba types* on page 122.)

Rumba should be played with an alla breve feeling. The foot is tapped on the counts of **1** and **3**.

Rumba 4 (Folklorico)

Explanation of the rhythm chart on the opposite page

Clave: 3/2. (*Rumba style.*) Refer to explanation page 128.

Cascara: Played on the side of *the conga* or on some other wooden object.
The rhythm is played from hand to hand as shown below the notes.
NOTICE: The same person often plays both *clave* and *cascara*. Both are played with a stick on the side of a *conga*.
In the beginning *the clave rhythm* is played and later on in the arrangement the rhythm is changed to *cascara*.

Tumba: *The tumba rhythm* is the »basic pulse« *(tumbao)*. This is the rhythm to be played when there is only one drum.

Conga: The rhythm is played from hand to hand. All the muffled strokes (+) which are not accentuated should be played in a relaxed manner near the edge of the head. »Slap« strokes can be used on the count of **and 2** in the second bar instead of the muffled strokes.

    ✱ This *conga rhythm* can be played in the following manners:
1. The two open strokes are played in the first bar – independent of the direction of the *clave*.
2. The two open strokes are played together with the *clave* beats on **1** and **2 and**, also in the *reverse clave rhythm (2-3)*. In this case the open strokes are played in the second bar.
3: The two open strokes are played as a balance for the *clave rhythm*. When playing in *3-2 clave* the two open strokes are played in the second bar and in *2-3 clave* the two open strokes are played in the first bar. This is the manner in which most Cuban *conga-drummers* play.

Quinto: The quinto plays solo – play with moderation to start with. Refer to page 134.

Clave: 2/3. (*Rumba style.*)

Cascara: Shown here for *2/3 clave rhythm*.

NOTICE! When *the claves* play *the Rumba style rhythm* as shown *the clave* and *the cascara rhythm* will hit the stroke on the count of **4 and** in the first bar together. This will produce more continuity in the rhythm.

The combination of *the tumba* and *the conga* in the example shown is just one possibility.
The alternative rhythms are just as characteristic and can be combined according to which sound and style is wanted.
Generally speaking, the less intricate rhythms should be used in fast tempi.

REMEMBER — *the tumba rhythm (tumbao)* should always be played.

Practicing the rhythm and rehearsing the rhythm section refer to page 99.

133

Rumba 4 (Folklorico)

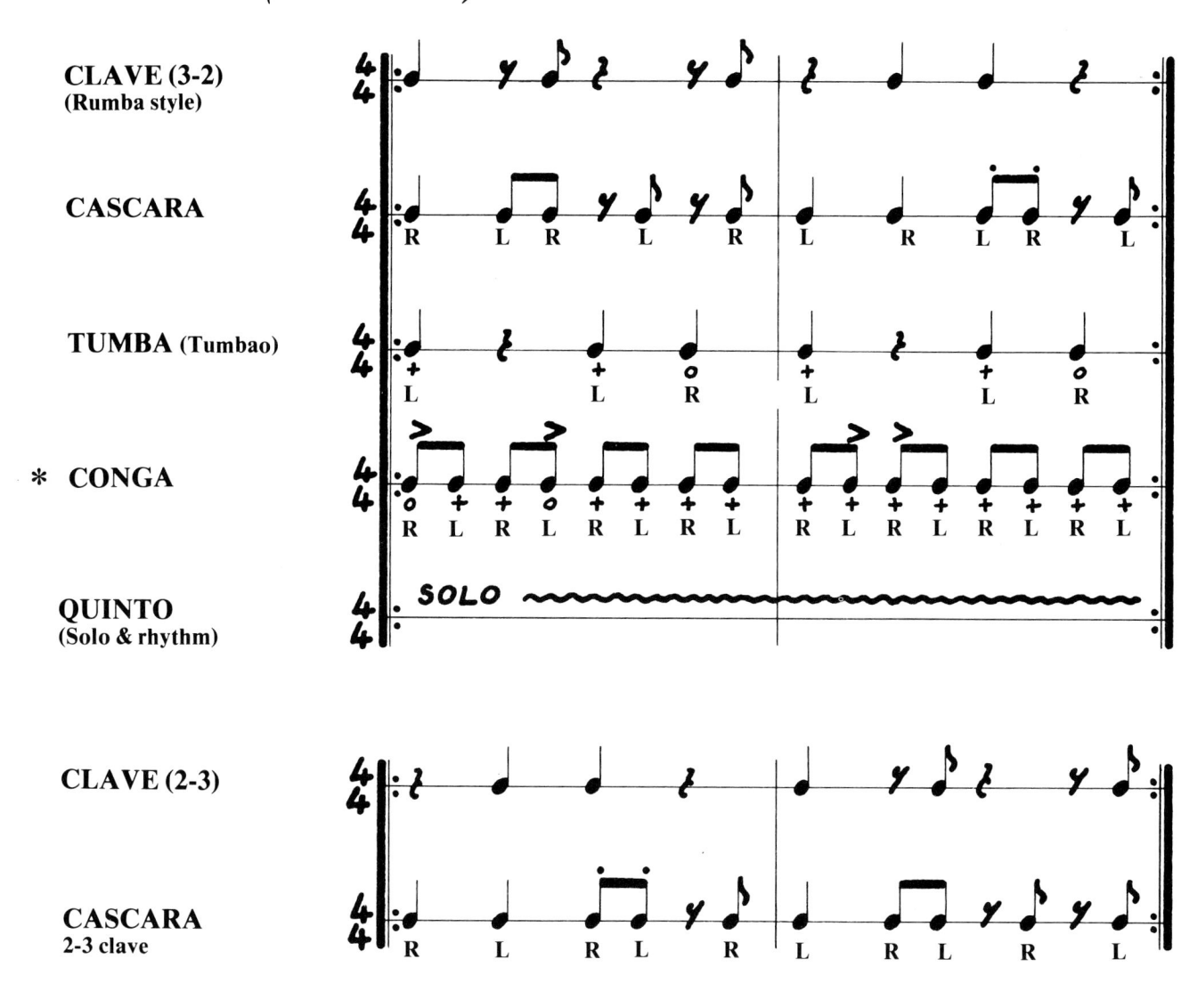

CLAVE (3-2)
(Rumba style)

CASCARA

TUMBA (Tumbao)

* **CONGA**

QUINTO
(Solo & rhythm)

CLAVE (2-3)

CASCARA
2-3 clave

Alternative rhythms

Cascara: See page 137.

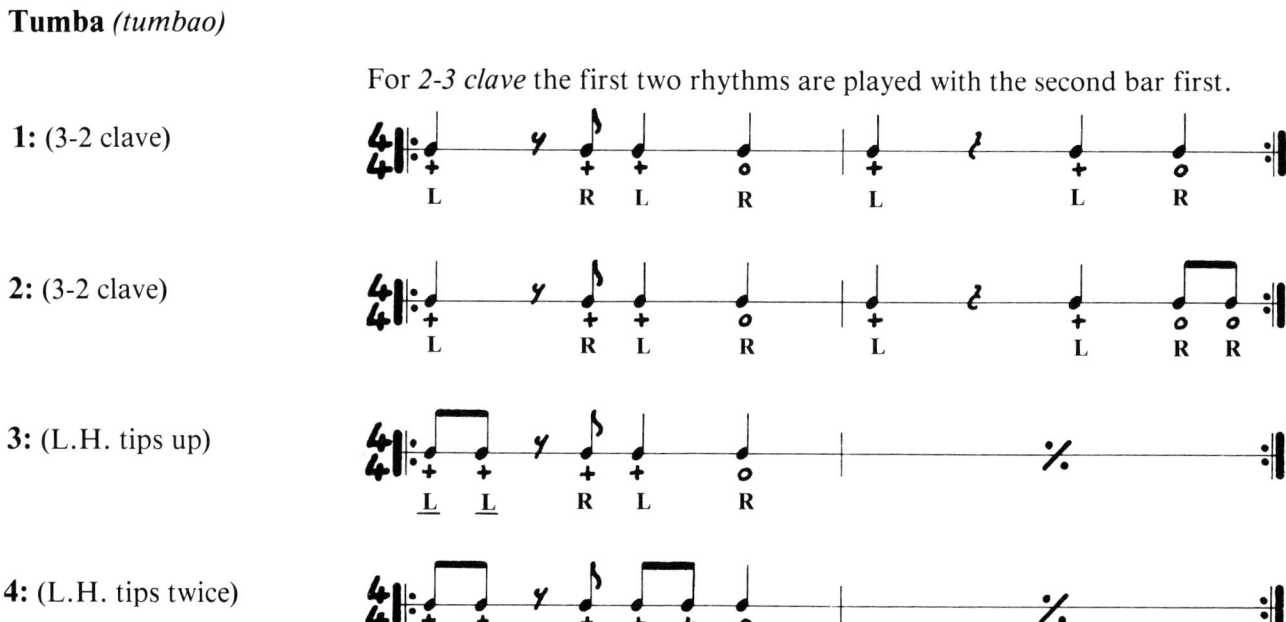

Tumba *(tumbao)*

For *2-3 clave* the first two rhythms are played with the second bar first.

1: (3-2 clave)

2: (3-2 clave)

3: (L.H. tips up)

4: (L.H. tips twice)

134

Conga (secondary rhythms played together with *the tumba-tumbao*).

The explanation on page 40 tells how to play the »slap« strokes with both hands. The places in which the left hand plays two consecutive muffled strokes – tip the hand upwards as in the *basic conga rhythm*.
See page 132 for playing *the conga* with *the clave* or in balance with *the clave*.

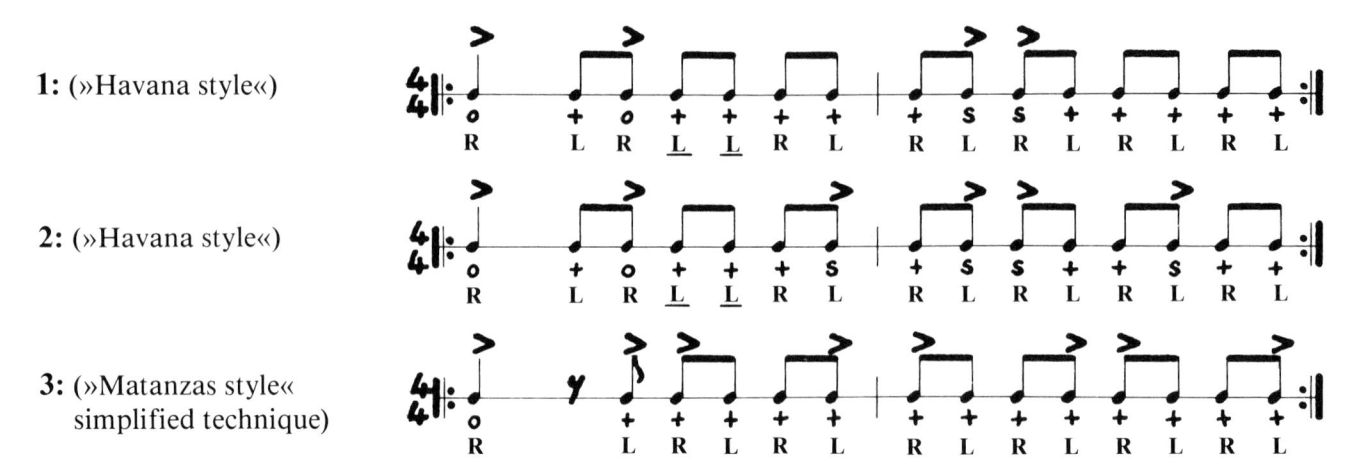

1: (»Havana style«)

2: (»Havana style«)

3: (»Matanzas style« simplified technique)

Quinto

The quinto solo should never lose touch with the rest of the rhythm section. Soloing of this type is not an exhibition of technical capabilities, but should be thought of as something to give inspiration to dancers and the rest of the group.
It is not possible to write *a quinto solo* note for note.
A *quinto solo* is a story — phrases and figures that fit the rhythm in different ways — filling out the open spaces in the rhythm — and creating dynamics in the group.

Start by playing fills every other bar. There is space in between the »open« strokes from *the tumba* and *conga* as shown here in a simplified example.
Alternate between accentuated and lightly played figures.

Once you get used to the rhythm and everybody begins to relax you can play phrases that span over a longer period.

Figures for the second bar

The figures are written with only heavy accentuations. The figures can be played, for instance, from hand to hand with a constant eighth-note feeling and using very relaxed closed strokes.

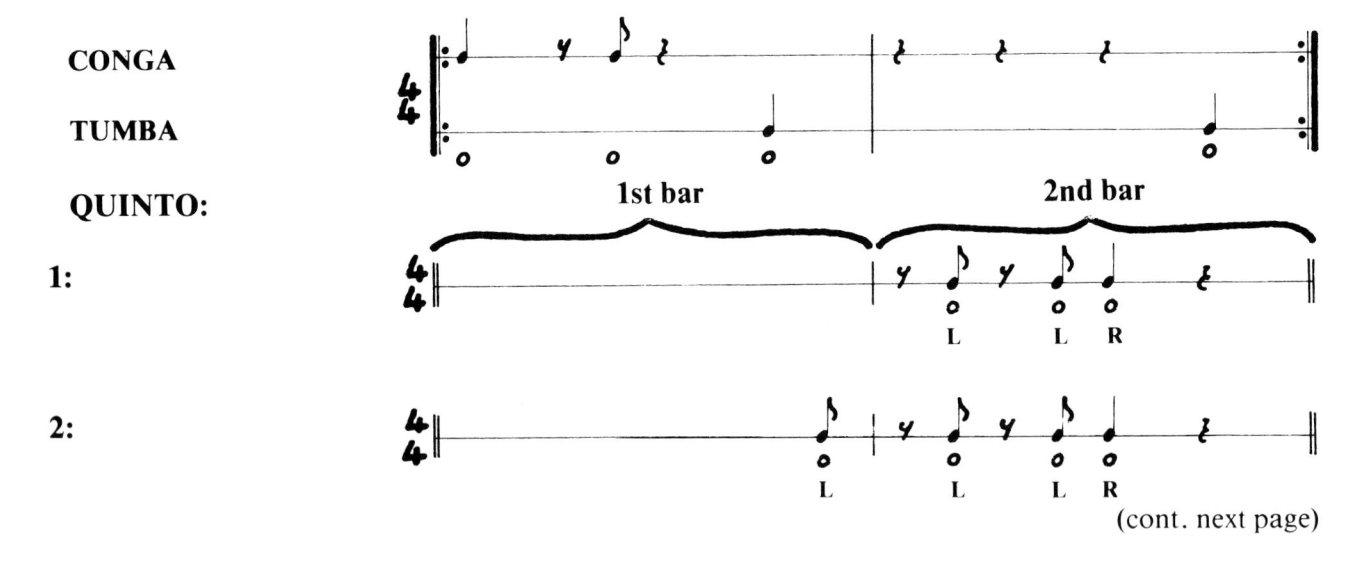

CONGA

TUMBA

QUINTO:

1:

2:

(cont. next page)

Quinto figures (cont.)

[Sheet music: CONGA and TUMBA pattern in 4/4, with 1st bar and 2nd bar marked]

QUINTO:

3: [2nd bar: L R L, open strokes]

4: [2nd bar: R L, R L, open strokes]

5: [2nd bar: R, R, R L, open strokes]

6: [2nd bar: triplet R L R, then L, open strokes]

7: [2nd bar: triplet R L R, then L R accented, open strokes]

Quinto figures using »slap« strokes

The explanation on page 40 shows how the »slap« strokes can be played with either hand. This technique gives a great choice of possibilities when playing solo. The open »slap« strokes are often used when playing in fast tempo. Refer to page 40.

All the examples shown from »1« to »7« can also be played with »slap« strokes instead of »open« strokes. Play each figure twice, the first time with »slap« strokes and the second time with »open« strokes.

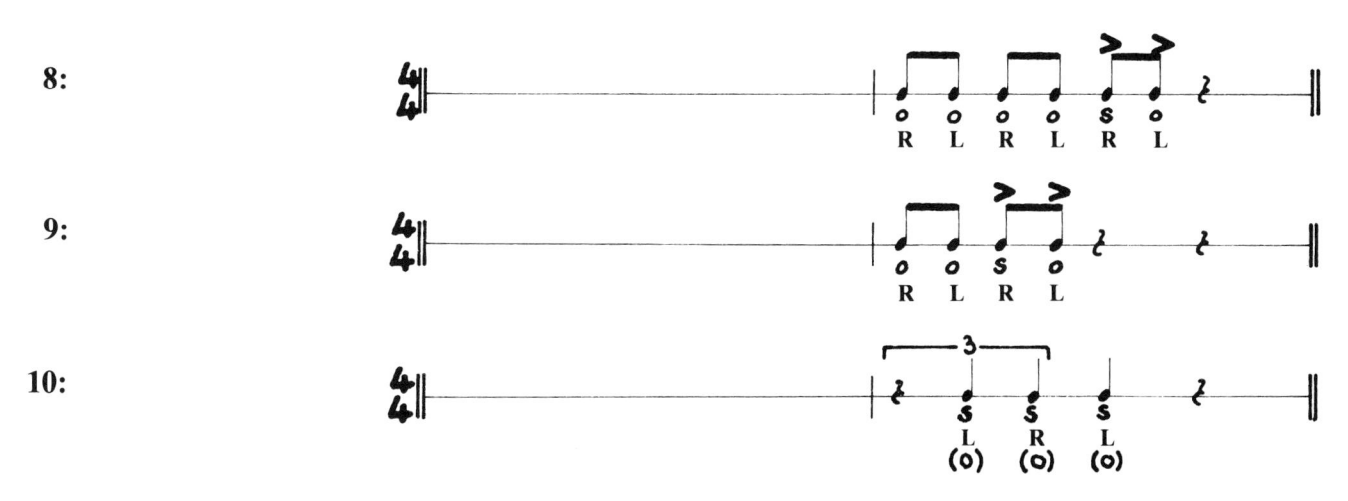

8: [2nd bar: R L R L R L, last two accented with slap-open]

9: [2nd bar: R L R L, with slap-open accented]

10: [2nd bar: triplet L R L, slap strokes with (o) below]

136

Three-bar quinto figures

The phrases start in **the second** bar of *the clave rhythm*.

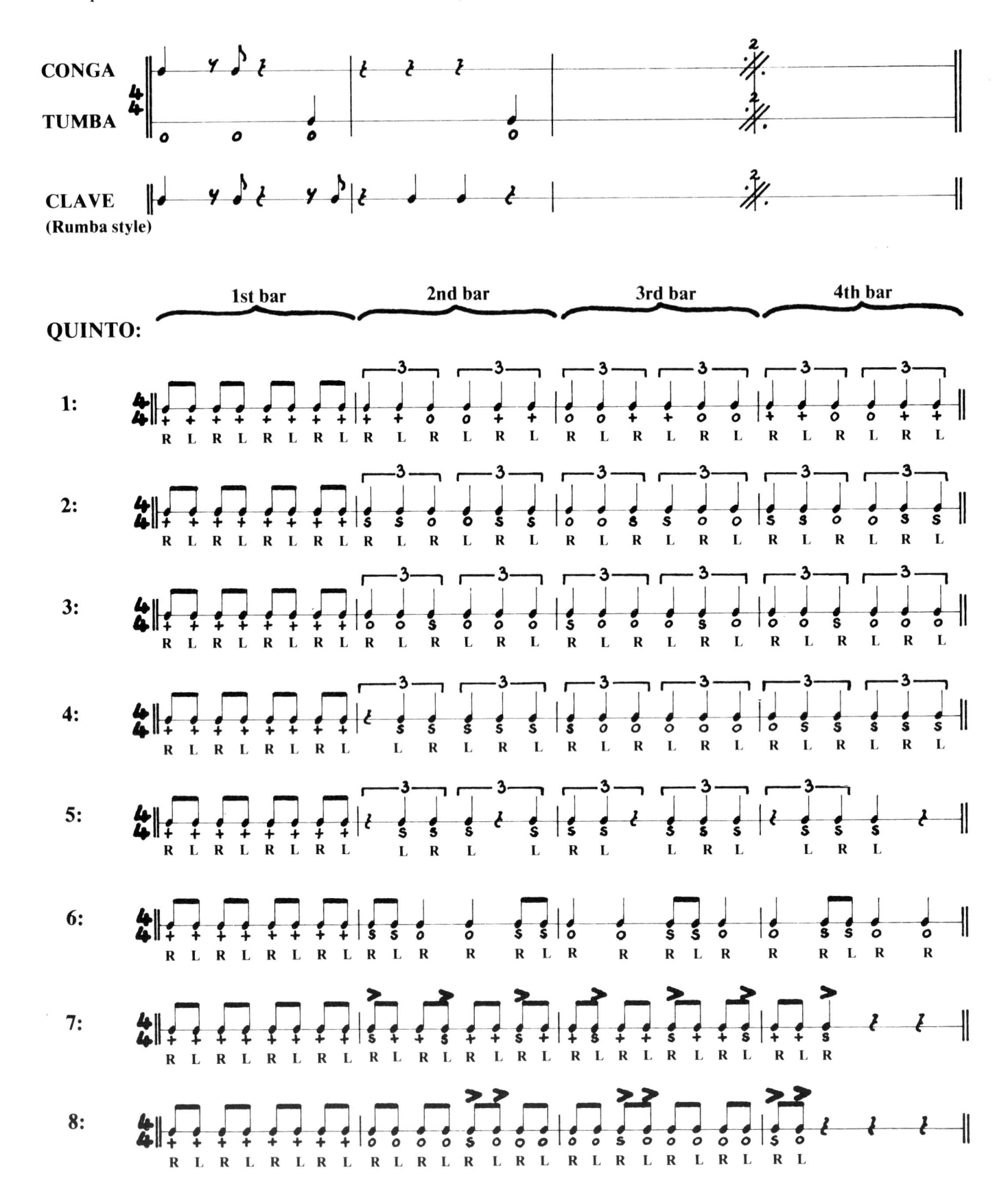

Alternative cascara-rhythms

3-2 clave

3-2 clave

When playing *2-3 clave*, start with the second bar first.
Notice that the right hand plays on **1** and **3** in each bar.

Breaks (»cierre«) for Rumba Folklorico

1

When hearing a cue from *the quinto* everybody plays *the break*.

3/2 clave *(Rumba-style)*

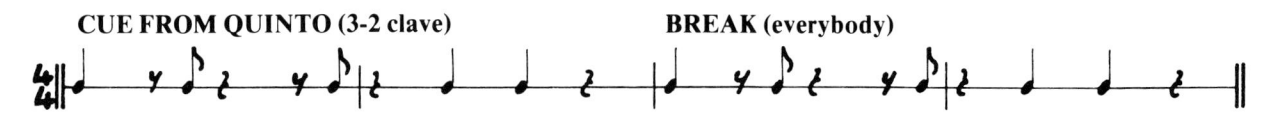

CUE FROM QUINTO (3-2 clave) **BREAK (everybody)**

2/3 clave *(Rumba-style)*

CUE FROM QUINTO (2-3 clave) **BREAK (everybody)**

The break can also be played as *the regular clave rhythm*.

2

After *the quinto* plays a cue *(the clave rhythm)* everybody plays: *the clave rhythm* and then the same rhythm as *cascara* which creates a four bar *break*.

QUE FROM QUINTO **BREAK (everybody)**

Or *the break* is played as *2-3 clave* and as the *2-3 cascara rhythm*. Refer to the rhythm chart.

Refer to »breaks« for *Rumba Popular* on page 131.

Afro-Cuban 6/8 1 *(Popular)*

The next section should be considered as advanced and requires that you feel at ease with the rhythms that have been shown up until now.

The 6/8 rhythms come from the musical rituals that the African slaves brought with them.

When *the 6/8 rhythms* are used by dance orchestras they are played as a simplified version of the folk music in the same manner as the other Cuban rhythms.

It's wonderful pulse makes *the 6/8 rhythm* ideal for improvising on, and apart from using it as a steady pattern *6/8* can be used as a *contrasting rhythm* when played together with, or in extension of, a *4/4 rhythm*. This is explained on page 143.

Afro-Cuban 6/8 is played over a two bar period in the same manner as *the 4/4 rhythms*.

The basic pulse of the rhythm is based on the counts of **1** and **4** and the foot is tapped on the same counts. (Refer to the left hand in the timbales rhythms shown on the opposite page.)

Explanation of the rhythm chart on the opposite page

Cowbell: Played if there are no timbales.

Timbales: The right hand plays C- or A-strokes on the *large cowbell* or *Paila*. The left hand plays the basic pulse on the counts of **1** and **4** in each bar with an accentuated »open« stroke on the count of **1** in the first bar and the rest muffled (+).

Conga/tumba: The rhythm is played from hand to hand.
There should be an evident difference between the accentuated strokes and the light strokes. (s) indicates that »slap« strokes can be used instead of the closed strokes (+).

Bongo: Alternately two strokes on the large drum (right hand) and two accentuated strokes on the small drum (left hand).

Guiro: Except for the accentuated strokes the stick should remain on the playing surface of the guiro throughout the rhythm. The accentuated strokes underline the basic pulse with the count of **1** in the first bar played loudest.

Reverse cowbell or *Paila rhythm:* Sometimes a melody will be written in a way in which *the cowbell rhythm* has to start with the second bar (refer to the basic rhythm shown above).

The necessary instruments for playing *Afro-Cuban 6/8* are: *cowbell* and *conga/tumba*.

Alternative rhythms refer to page 142 and the opposite page.

Afro-Cuban 6/8 1 *(Popular)*

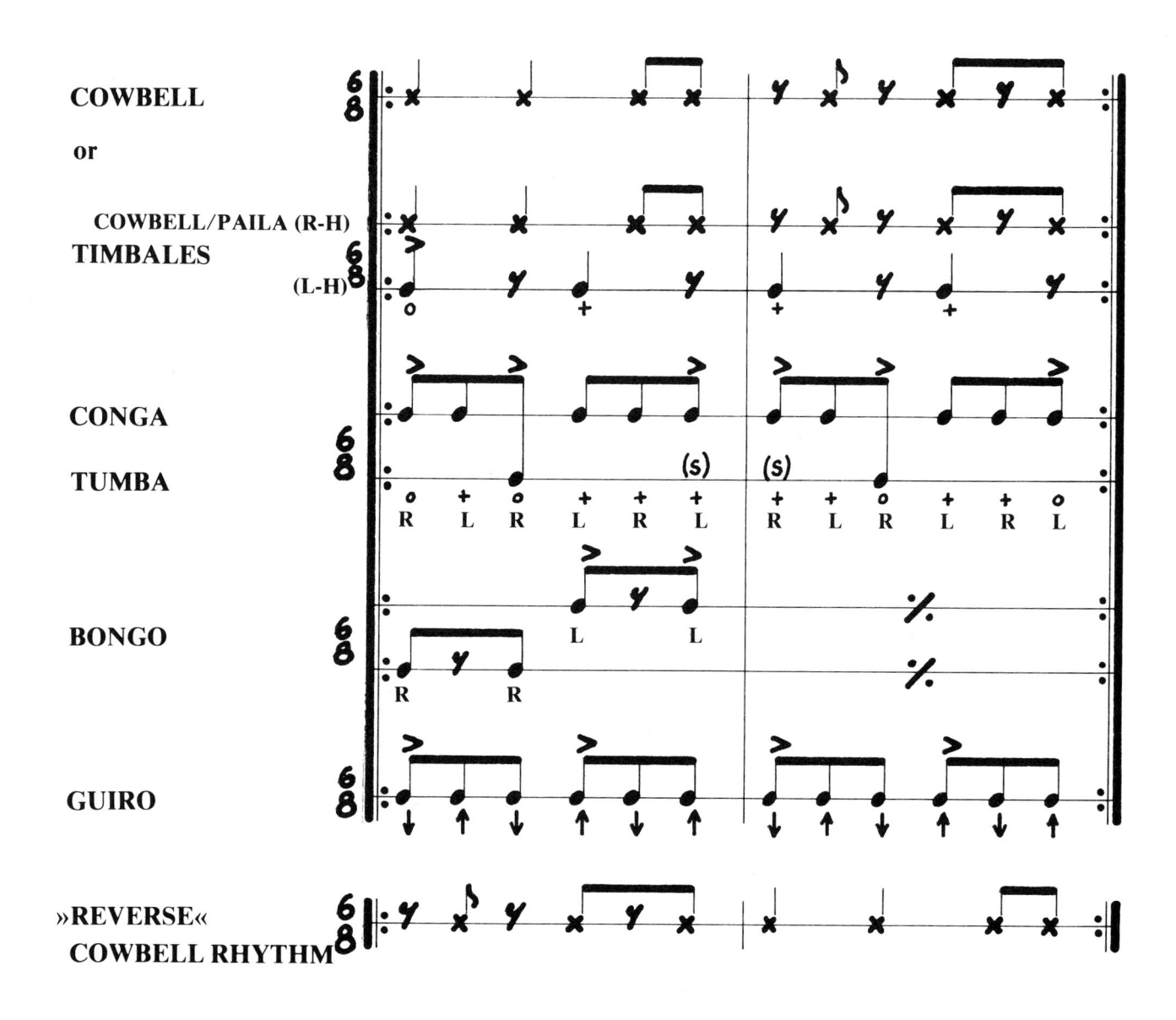

Variations for conga/tumba

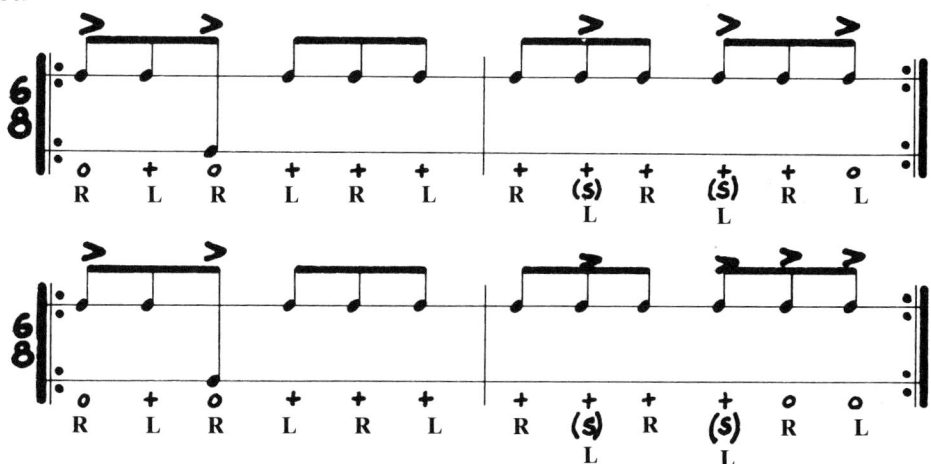

Alternative guiro rhythm

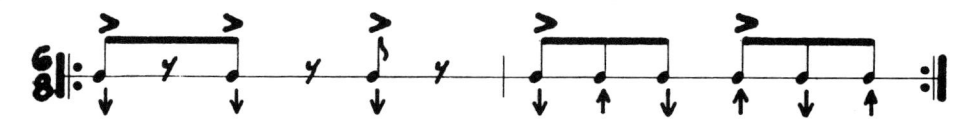

Afro-Cuban 6/8   2 *(Popular)*

Explanation of the rhythm chart on the opposite page

Cowbell: Played if there are no *timbales* (A-strokes).
Timbales: The right hand plays C- or A-strokes on *the large cowbell,* or *Paila.*
 The left hand plays *the basic pulse* on the counts of 1 and 4 in each bar. An accentuated »open« stroke on the count of 1 in the **first** bar and the rest of the strokes muffled.
Conga/tumba: The rhythm is played from hand to hand. The rhythm can be played on one drum.
 The »open« stroke which is usually played on *the tumba* is played on *the conga* instead.
 (s) indicates that »slap« strokes can be used instead of the closed strokes (+).
Bongo: Alternately two strokes on the large drum with the right hand and two accentuated strokes on the small drum with the left hand.
Maracas: The rhythm is played from hand to hand. Evenly accentuated strokes.

Reverse *cowbell* or *Paila* rhythm:
 Sometimes a melody will be written in a way in which *the cowbell rhythm* has to start with the second bar.

The necessary instruments for playing *Afro-Cuban 6/8* are: *cowbell* and *conga/tumba.*

Alternative rhythms refer to page 142.

Afro-Cuban 6/8   2 *(Popular)*

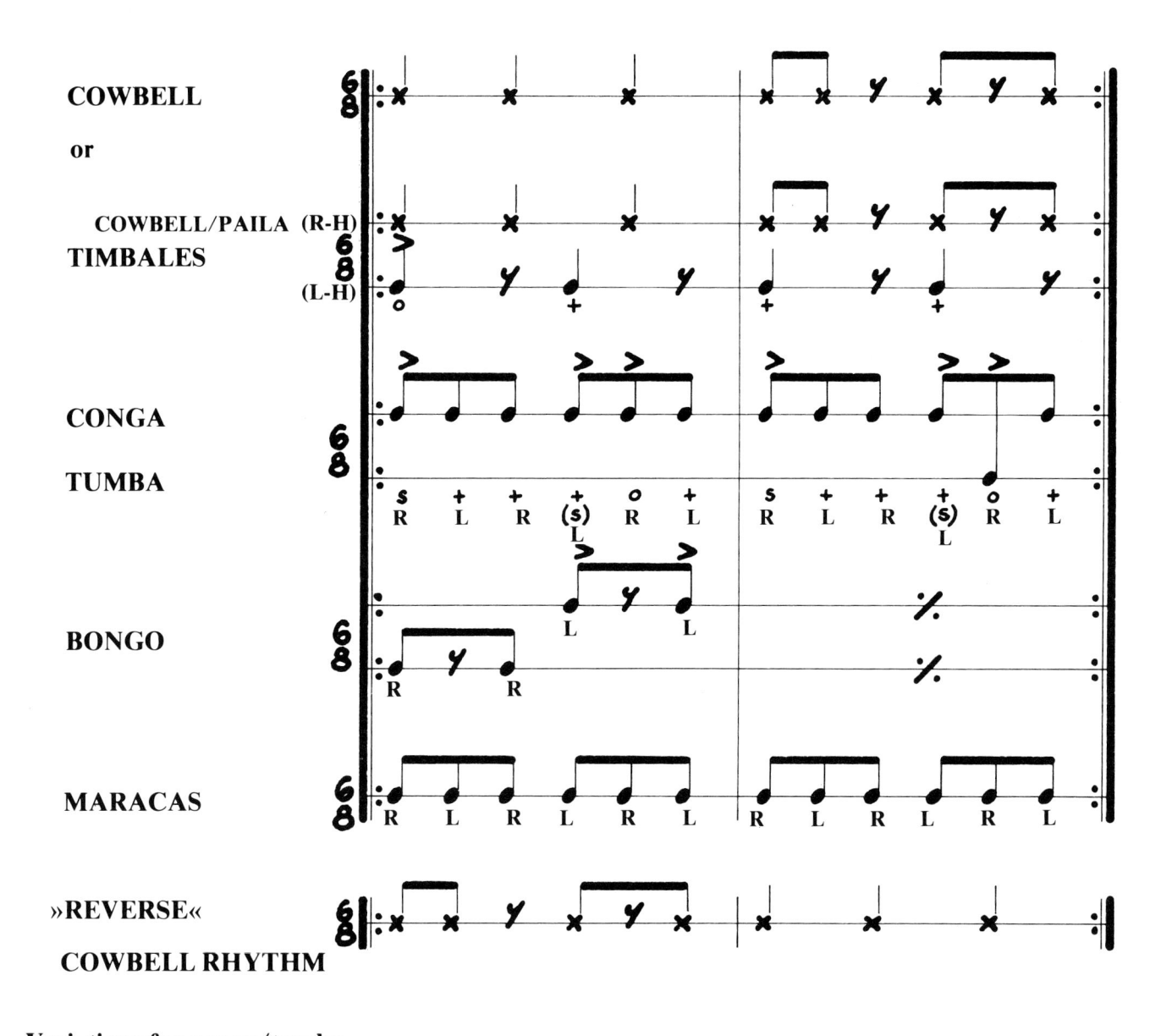

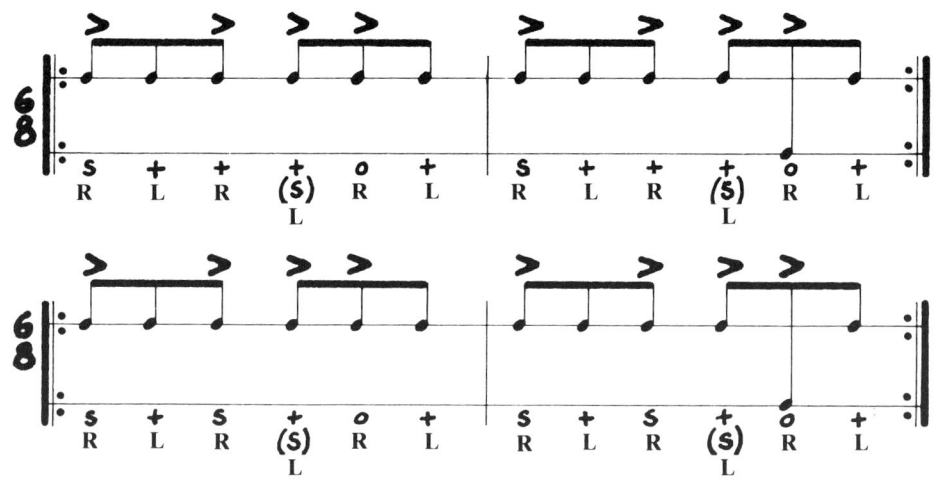

*The rhythms can be played on one drum. The »open« stroke that is usually played on *the tumba* is played on *the conga* instead.*

(s) indicates slap strokes as an alternative.

Alternative rhythms for Afro-Cuban 6/8

The next two rhythms are used as a contrast for *the cowbell rhythms* shown in the rhythm chart.

The instruments can be combined in the following ways:
1: *The hand cowbell* plays the basic rhythm and *the timbales* play the contrasting rhythm on *the small cowbell* using C-strokes.
2: Vice versa: *Timbales* plays on *the large bell* using C- or A-strokes and *the hand cowbell* plays B-strokes.
3: *The timbales* or *the hand cowbell* play the basic rhythm and *the guiro* plays the contrasting rhythm.

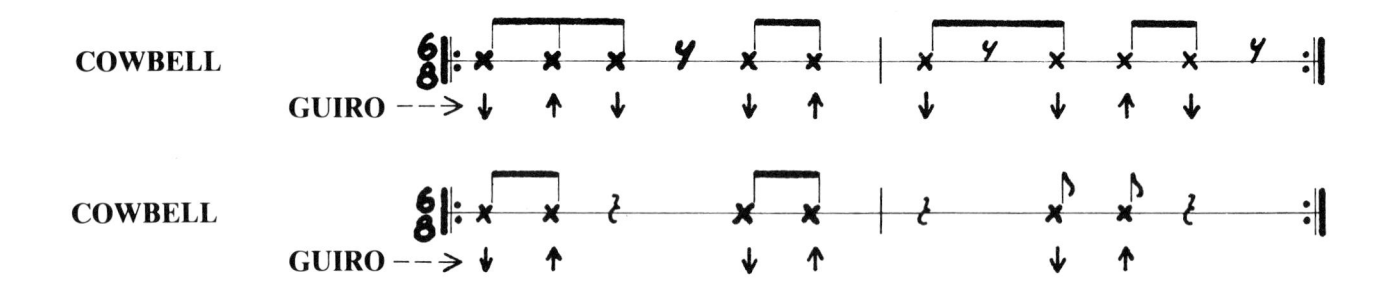

Conga/tumba

A more fluid type of rhythm which also will work well when playing *Rock* or *Jazz*.

6/8 and 4/4 combined or in continuation

6/8 is used as a contrasting rhythm to *4/4*.
Sometimes an arrangement will change from *6/8* to *4/4* or vice versa.
Parts of the rhythm section can also change to *6/8* while the rest continues in *4/4*. This can also be done by the *conga, bongo* or *timbales*, using *6/8 feeling* when playing a solo.
In practice this is the method used:
In *6/8* the foot is tapped on the counts of **1** and **4** (remember you are now counting six to the bar and not four).

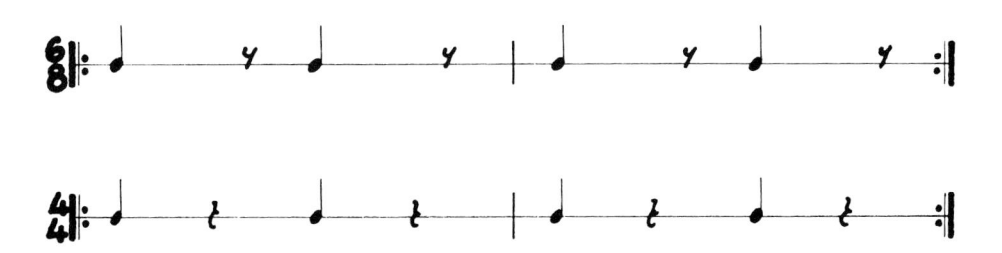

When playing a fast *4/4 rhythm* such as *Mambo* or *Rumba* the foot is tapped on the counts of **1** and **3**. *6/8* is played and felt with a triplet feeling in conjunction with *the 4/4 rhythm*, and the **basic pulse** (the counts on which the foot is tapped) **is the same**.

When a medium tempo *4/4 rhythm* such as *Cha-cha-cha* is played together with a *6/8* then the foot is tapped on the counts of **1-2-3-4** in *4/4 rhythm* and there will be two bars of *6/8* to one bar of *4/4*.

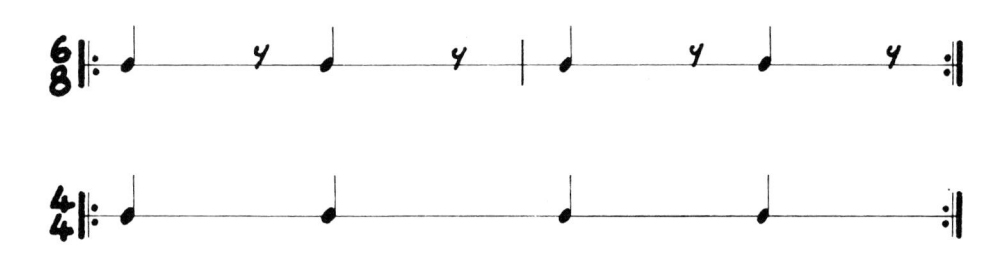

Brazilian rhythms

Introduction

Brazilian music is a fascinating mixture of many cultures which manifests itself in the vast number of instruments and musical styles which exist in the country.
The important influences are from the African slaves, the European colonists from Portugal and the Brazilian Indians, all of which have contributed both instruments and music forms to Brazilian culture.

The rhythms have come into being in different parts of the country and at different times. The two largest sources of music are the state of Bahia towards the north, and Rio de Janeiro.
Since it is not possible to distinguish between Brazilian folk music and popular music, both types of music have been given the single term »Musica Popular Brasileira«.

The rhythms we will be working with here are the most well known and popular, but they are still only a few of the many rhythms that are to be found.

Types of orchestras

The combination of instruments in the Brazilian orchestras and groups is somewhat more varied than the Cuban.

The guitar, »*violão*«, is the most popular instrument in popular and folk music. The guitar is accompanied by either one or more vocalists or by rhythm instruments, the *pandeiro* being the most commonly used.

A smaller group may also use an accordion — »*Acordeon*« or »*Sanfona*« which is also used in popular and folk music. (Refer to *Baion* on page 164.)

Apart from stringed and percussion instruments, flutes of various types are the next most important ingredient.
At gatherings in Northern Brazil, the small orchestras use flutes and percussion (folk musik) but the flute is best known from **the Samba** and **Bossa Nova orchestras.**

»**Escolas de Samba**« or Samba schools are associations in which the people, especially from the hill country called »Morros« around Rio de Janeiro, meet and practice vocal, rhythm and dance arrangements for the annual four-day long carnival. Each year the various Samba schools compete at the carnival to decide which school has the best costumes, arrangements etc.
Apart from the large array of rhythm instruments, an instrument called *the »cavaquinho«* is used for accompaniment. *The »cavaquinho«* is a small four stringed instrument resembling the ukulele.

Marching bands have participated right from the beginning in producing many competent instrumentalists and at the same time have popularized such instruments as the trumpet, saxophone and the snare drum, »*caixa*«, within Brazilian popular music.
These orchestras also play carnival rhythms such as *Marcha Carnevalesca (Marcha de Carnival)* and *Marcha Rancho*.

Many Brazilians today are connected with various **religious cults**, of which *Candomblé* and *Macumba* are the most well-known.
Elements from this magical music and the rhythms especially, have given evident inspiration to much of the popular music.
At these religous ceremonies the rhythm is played by *atabaques, pandeiro* and other percussion instruments. *The cavaquinho* and *guitar* are used as melody instruments.

»**Capoeira**« is the name of another Afro-Brazilian ritual which is a dance and at the same time a martial arts form. The slaves practiced this »dance« in order to be able to use their feet for defending themselves when their arms were chained or tied. This ritual is still practiced, in which two or more dancers, by using circling movements around each other try to launch kicks at each other. The hands are used only to keep balance during the acrobatic movements. The »dance« is executed with rhythmic steps accompanied by *atabaques* and »*berimbau*« (refer to page 93).

»**Batuque**« is often used as a general name for the Afro-Brazilian dances and rhythms.

»**Choro**« is the name of a type of music that, to this day, is very popular in Brazil. *The Choro groups (Choro conjuntos)* began by playing old, well-known types of music such as *Polka, Maxixe* and *Schottisch* in technically advanced instrumental renditions.
In the beginning, the groups consisted of *ebony flute* (melody), *cavaquinho* (harmony) and the guitar which played the melodic bass line which is characteristic of this style.
Later on the groups expanded with instruments such as four and six stringed guitars, banjo, »*bandolim*« – a type of mandolin – *clarinet, saxophone* and percussion – especially *reco-reco* and *pandeiro*.
(The rhythm instruments use the same rhythms as shown under *Samba*.)

The **Samba groups and orchestras** are found in a large number of variations but all of them use percussion as the dominating element.

When studying the Cuban rhythms, you will notice that they all, except *Afro-Cuban 6/8*, have the *clave rhythm* as a foundation-»key«.
Another characteristic is the accentuated **2** and **4**, or **2** and **4 and** feeling. This means that the rhythms are not generally based on **1** and **3**.

For instance:

CONGA

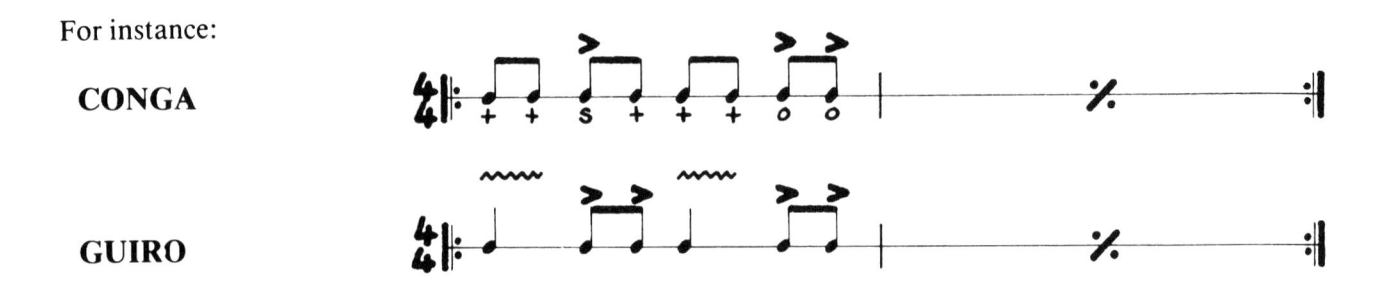

GUIRO

Contrary to the Cuban rhythms, the Brazilian rhythm foundation is based on the counts **1** and **3**.
There is no basic *clave rhythm*, but an equivalent *basic pulse* constructed by various instruments.
Samba is the most well known of the Brazilian rhythms and will be the first we will work with.
There are many different types of *Samba*, but they all have the same *basic pulse*.
Samba is split up into three parts or functions:

1: »Basic rhythm«. Rhythms that accentuate the counts of **1** and **3** or **and 1** and **and 3**.
2: »Balance rhythm«. Rhythms that accentuate the counts of **2** and **4** in order to balance and stabilize the rhythm.
   The »basic« — and »balance« rhythm combined produce the »basic pulse« or feeling.
   The strokes on the counts of **1** and **3** are more heavily accentuated than strokes on the counts of **2** and **4**.
3: **The third part** of the rhythm is the various types of instruments that play **rhythms that span over two bars**. These instruments will not sound and feel right unless the »**basic pulse**« is stated.

Just like in the Cuban rhythms, the flow of the melody can sometimes require the two-bar figures to start with the second bar first. This rhythmic adjustment can be acquired with practice, but sometimes even the real masters can be in doubt.

Rehearsing the rhythms and the rhythm section

Rehearsing the rhythm section

Begin by playing the rhythms with the rhythm section only — without piano, bass or guitar.
By rehearsing in this manner you will learn to think of the rhythm as music in itself — as an independent element.

When each person has learned the figures to be played on his/her own instrument, begin to build up the rhythm one instrument at a time, so that you can hear what each person is playing. This will make you concentrate on what is going on and will make the rhythm steadier.
When everybody is concentrated and relaxed the rhythm can start to swing.
Remember to play as simply as possible, it is the rhythm as a whole and the correct combination of instruments – the sound itself that is important, not each person's individual solo performance. Just one ego-tripper can ruin everything.

Structuring and rehearsing the rhythms

Use this structure for all the rhythms:
1: Build up the rhythm one instrument at a time.
   It is best to start with *the surdo*.
   Even though many of the instruments play the same rhythm in the first and the second bar it is important that they start on the count of **1** in the first bar. It is important that everybody can hear the two-bar period, even before the instruments that play over a two-bar pattern, such as *the tamborim* and *ago-go* are added.
2: Once the rhythm starts to function correctly, rehearse periods and rests. Agree on a certain number of bars to be played and then stop, or give *a cue* to stop while the rhythm is still being played.
   Make a two or four bar rest and then start playing again together on the count of **1** in the first bar.
   The rhythm should be tight immediately upon starting again, this is where you can tell whether you have practiced enough or not!
3: Instead of rests, practice some simple breaks which everybody should play.
   You can also practice a combination of rests and breaks.
4: The rhythm section should now be ready to rehearse together with the melody instruments.
   If you wish to work more with the rhythm section alone, then you can set up an arrangement with a beginning, several breaks along the way and an ending.

Apart from this structuring and rehearsal of the rhythms, which is the same for all the rhythms, you will find that they differ from each other in many ways.
These differences are explained in conjunction with the individual rhythms.

Samba

The Samba is without a doubt the most well-known and popular of the rhythms from Brazil.
The Samba rhythm is played in different ways and in various tempi, right from very slow to very fast.

The first officially registered *Samba* was a »*Samba Carnevalesco*« from 1917. This carnival hit was called »*Pelo Telefone*« and was written by Ernesto dos Santos — also known as »Donga«.

The basic Samba rhythm and style is no recent invention and there are many theories as to where the rhythm and the name »*Samba*« come from, and that being the case, I will refrain from further attempts at the same.

The most well-known *Samba types* are: *Samba Batucada (Samba Carnevalesco, Samba de Morro).*
Samba Moderno (Samba do Salão).
Samba Choro.
Samba Canção.
Bossa Nova.

The basic rhythmic pulse and the structure is fundamentally the same in all *the Samba styles* — refer to page 146.

Samba should have a definite »*alla breve*« feeling (the foot is tapped on the counts of **1** and **3**).

Samba Batucada

(Samba Carnavalesco, Samba de Morro)

The first, and at the same time, the most well-known *Samba* we are going to work with here has various names:

Samba Batucada: Batucada is the name of the group of rhythm instruments used and also the name of the rhythm.
Samba Carnavalesco: The rhythm that is played at the famous annual carnival in Rio de Janeiro.
Samba de Morro: Samba from the hill country *(Morros)* around Rio de Janeiro.
It is primarily the population of this area that gather in their »*Escolas de Samba*« to rehearse the new songs and arrangements for the next carnival — refer to page 144.

The great thing about this rhythm is the more people participating, the merrier!

The rhythm is either played with vocals and vocal choruses or purely instrumental, with percussion only, and in certain cases with the »*cavaquinho*«.

There is a large selection of records from the various »*Escolas de Samba*« — listen and enjoy!

Samba Batucada 1

»*Samba Batucada 1*« has a very simple structure but is still a typical rhythm construction. »*Samba Batucada 1*« is based on a structure using the instruments that are easiest to play, which makes this rhythm a good place to start.

The rhythm can be played in all tempi but is most often played in a fast tempo.
Samba should have a distinct »alla breve« feeling — the foot is tapped on the counts of **1** and **3**.

All the instruments are explained in part one.

Surdo: Plays the basic rhythm.
              The left hand muffles on the count of **4** without counting the movement as a stroke.
              It is better to use too many *surdos* – than not enough.
Chocalho: Accentuated on **1** and **3** *(basic rhythm)*.
Reco reco: Accentuated on **2** and **4** *(balance rhythm)*.
Tamborim: If possible, there should be several *tamborims* played at the same time in various pitches.
              Start one at a time, this produces a nice effect.
Ago-go: There should not be too many at once – one is enough.
Apito: Refer to page 147.

Alternative rhythms, refer to page 152.

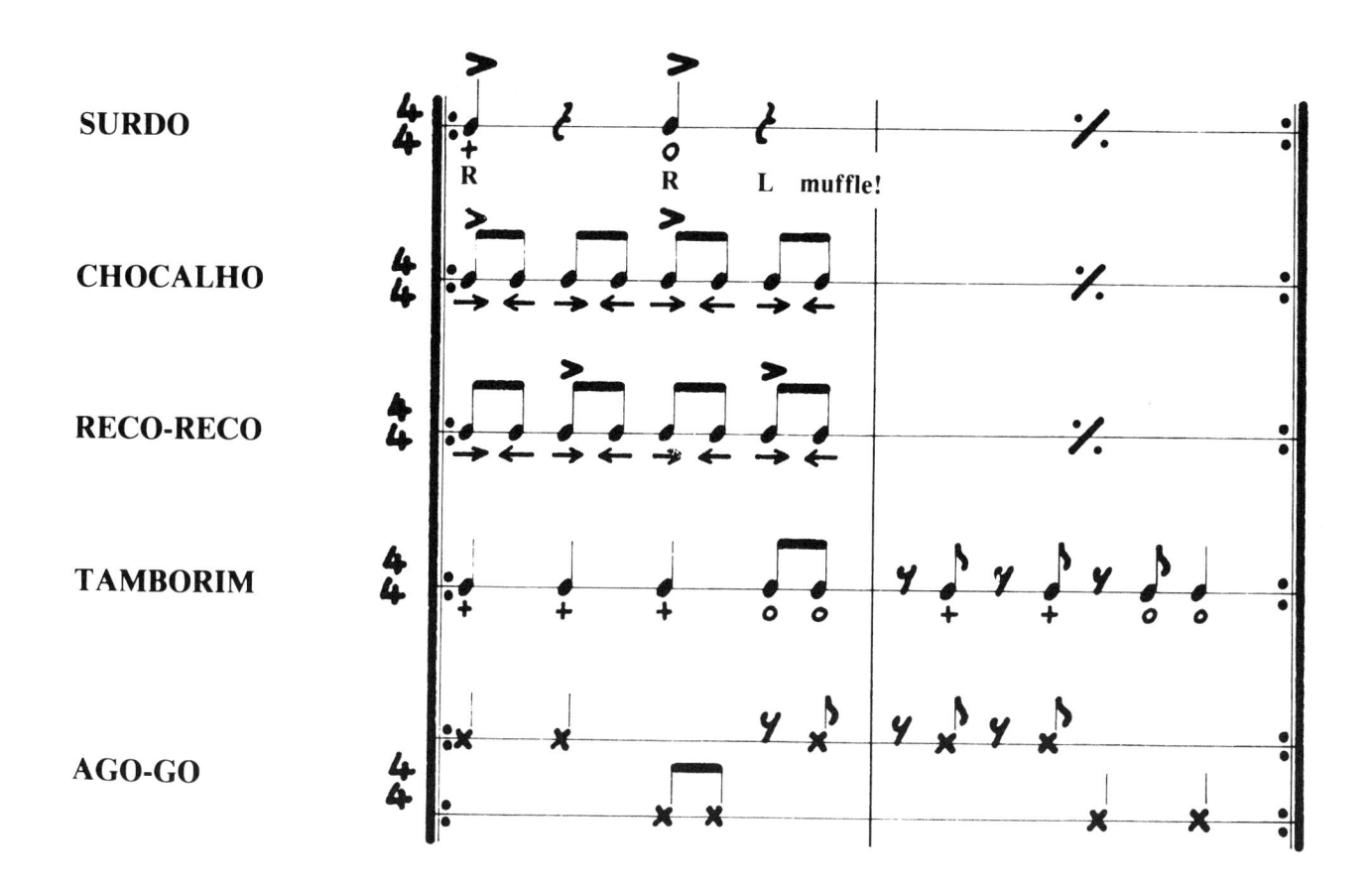

SURDO

CHOCALHO

RECO-RECO

TAMBORIM

AGO-GO

+ APITO

Samba Batucada 2

This is *Samba Batucada* using the complete orchestration.

Explanation of the rhythm chart on the opposite page:

Surdo: The strokes in this rhythm are played with both hands. The left hand plays the strokes with the palm of the hand. The right hand plays with a mallet. Refer also to page 152.
Remember that it is better to use too many *surdos* than not enough, and that the instruments playing two-bar figures can start with the second bar first. (Refer to page 146.)

Chocalho: Accentuated on **1** and **3**.

Reco reco: Accentuated on **2** and **4**.

Tamborim: Plays over a two-bar period. Refer also to page 152.

Pandeiro: »National instrument« of Brazil, which requires diligent practice.
The *pandeiro* plays the basic rhythm, accentuations on **1** and **3**.

Caixa: Snare drum. Notice that the rhythm of *the caixa* is similar to the rhythm of *the tamborim* and these rhythms must function well together. Refer also to page 152.

Caixeta: Plays a simple rhythm over a two bar period.

Ago go: Refer to the method of closing on page 72.

Cuica: The funny yet irreplacable instrument of *Batucada*.
Keep on playing the rhythm until you can execute it with ease then try improvising on the rhythm.

Pratos: Marching cymbals. Used only in certain parts of the arrangement and rarely from the beginning.
They produce a nice effect for pepping up the rhythm section.

Apito: The whistle is used as a rhythm instrument and also as a signal for breaks and changes.

Rehearsing the rhythm section and the rhythm, refer to page 147.

Atabaque is also used in *the Batucada*, refer to page 88 and 89.

Alternative rhythms refer to page 152 and to each instrument in part one.

Samba Batucada 2

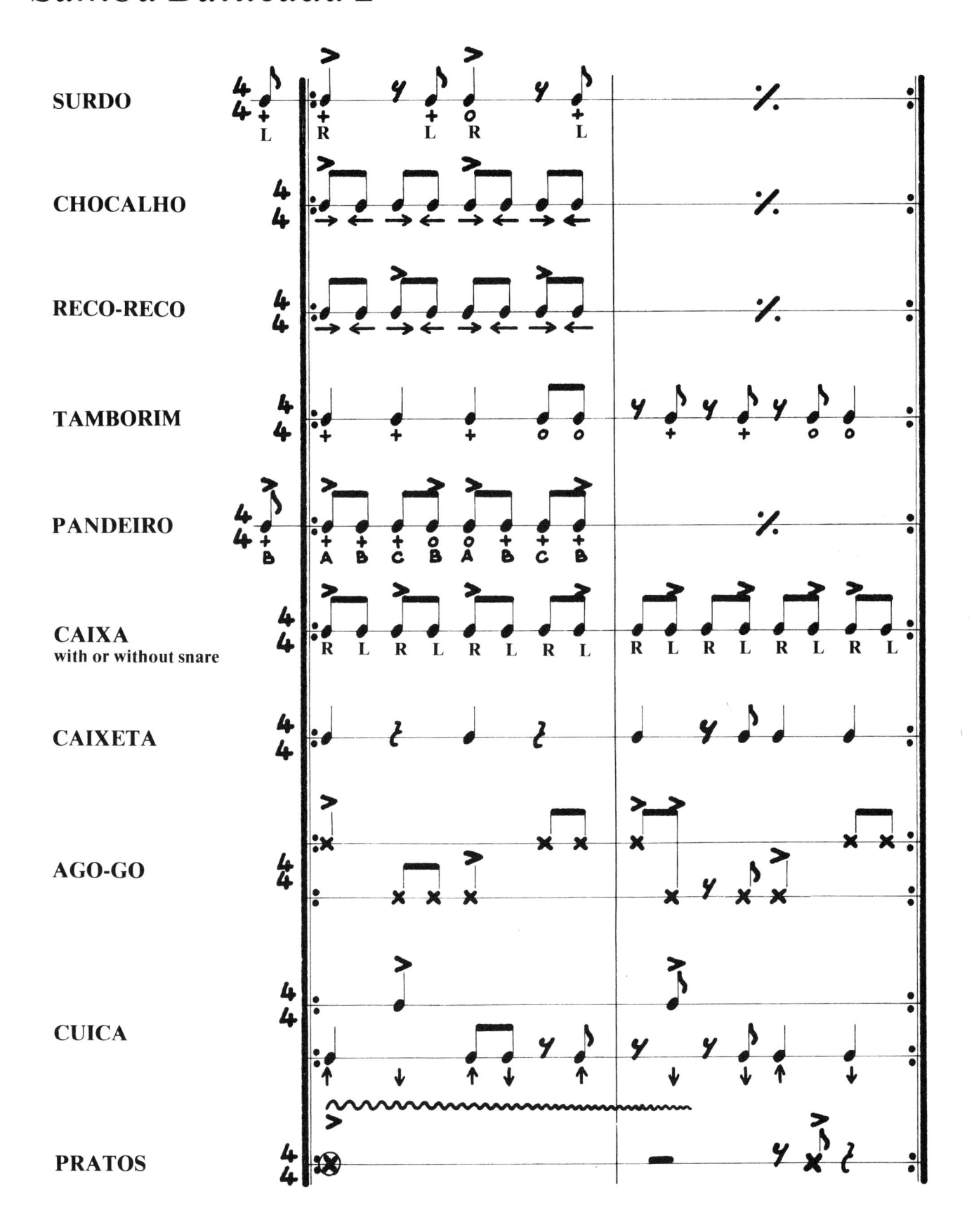

+ APITO

Alternative rhythms for Samba Batucada

Surdo

1

This rhythm, with an open stroke on the count of <u>1</u>, should be played on a higher-tuned *surdo*. The rhythm is played together with the *surdo rhythms* shown in both »*Samba Batucada* 1 and 2«.

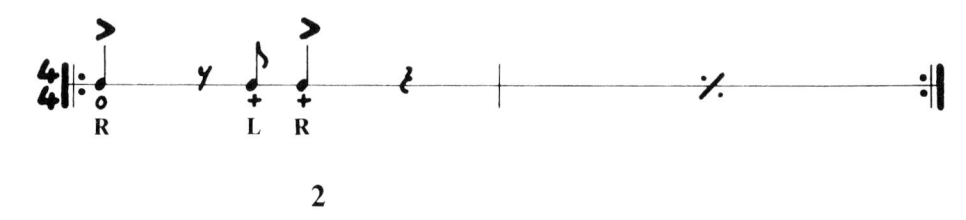

2

Variation of the rhythm shown in the rhythm chart »*Samba Batucada 2*«.

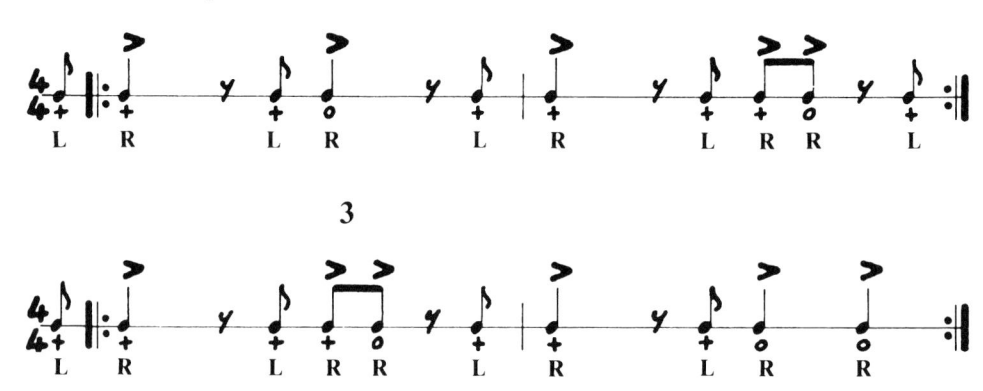

3

Reco-reco

Here the *reco-reco* plays strong accentuations on the counts of <u>1</u> and <u>3</u> *(basic rhythm)*.

Tamborim and caixa

During the arrangement *the tamborim* often changes to this rhythm. Notice the offbeats which are played with the fingers of the left hand.
The rhythm goes together with the *caixa rhythm* which is also shown below, but is not necessarily played at the same time.

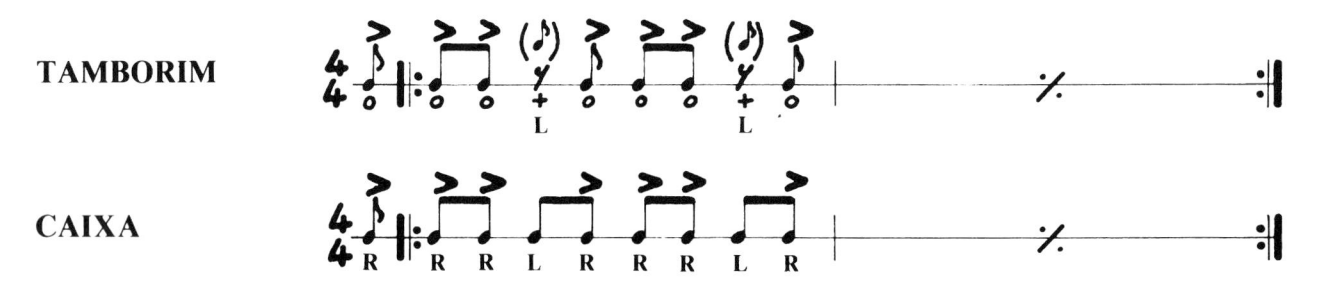

TAMBORIM

CAIXA

The strokes with the left hand should be played in a relaxed manner.

Remember to play the two-bar figures correctly together with the other instruments fitting to the flow of the melody. Refer to the explanation on page 146.

Breaks

Each *Samba group* has its own sound and way of arranging the rhythms.
Some play without breaks at all, and others use a variety of breaks when playing.

A signal from the whistle, »*apito*«, is used to call a break. This can be done with a long tone over a two-bar period.

1: The whole section stops on a signal from the whistle, and one instrument continues on its own.
   The instrument can either continue the rhythm or improvise a solo.
   If there are several people playing the same instrument, they all play their basic rhythm with possible variations that are agreed on beforehand.

   The whistle again plays a signal and the section starts once more, usually by playing a break.

   When the rhythm starts again after a break or stop, the tempo can be changed. This is done by letting *the surdo* play the new tempo for two or four bars.

2: *The surdo* is shown seperately to show the »open« (o) and muffled (+) strokes. The break can be played by everybody or by *the surdo* only.

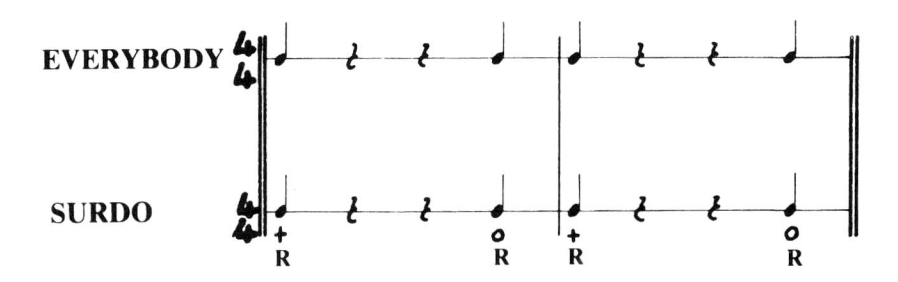

3: The break can be played by everybody or by *the surdo* only.

Fast tempo:

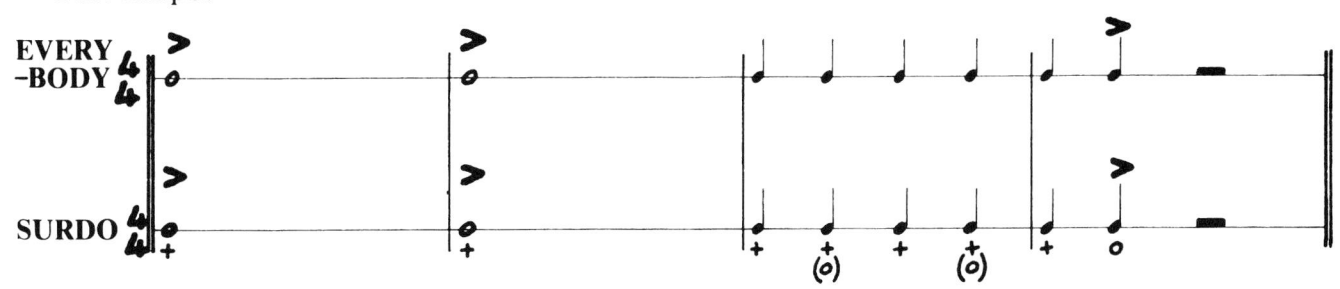

Medium and slow tempo:

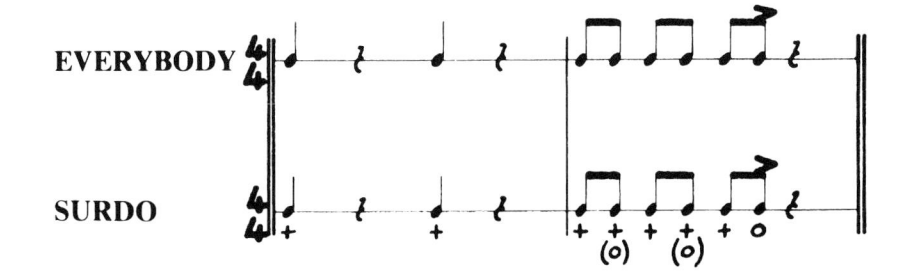

(**Breaks** cont.)

4: The break can be played by everybody or by *the surdo* only.

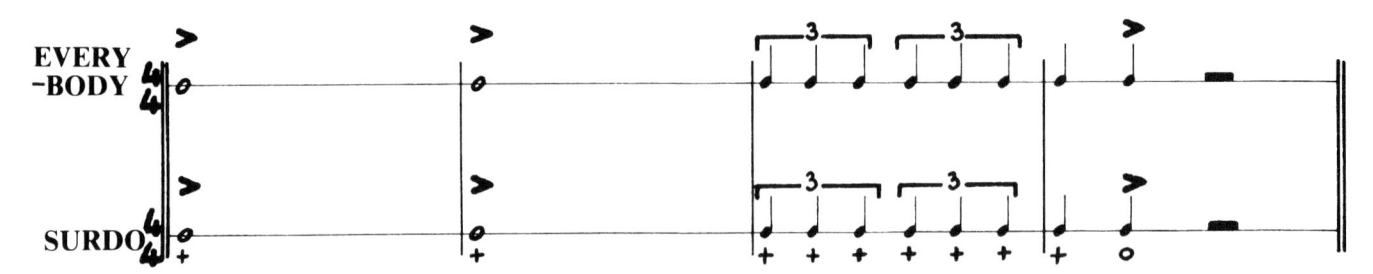

Alternative: Everybody plays the first and second bars and *the surdo* plays the third and fourth bar alone.

5: Notice the uneven period.

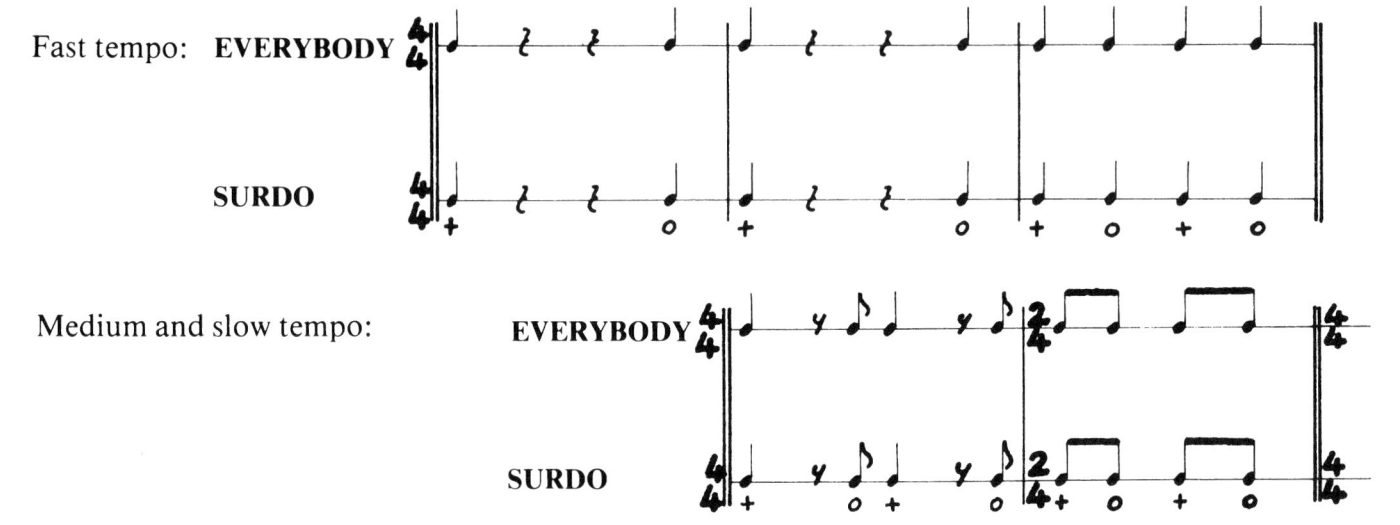

Fast tempo: **EVERYBODY** / **SURDO**

Medium and slow tempo: **EVERYBODY** / **SURDO**

6: The instruments are dealt up into two groups for this break:
  1) »Call«: *surdo, chocalho, reco-reco, pandeiro* and *caixeta.*
  2) »Answer«: *tamborim, ago-go* and *cuica.*

The surdo plays with both groups in the last two bars.

Samba Choro and Samba Canção

Samba Choro and *Samba Canção* are rhythmically the same as the other types of Samba.
The difference is in the musical style.

Samba Canção

The vocals are the basic element in *Samba Canção*, the rhythm instruments being less predominant in this style.
The melody instruments used are most often the guitar and the cavaquinho.

Samba Choro
(Refer to Choro on page 145.)

This style is a mixture of *Choro* and *Samba*.
These melody instruments are taken from *Choro*, and the vocals and percussion are taken from *Samba*.
(Refer to *Samba Moderno* and *Samba Batucada*.)

Samba Moderno (Samba do Salão)

Samba Moderno is a more sophisticated style of *Samba* played at dance halls. Rhythmically it is structured in the same manner as *Samba Batucada* but this more stylized version gives more room for instruments with less playing volume such as *the cabasa* and *the triangle*. *The drum set* is often used with these orchestras but the rhythms shown here are shown for *the surdo*.

As to *Samba* for *the drum set* — refer to the recommended drum guide books on page 181.

When the drum set is used in *Samba the bass drum* plays the counts of **and 1** and **and 3** and the *hi-hat* (left foot) plays the counts of **2** and **4**. Refer to *Bossa Nova* on page 161.
This means that *the drum set* plays *the »basic pulse«* and you have more freedom to choose various instruments for percussion.

This style is good to use when arranging a *Samba* for a smaller group.

Samba Moderno 1

Explanation of the rhythm chart on the opposite page:
(All the instruments are explained in the first part of the book.)

Surdo: Plays the *»basic rhythm«*. Muffled stroke on the count of **1** and »open« stroke on **3**. The left hand muffles on **4** — without considering this an actual stroke.
Triangle: Accentuated »open« strokes on **and 1** and **and 3**, the rest are muffled.
Cabasa: Accentuated on **2** and **4**.
Tamborim: If there is only one *tamborim player* it is possible to vary the rhythm. Try to follow the guitar or piano rhythm.
Pandeiro: The essential instrument in an original *Samba*.
Chocalho: *Basic rhythm.* Accentuated on **1** and **3**.
Reco-reco: *Balance rhythm.* Accentuated on **2** and **4**.

There will sometimes be room for *the ago-go* and *cuica* in some arrangements.

Rehearsing the rhythm section and rhythm refer to page 147.

Alternative rhythms refer to each instrument in part one, and to page 152.
Breaks for *Samba* refer to page 153.

Samba Moderno 1

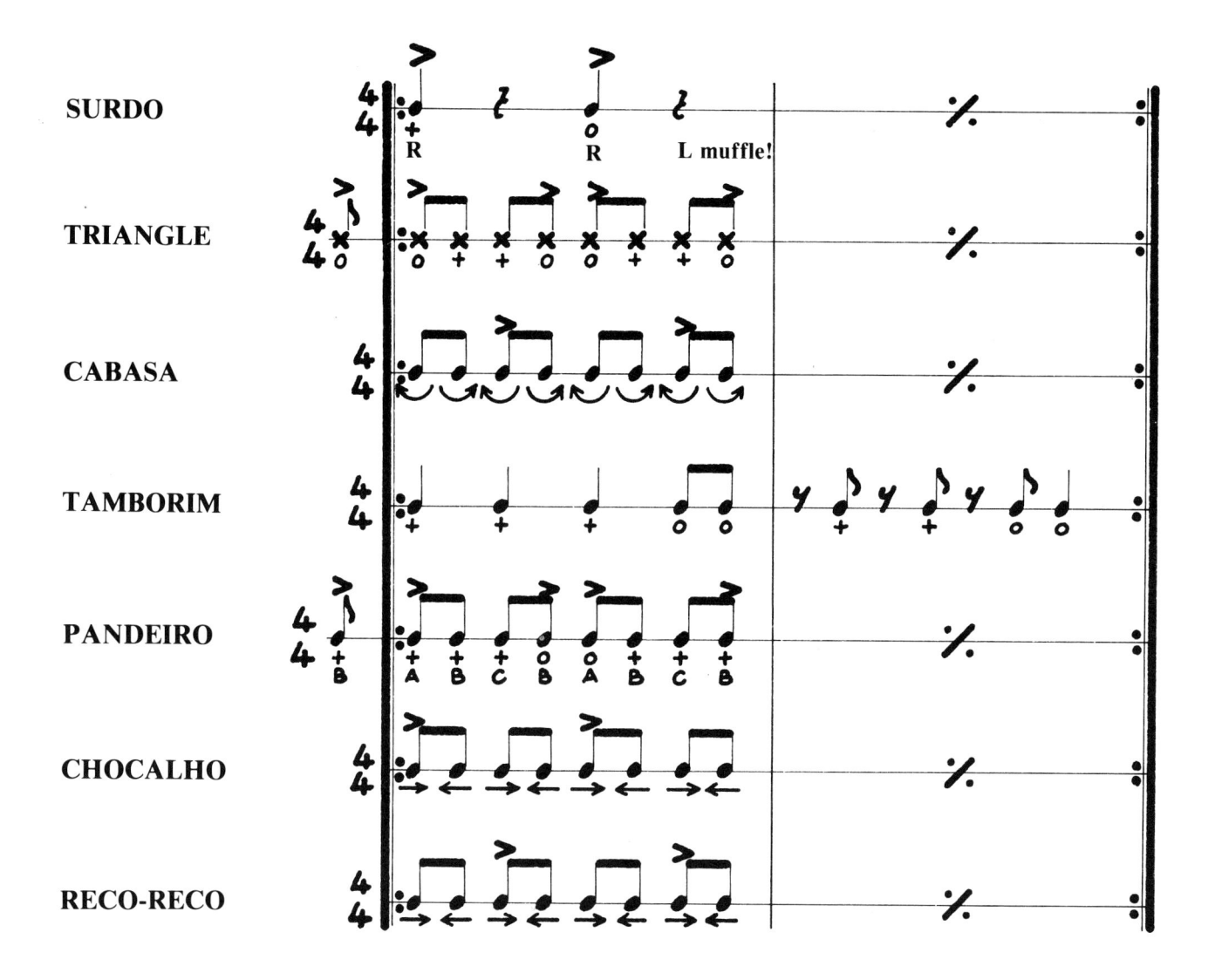

Samba Moderno 2

The Brazilian *congas (atabaques)*, the Cuban *bongos* and *the cowbell* are introduced in this example. These instruments have become a regular part of *the modern Samba*.

Explanation of the rhythm chart on the next page:

Surdo: Both hands are used in this rhythm.
Chocalho: Accentuated on **1** and **3** *(basic rhythm)*.
Reco reco: Accentuated on **2** and **4** *(balance rhythm)*.
Cowbell: This is one of the most common *cowbell rhythms*.
The cowbell can also play *the tamborim* rhythm by using muffled and »open« strokes (refer to *cowbell*, page 24).
The small cowbell is recommended for this *Samba*.
Bongo: Accentuated on **and 1** on the large drum and on **and 3** on the small drum.
The rest of the strokes are played lightly.
Atabaque (conga): Accentuated »open« strokes on **and 1** (notice the left hand plays the »**and**«-stroke) and accentuated »closed« strokes on **and 3**.
The rest of the strokes are played lightly.

The other instruments for *Samba Batucada* can also be used.

Rehearsing the rhythm section and the rhythm refer to page 147.

Alternative rhythms refer to each instrument in part one, and to page 152.
Breaks for *Samba* refer to page 153.

Samba Moderno 2

Bossa Nova

Bossa Nova means »*the new rhythm*«, a type of sophisticated *Samba* which has been influenced by other musical styles.
The Cuban *Bolero*« and »*cool jazz*« from the U.S. became popular in Brazil, influencing the Brazilian music.
With *the Samba Canção* as a starting point, *the Bossa Nova* became a mixture of the different musical cultures mentioned before and was at its most popular stage during the years 1958 to '64.
The first *Bossa Nova* compositions were written by Antonio Carlos Jobim (Tom Jobim), of which the most well-known are »Desafinado« and »Samba de uma nota so« (One Note Samba). João Gilberto is also an influential person, contributing to this musical style with his special type of syncopated guitar playing.
The Bossa Nova made its major debut in the movie »Orfeo Negro« (Black Orpheus) in which the rhythm was used for the title track. Charlie Byrd and Stan Getz recorded the album entitled »Jazz-Samba« which became extremely popular. This record title gave *the Bossa Nova* the synonym »*Jazz-Samba*« but the latter term is mainly used outside of Brazil.
This new way of playing created a change in the structure of the *Samba groups:* guitar, bass, drum set and piano. Percussion and vocals became a regular part of the ensembles from then on.
Bossa Nova has the same basic rhythmic pulse as *Samba* but with a more evident 4/4 rhythm – refer to page 9.

The rhythm that is played on the snare drum is very characteristic of *the Bossa Nova*. Except for one stroke, the rhythm is identical to the Cuban *clave rhythm*.
The stroke on the count of **3** in the second bar in the *3/2 clave rhythm* is played on the count of **3 and** instead when playing *Bossa Nova*. In other words, that stroke is played one eighth note later.

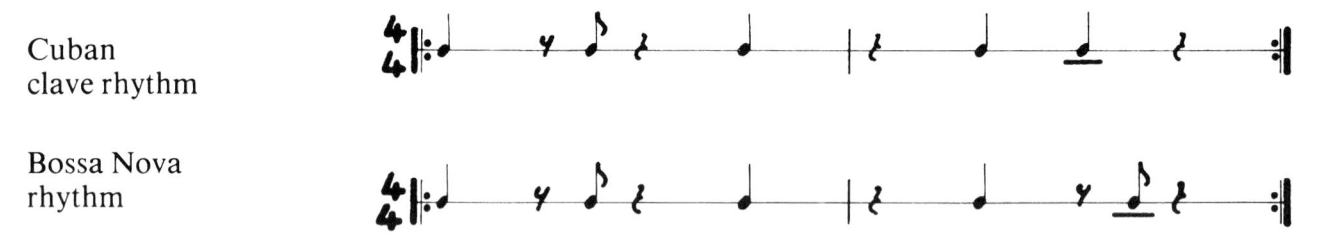

Cuban clave rhythm

Bossa Nova rhythm

Contrary to the Cuban *clave rhythm,* **the Bossa Nova rhythm is often varied when played.**
The rhythm is played using cross-rim on the snare drum. (Refer to the explanation and picture »*timbales*« on page 53.)
Here the rhythm is written with the second bar first in comparison to the Brazilian rhythm instruments playing two-bar figures shown earlier – the *tamborim* for instance. Refer to page 146.

Bossa Nova is usually played in medium tempo but can also be used in slow and fast tempi.

The mixture of musical styles that are the foundation for *Bossa Nova* make the use of Cuban percussion instruments possible when playing the rhythm.

The drum set

As mentioned before, the drum set is an important part of *the Bossa Nova group*.
The bass drum plays on the counts of **and 1** and **and 3**, and *the hi-hat* plays on the counts of **2** and **4** but is otherwise held closed. This *(Samba) basic pulse* is played without variation.

The right hand plays eighth notes on either *the ride cymbal* or *closed hi-hat* when playing with sticks, or on *the snare drum* when playing with brushes.
(In the list on page 181 there are references to various drum guide books for further information about *the drum set*.)

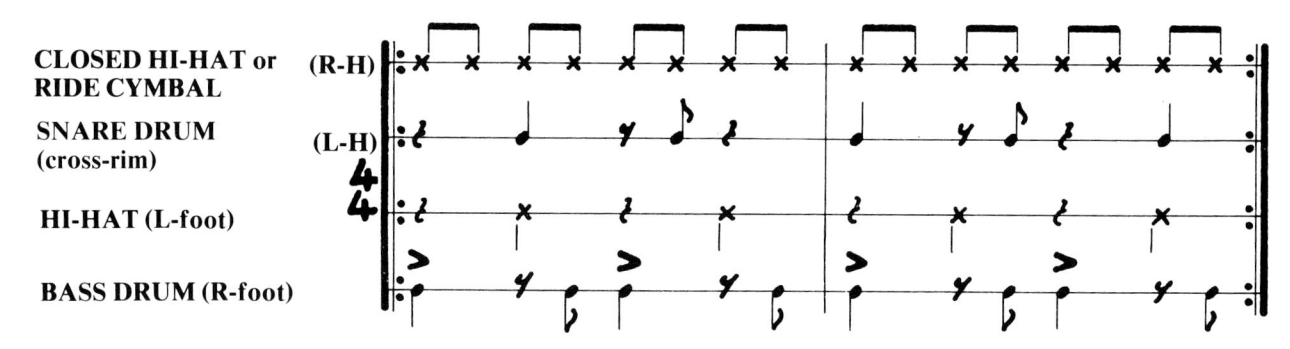

CLOSED HI-HAT or RIDE CYMBAL (R-H)
SNARE DRUM (cross-rim) (L-H)
HI-HAT (L-foot)
BASS DRUM (R-foot)

The rhythm played on *the tamborim* can also be used as a *snare drum rhythm*.

Variations for Bossa Nova (snare drum)

1:

2:

3:

Percussion

Apart from *the drum set* in the smaller *Bossa Nova groups* there is usually only one percussion instrument, but various other percussion instruments can be added as long as they do not dominate the sound of the melody instruments of the groups.

The cabasa, maracas and *triangle* are the rhythm instruments that are used in this type of group because of lighter pitch and tonal quality.

If there is only one percussion instrument played in the group, the instrument should accentuate the counts of **2** and **4**, as *the bass drum* is accentuating the counts of **and 1** and **and 3**.

Percussion for Bossa Nova (continued)

Shown here are two examples of combinations for the rhythm instruments that are normally played in *Bossa Nova*, but each instrument can also be played separately.

1

Cabasa: Accentuations on the counts **2** and **4** *(the balance rhythm).*
Triangle: Accentuated (»open«) on counts **and 1** and **and 3** *(the basic rhythm).*
Maracas: Evenly accentuated eighth notes.

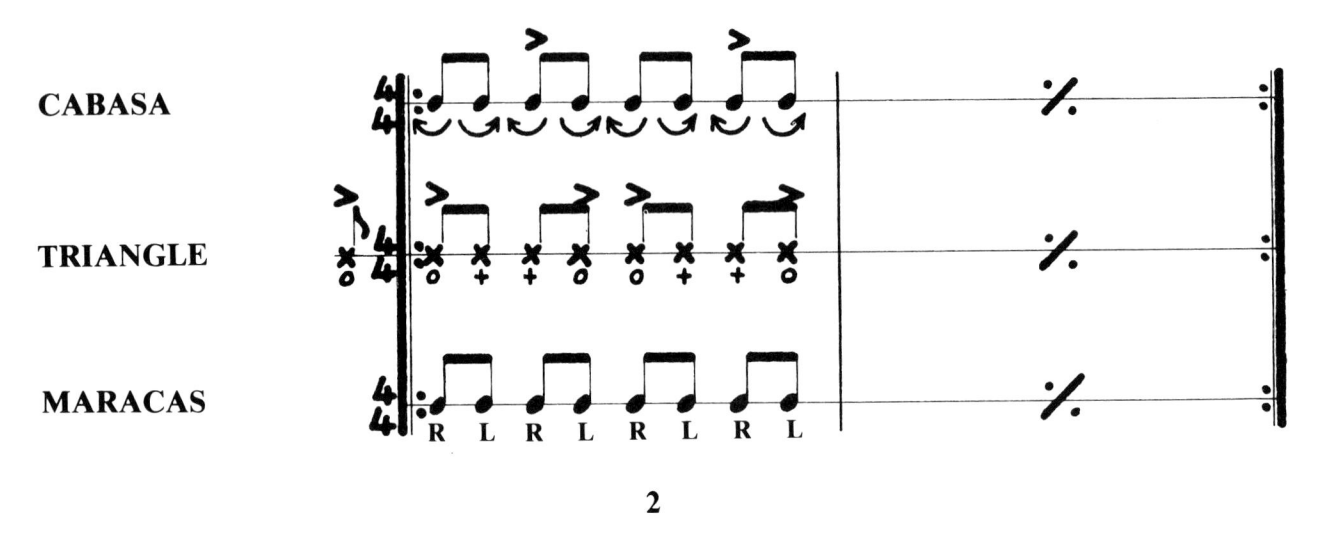

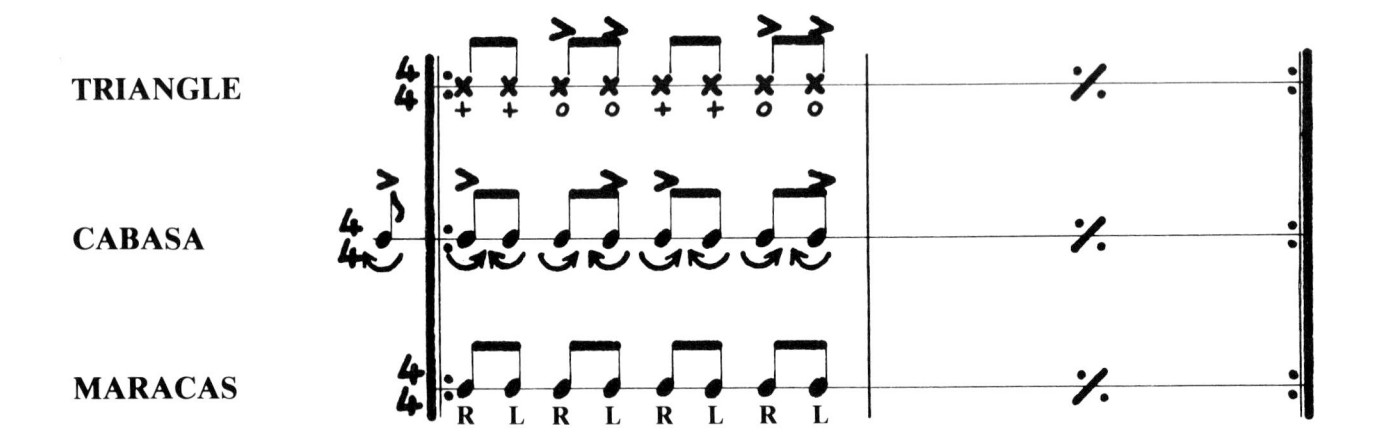

2

Triangle: Accentuated on counts **2 and** and **4 and** *(the balance rhythm).*
Cabasa: Accentuated on counts **and 1** and **and 3** *(the basic rhythm).*
Maracas: Evenly accentuated eighth notes.

Alternative rhythms and instruments

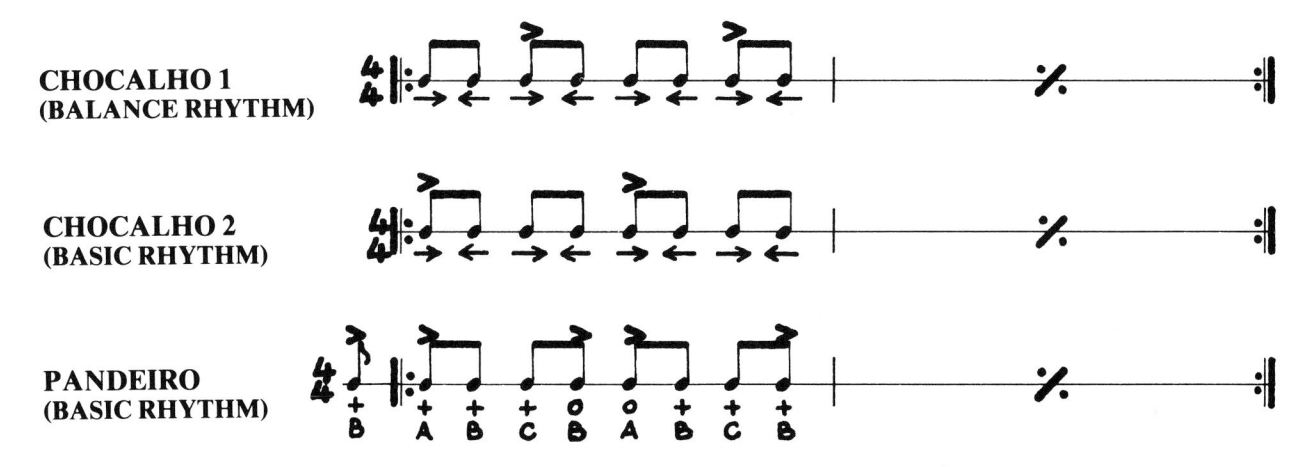

CHOCALHO 1 (BALANCE RHYTHM)

CHOCALHO 2 (BASIC RHYTHM)

PANDEIRO (BASIC RHYTHM)

In louder arrangements, generally those played with a larger orchestra, *the congas (atabaques)* come into use. These are either played in the Brazilian style *(Samba)* or in the Cuban style.

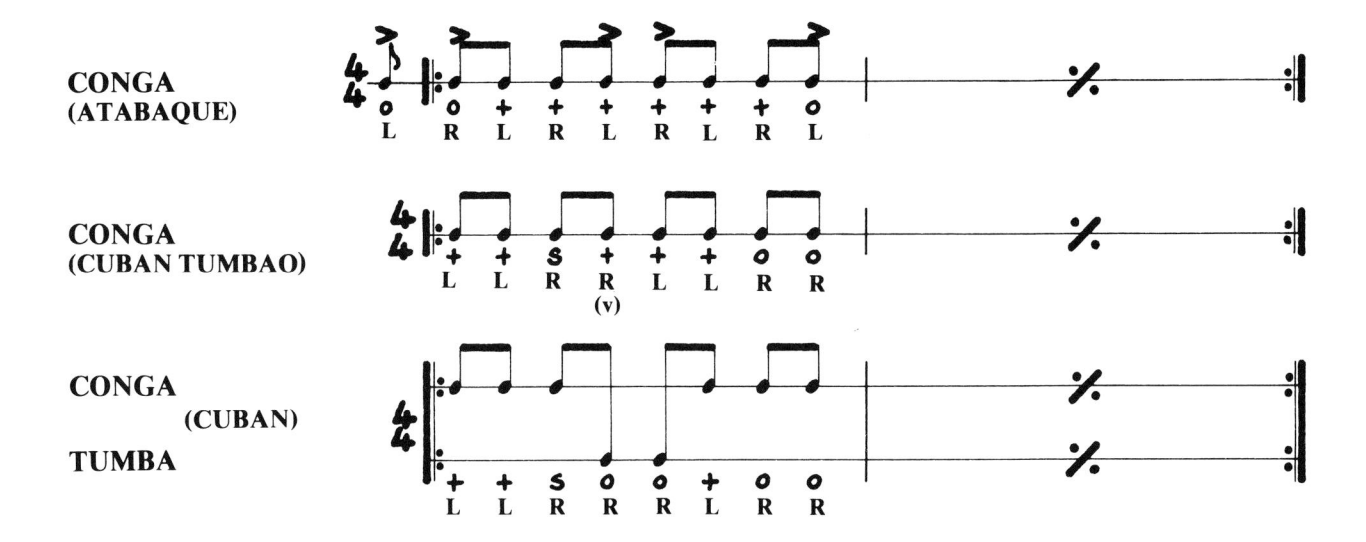

CONGA (ATABAQUE)

CONGA (CUBAN TUMBAO)

CONGA (CUBAN) TUMBA

Using *the tamborim* or *ago-go* can also be a nice effect but it should not destroy the characteristically sophisticated sound of *the Bossa Nova style*.
Refer to »*Samba*« and in the first part of the book for more about these instruments.

Baion *(Baião)*

Baion took over the popularity of *The Samba* — also outside Brazil.
The Sanfona-(accordion) player named Luiz Gonzaga popularized the rhythm in 1945, but this rhythm had been known and used long before that in the folk music from the north eastern part of the country.

The traditional Baion group consisted of *Sanfora* (accordion), *guitar, triangle* and »*zabumba*«. Zabumba is a regular marching bass drum played with the heads turned horizontally.

The right hand plays the accentuated strokes with a mallet and the left hand muffles the bottom head – and plays contrasting strokes with a small stick at the same time. As an alternative, the strokes can be muffled by pressing the beater onto the head after playing the stroke.
The bass rhythm is now usually played by *the surdo* and the contrasting strokes are played by *the caixeta*.

Baion is played by all types of orchestras, right from the large carnival orchestras to the more sophisticated dance bands.

Baion is played from medium tempo to fast tempo and should have a distinct »alla breve« feeling — the foot is tapped on the counts of **1** and **3**.

Explanation for the rhythm chart of the next page:

Surdo: Muffled stroke on the count of **1** and »open« stroke on the count of **2 and**.
The left hand muffles the head on **4**.
Triangle: »Open« stroke on the counts of **2 and** and **4 and**. The other strokes are muffled.
Ago-go: Stroke on the large bell on the count of **1** and on the small bell on **3**.
The closing method is not used in this rhythm.
Caixeta and/or *Caixa:* Choose one or the other, or both instruments depending on the style and the size of the orchestra. Strokes on the counts of **2** and **4**.
Pandeiro: Played as regular basic rhythm but the strokes on **2** and **4** are more accentuated.
Reco reco: The **4 and 1-** and **2 and 3**-movements are performed without lifting the stick from the surface of the instrument. **1** and **3** are accentuated.
Chocalho: Accentuated on **2** and **4** the rest performed with even eighth note movements.
Cabasa: Accentuated on **1, 2 and** and **4**.

The necessary instruments for *Baion* are: *Surdo* and *triangle*.

The surdo is replaced by *the bass drum* of the drum set in the modern groups.

Rehearsing the rhythms and the rhythm section refer to page 147.

Baion (Baião)

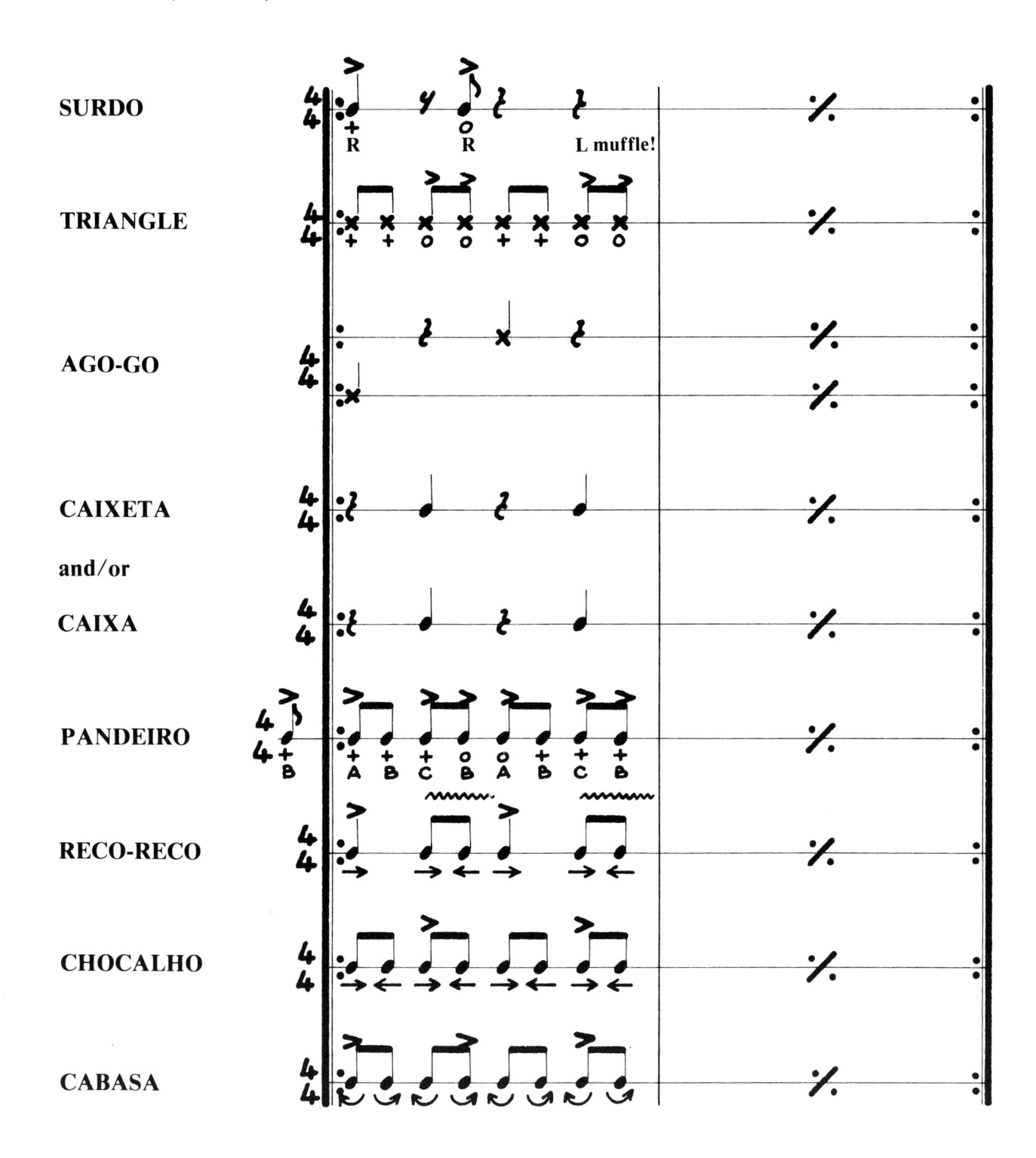

Alternative rhythms for Baion

Surdo

1

Instead of muffling the head on the count of **4** with the left hand (as shown in the rhythm chart), the head is now muffled on the count of **3**. The »open« tone is now shortened.

Both methods may be used in the following examples.

2

Variation of example »1«, which can be used in the second bar.

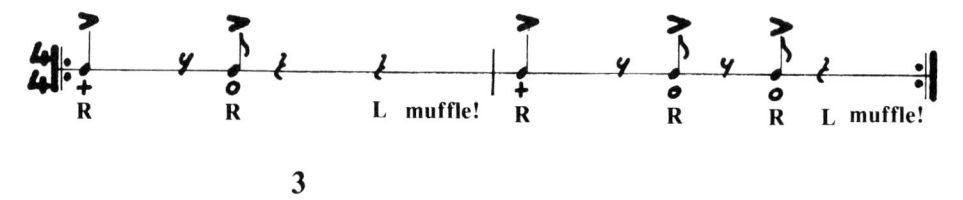

3

This rhythm is also used for Samba, and certain types of *Maracatú*.

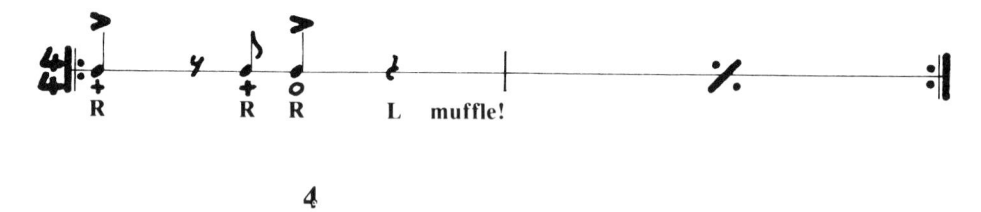

4

Variation of example »3«, which is used in the second bar only.

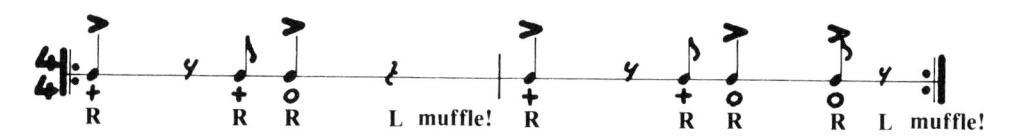

Triangle

Ago-go

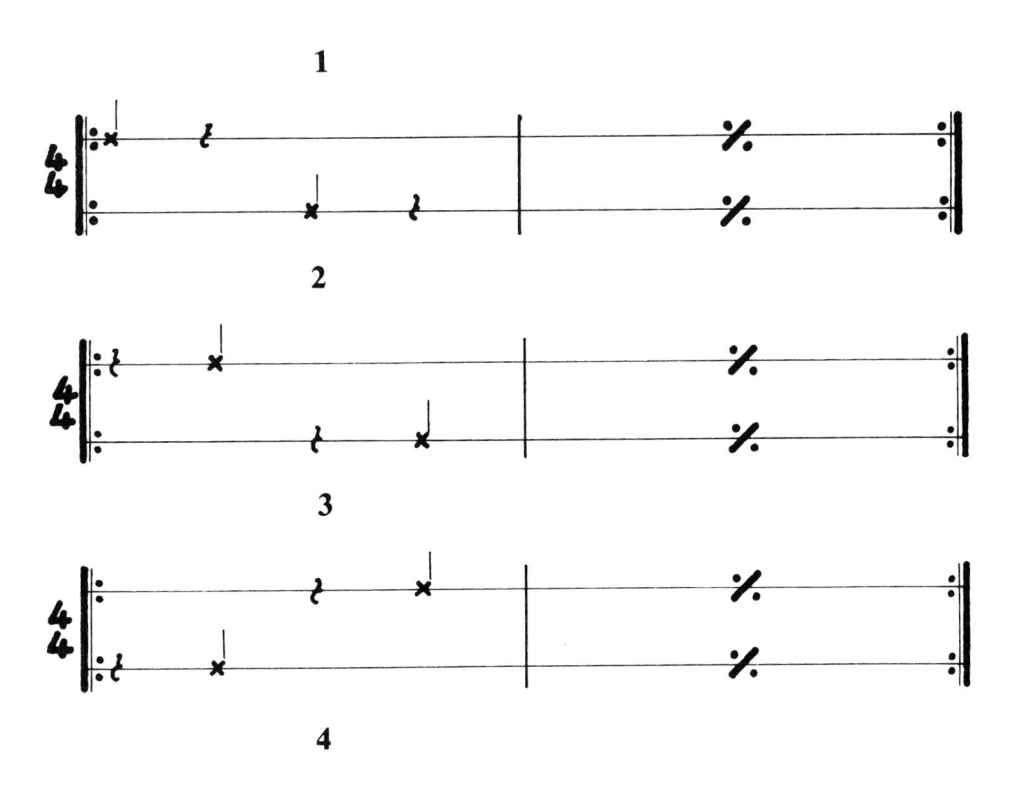

1

2

3

4

Used as a separate rhythm or as a variation of the rhythm shown in the chart.

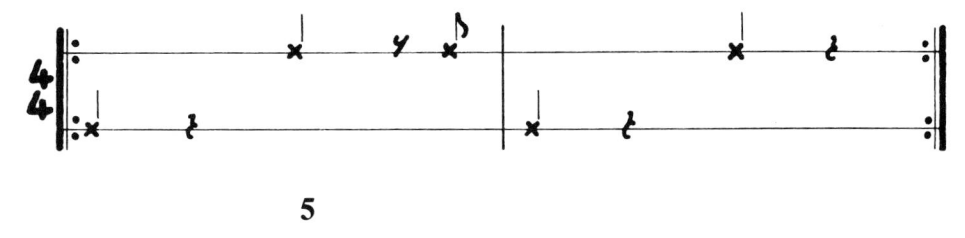

5

Used as a separate rhythm or as a variation of the rhythm shown in the chart.

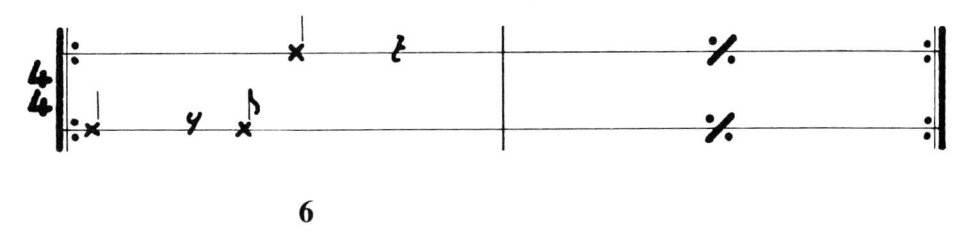

6

Used as a separate rhythm or as a variation of the rhythm shown in the chart.

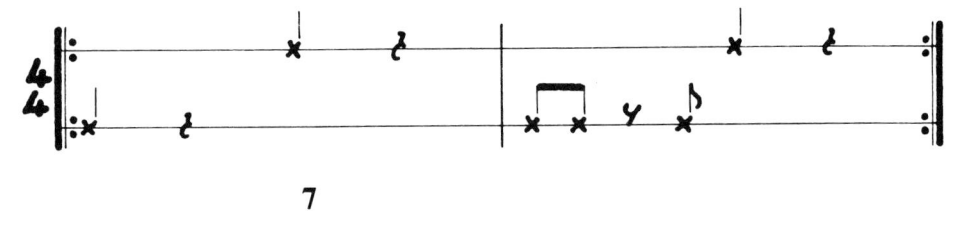

7

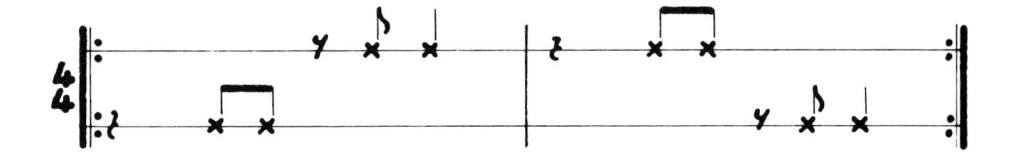

Caixa

This rhythm is used together with *the ago-go rhythm*, example »7«.

Reco-reco

Atabaque (conga)

1

2

3

> 169

Maracatú

Maracatú came into being as a dance and a rhythm for the Brazilian Folk Theater. The rhythm is of *the Baion family* and is very popular in Brazil.
Even though *Maracatú* is not well-known outside of Brazil in its original form, there are parts of the rhythm that are used in other contexts.
The characteristic *ago-go rhythm* is often used in *Rock* and *Jazz* rhythms by such percussion artists as *Airto Moreira,* among others.

Maracatú is played from medium to fast tempo and should, as in *Samba* and *Baion*, be played with a distinct »alla breve« feeling — the foot being tapped on the counts of **1** and **3**.

Maracatú 1

Surdo: All strokes are played with the right hand, the left hand muffles on the count of **4** in the second bar — as a stroke.
Ago-go: The rhythm is played without variations throughout the number.
Triangle: »Open« strokes on the counts **2 and** and **4 and** in each bar.
Caixeta and/or *caixa:* Strokes on counts **1** and **2 and** in the first bar.
Reco reco: A long scraping movement starting on the count of **4** in the second bar.

Rehearsing the rhythm section and the rhythm refer to page 147.

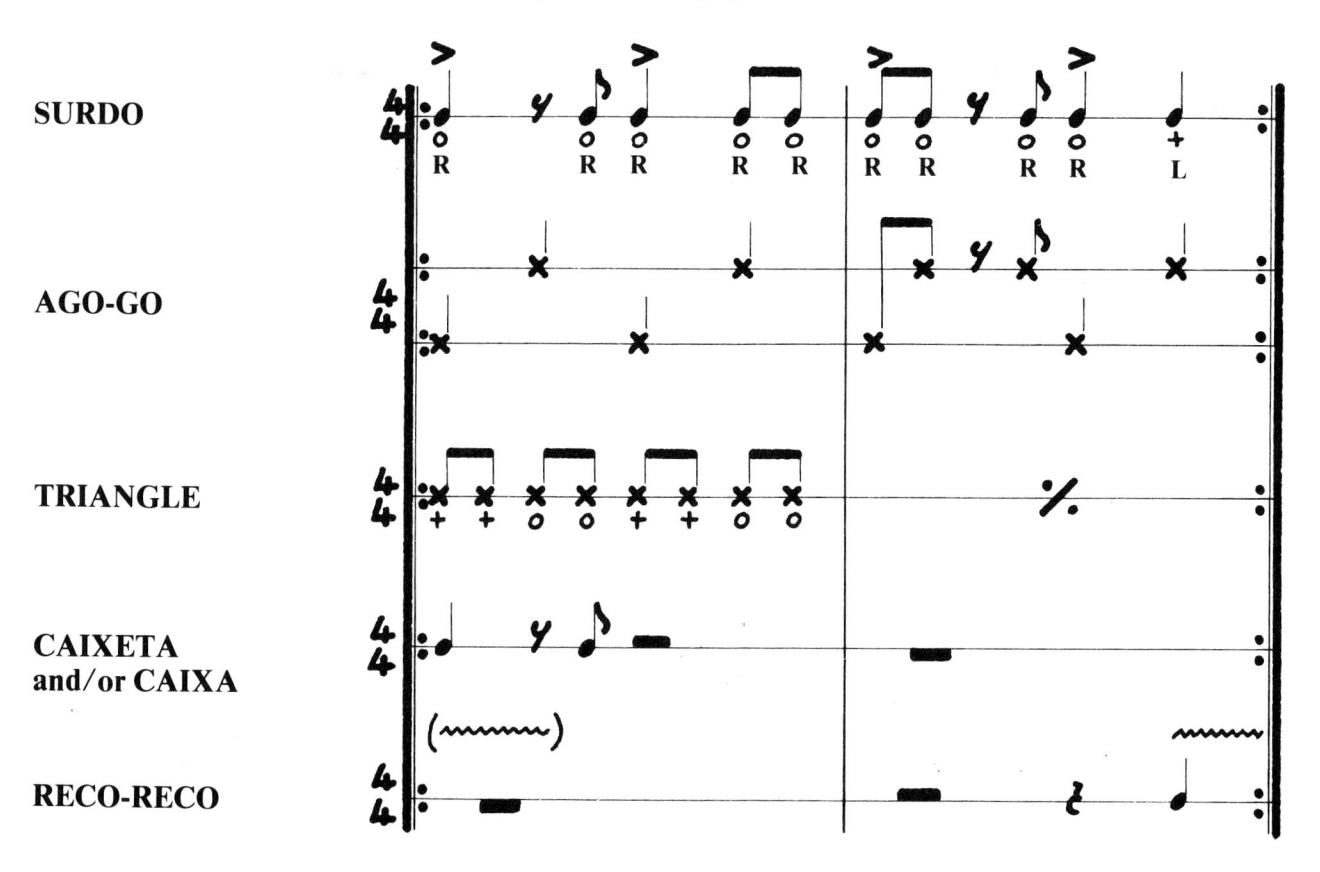

Maracatú 2

Surdo: Plays the same rhythm as in certain types of *Baion* and *Samba*.
Ago-go: The primary rhythm for *Maracatú* — played without variations.
Atabaque (conga): As great a difference as possible between accentuated and unaccentuated strokes.
Triangle: »Open« strokes on counts **and 2** and **and 4** in each bar.
Reco reco: Accentuated on **2** and **4**.

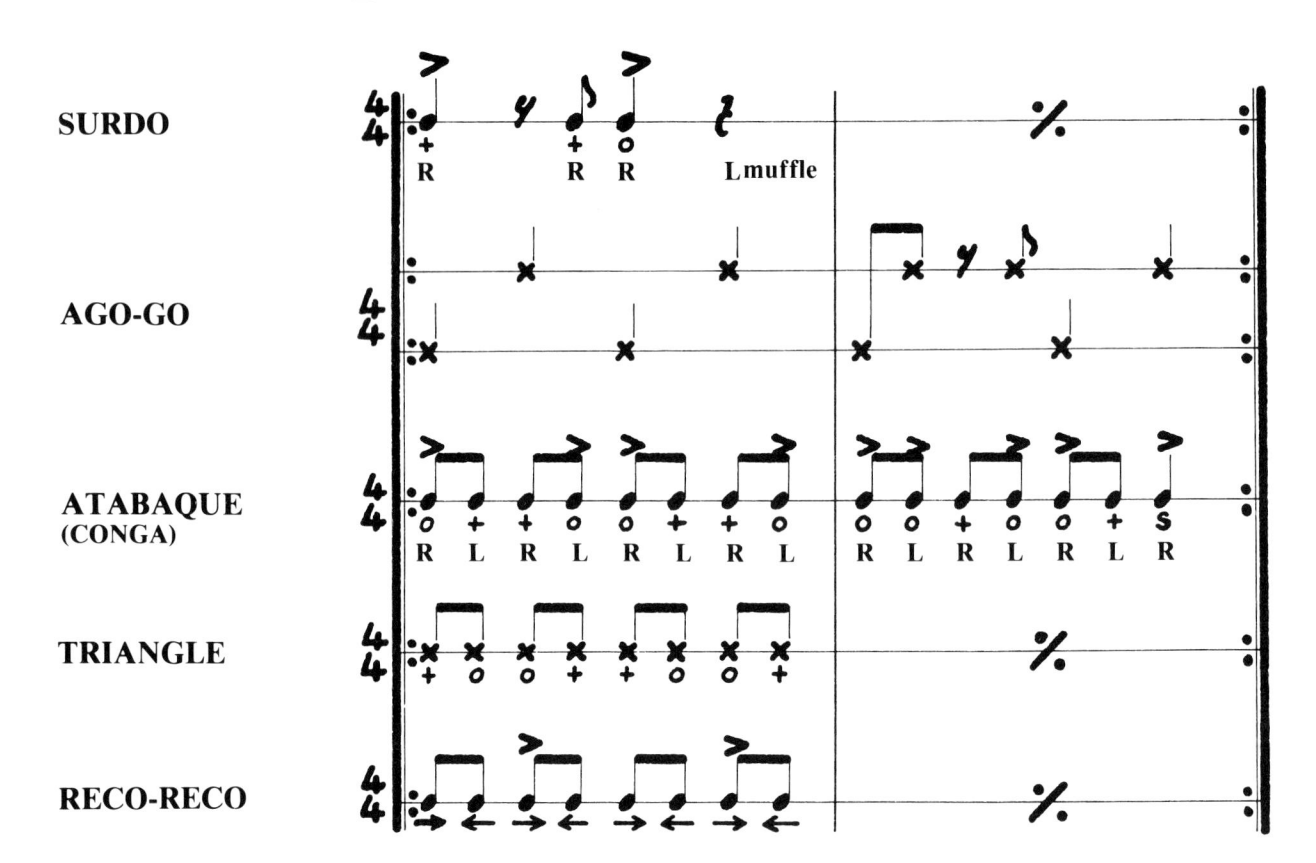

Alternative rhythms for Maracatú

Surdo

The stroke is played with the flat of the left hand.

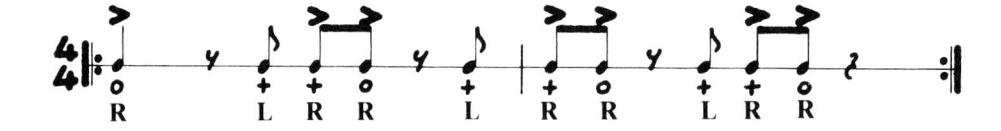

Pandeiro

Basic rhythm — refer to part one of the book.

Calypso from Trinidad

The Calypso rhythm cannot actually be classified along with the other rhythms and types of music that have been studied in this book. The rhythm is very popular though, and I will show a couple of examples on the next pages.

The most well-known *Calypso style* comes from *Trinidad* which is a part of the English-speaking section of the Caribbean islands.
The music from these parts is more difficult to define than the music from Cuba and Brazil.
The style of singing is very characteristic of *the Calypso*. The lyrics are made up on the spot and deal with topical events in a satirical manner — preferably events of a scandalous nature.

Apart from being played as a basic rhythm, *the Calypso* is also incorporated into *Rock* and *Jazz rhythms*.

The Calypso is played in all tempi and is inspired by various types of music. The most well-known style of *Calypso* is played in medium and fast tempi, and is of the same rhythmical style as *the Rumba* — refer to »*Rumba 2*« on page 125.

The Calypso uses the same basic *tumba rhythm (tumbao)* as in *Rumba* — but without the Cuban *clave rhythm*.
The foundation of *the Calypso* is equivalent to the first bar of *the clave rhythm*. This rhythm is repeated in both bars.

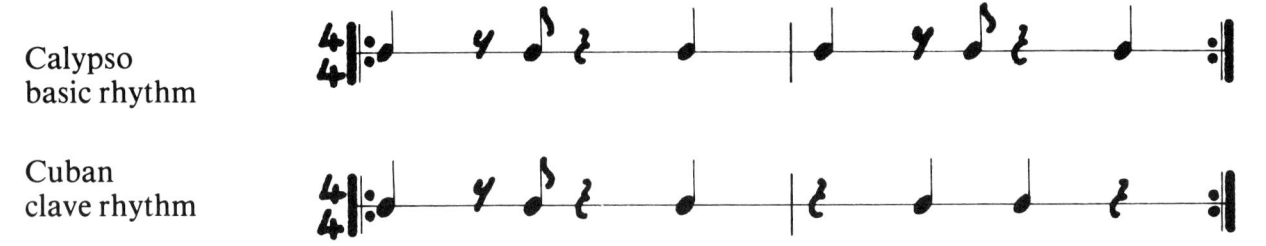

Calypso
basic rhythm

Cuban
clave rhythm

The Calypso is played with a distinct »alla breve« feeling — the foot is tapped on counts **1** and **3**.

Explanation of the rhythm chart on the opposite page:

Clave: The rhythm can also be played on *the bass drum* of the drum set.
Maracas: Played hand to hand.
Tumba and *conga* played by two persons:
    The tumba plays the same rhythm as in *Rumba*.
    The left hand plays »closed« strokes (+) on counts **1** and **3** and the right hand plays an »open« stroke (o) on **4**.
Conga: The rhythm is played hand to hand with accentuated »open« strokes (o) on counts **1** and **and 3**.
    The other strokes should be played lightly as »closed« strokes.
Conga and *tumba* played by one person:
    Except for the stroke on *the tumba* on **4**, all the strokes are played on *the conga*.
Bongo: The rhythm is played hand to hand with the fingertips. Accentuated on counts **1** and **and 3** (small drum) and on **4** (large drum). The other strokes are played lightly. The Cuban *Martillo* can be used.
Timbales: *Paila rhythm* played hand to hand. The same rhythm as *the maracas*.
Cowbell: The rhythm is played with B-strokes on *the hand cowbell*.

Calypso

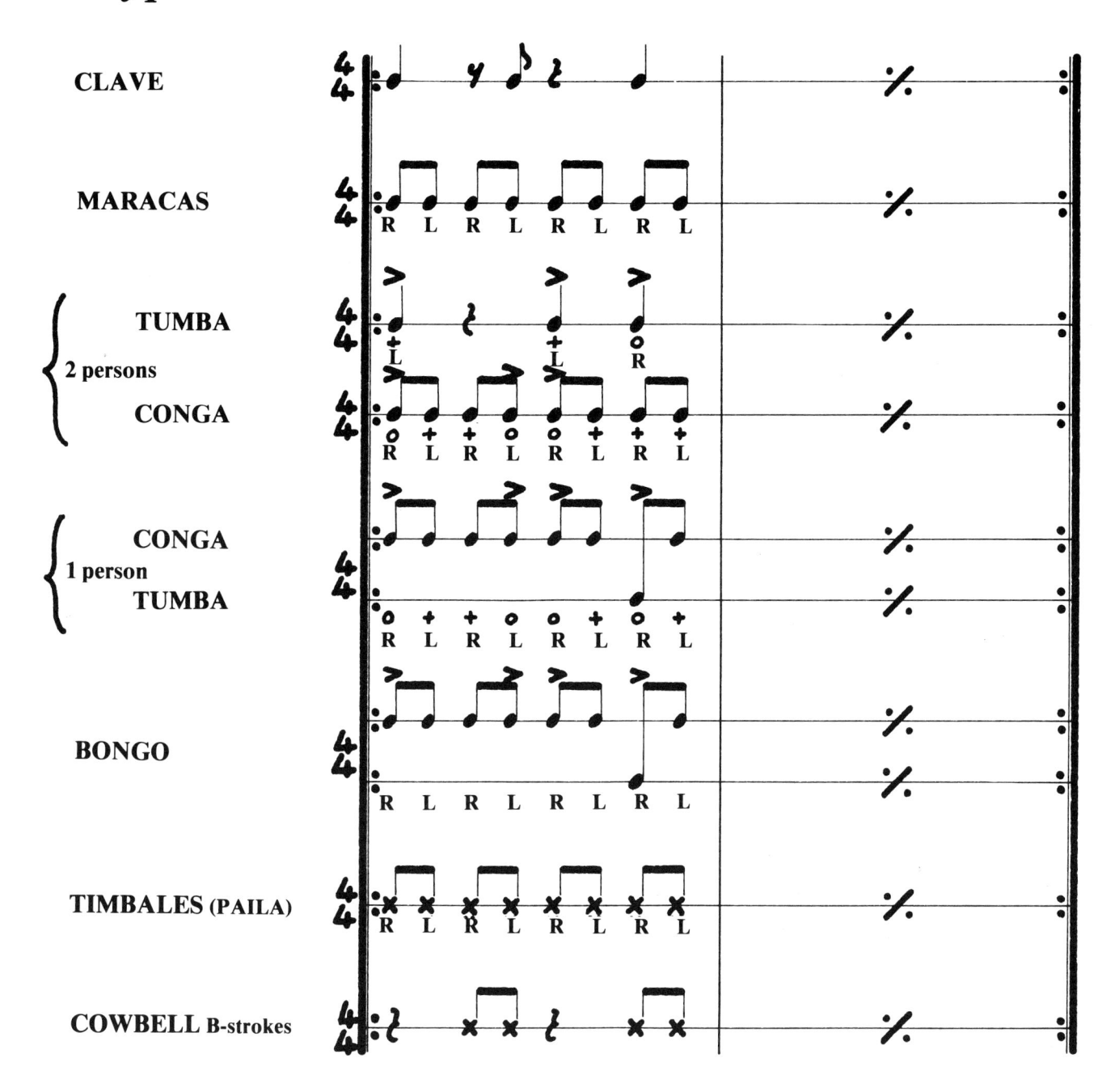

Alternative rhythms

Maracas and timbales (Paila): As *Bolero* and *Rumba* — refer to page 59.

Timbales:

The rhythm is played on *the large cowbell* as C-strokes, or as *Paila* using the right hand on the side of *the small timbale*.
The left hand plays a muffled stroke (+) on the count of **2** and an open stroke (o) on **4** *(large timbale)*.

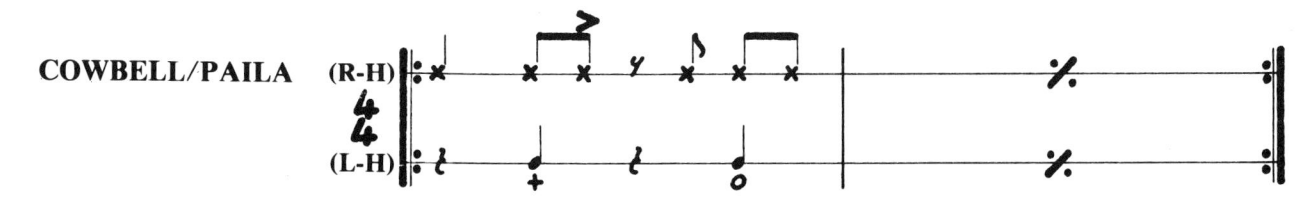

Alternative rhythms (cont.)

Conga/tumba

Examples »1« and »2« can either be used as separate rhythms or as variations of the rhythm shown in the chart.

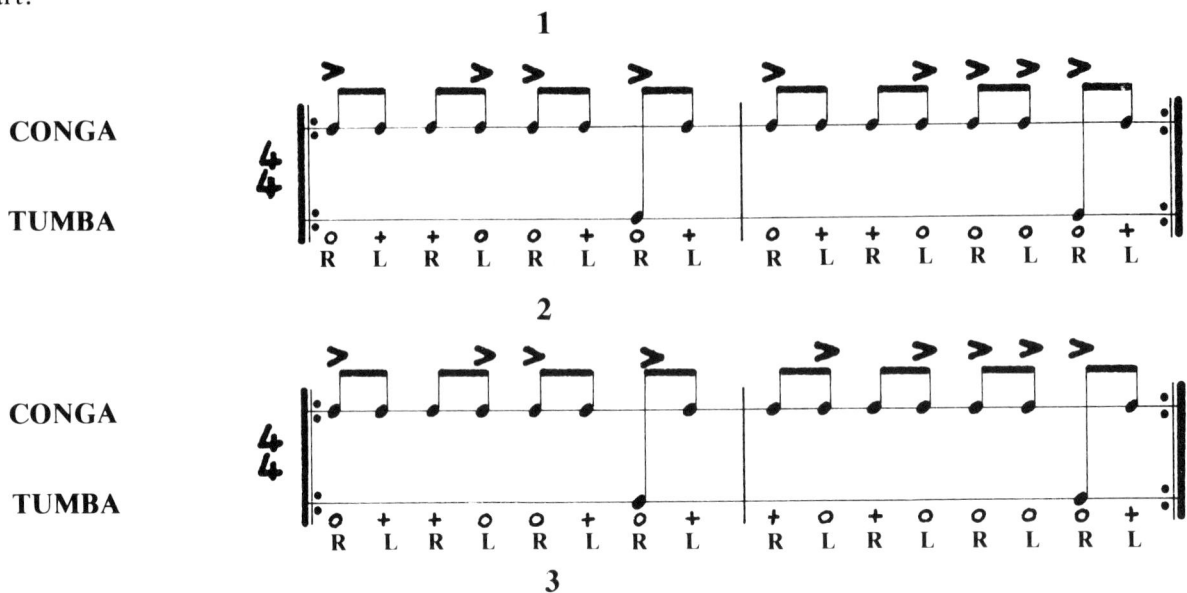

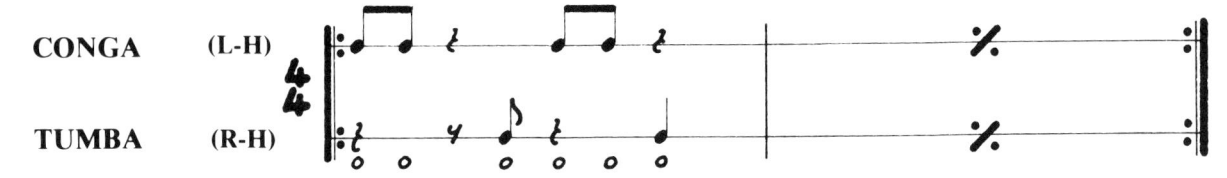

Bongo

The rhythms shown here can be used as separate rhythms or as variations of the rhythm shown in the chart. The Cuban *Martillo* rhythm is also used for *Calypso*.

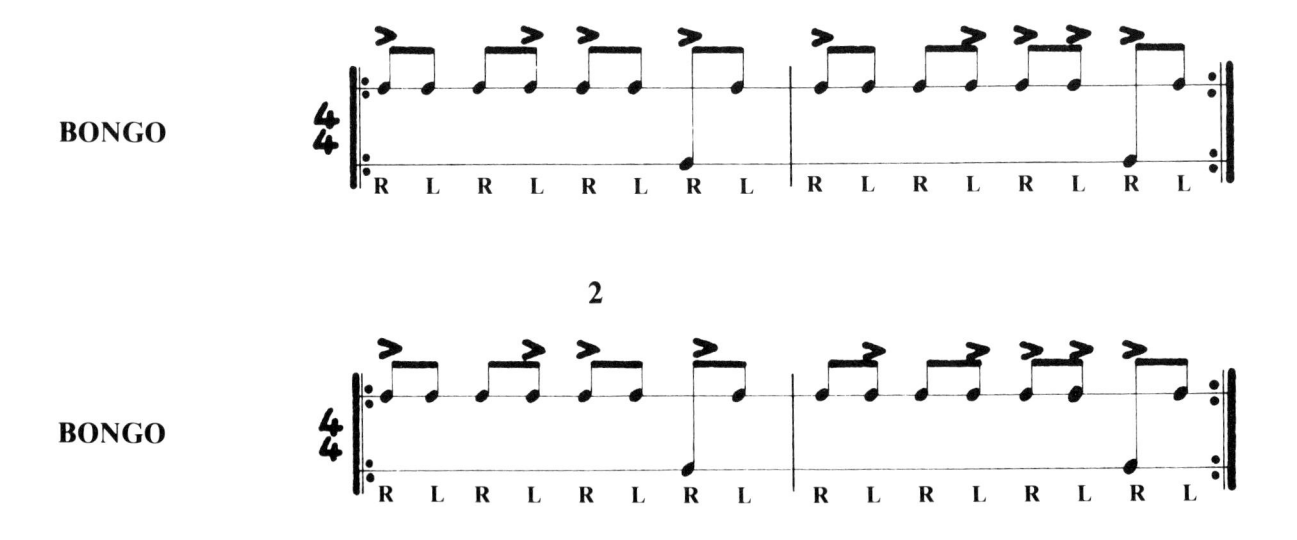

In this rhythm the right hand stays on *the tumba* and the left hand on *the conga*.

Tuning and maintenance of congas and bongos

Congas

You must tune *the conga drum* circularly.
This is done by tightening the first lug a quarter turn, then tighten the lug next to it and so on.

This will even out the tension exerted on the tuning lugs and the head.

If you tune the head by tightening the lugs diagonally opposite each other, you will be putting too much pressure on one lug at a time and the drum can become oval-shaped.

This tuning technique can be used on regular drums with thinner heads.

The drum is tuned up until the head is tight.
Hit the rim of the head with a fingertip alongside each tuning lug and try to tune the head so that the tone of the head is as even as possible. But keep in mind that a natural head made of skin is not of equal thickness all over so the difference of the pressure on the tuning lugs should not be too extreme.

> When a drum is new, the head will make certain popping noises when being tuned up — don't worry! It's supposed to! This only means that the head is being stretched into place. Many people stop tuning when they hear these sounds and the drum never gets tuned up properly.

The drums are not usually tuned to certain pitches and there is usually no certain set of tones for *the quinto, conga* and *tumba*.

Each person tunes the drums differently and this may change from day to day and even from room to room.
Listen to different records and compare the sounds of the different »*congueros*« — *conga players*.

Loosen the heads when you have finished playing.

After being used a while the heads may tend to be slightly dirty.
For cleaning, remove the head by loosening the lugs a little at a time, and one at a time around the drum. The bolts are taken off and the rim is removed. Now the head can be lifted off the drum and the heavy skin will not lose its shape.

By using a nail-brush, regular soap and COLD water you can now wash the head.
Dry the head with a cloth after washing and mount it on the drum immediately afterwards.
Mount the rim and the bolts but do not tighten the bolts any more than is possible by hand.
Let the head dry by itself and then procede to tune the drum up.

Very thin heads can be washed while on the drum. Remove the bolts and rim.

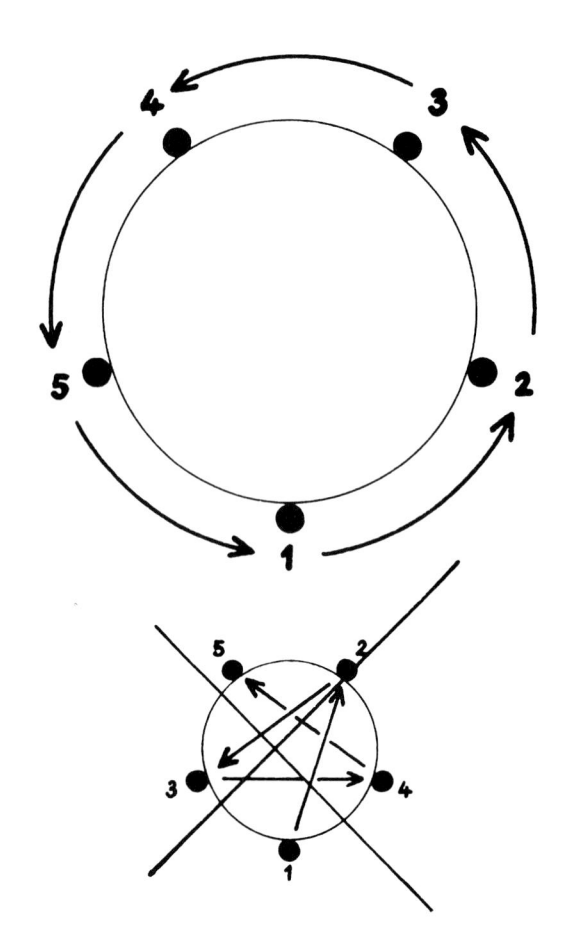

The heads are cured beforehand with oil and do not need extra oil, cocoa butter etc. after being washed. The sweat and oils from the hands are enough to take care of the heads.

Old and dried-out heads may be in need of special care, however.
Apply a small amount of linseed oil with a cloth onto the head in an even layer and let the drum sit for 24 hours.
Dry the head off with a clean cloth and the drum will be ready for action again.

Bongos

Bongos are tuned in the same manner as *congas*. The small head is so thin that it will not suffer from being tuned across the head.

The heads of *the bongos* are tuned to a high pitch, especially the small drum.

The heads are slackened after use.

When washing the heads, the bolts and rim are removed from the drum but the head is left on.
Mount the rim and bolts back on the drum immediately after washing so that the drum does not become mis-shapen.

Otherwise follow the same procedure as with *the congas*.

Discography

All the records mentioned are imported for Europe. The Cuban style include records from New York and Puerto Rico.

Cuba:

Carnival
»*Carnaval — A Santiago de Cuba*«. Le Chant du Monde, LDX-A-4250.

Folklorico
Los Papines, »*Tambores Felices*«. Areito LD-3468 (EGREM, Cuba).
Los Papines, »*Te Canta Mi Tambo*«. Areito LD-3194 (EGREM, Cuba).
Carlos »Patato« Valdez, »*Authority*«. L.P. Ventures LPV-393.
Carlos »Patato« Valdez, »*Ready for Freddy*«. L.P. Ventures LPV-419.
Conjunto de Guaguancó de Carlos Embale, »*La Gran Tradición Musical Cubana*« — »*La Rumba*« *(Vol. XII)*. Areito LD-3428 (EGREM, Cuba).
Mongo Santamaria, »*Drums and Chants*«. Vaya JMVS 56 — series 0698.
»*La Musica del Pueblo de Cuba*«. Areito LD-3440/LD-3441 (Two records). (Includes: *Afro/Cuban, Rumba, Comparsa* and *Son*) (EGREM, Cuba).

Son
Septeto Nacianal de Ignacio Piñeiro, »*La Gran Tradición Musical Cubana*« — »*El Son*« *(Vol. XV)*. Two more Vol. available. Areito LD-3427 (EGREM, Cuba).
Septeto Nacional de Ignacio Piñeiro, »*Glorias de Cuba*«. WS-Latino WS-4085.

Conjunto
Arsenio Rodriguez, »*Y su Conjunto*«. Ansonia ALP 1337.
Arsenio Rodriguez, »*Y su Conjunto — Vol. 2*«. Ansonia SALP 1418.
Conjunto de Chapottin y sus Estrellas, »*El Gran Chapottin*«. Areito LD-3126 (EGREM, Cuba).
»*Sonora Mantancera*«. Ansonia ALP 1225.
Sonora Mantancera, »*Fiesta*«. Orfeon 16H 5164.
Conjunto Caney, »*Rico Vacilón*«, Areito LD-3309 (EGREM, Cuba).

Conjunto (new style)
»*Conjunto Rumbavana*«. Areito LD-3872 (EGREM, Cuba).
Conjunto Cache, »*Por Primera Vez*«. Criollo C-471.
Conjunto Clasico, »*Los Rodriguez*«. Lo Mejor Records LMR 801.
Celia Cruz, »*Celia, Johnny, Justo & Papo — Recordando el Ayer*«. Vaya JMVS 52.
Alfredo »Chocolate« Armenteros, »*Chocolate Prefiero el Son*«. S.A.R. SLP 1009.

Charanga (Tipica)
Orquesta Aragon, »*Cha-cha-cha*«. Arcaño DKL 3057.
»*Orquesta Aragon*«, Cariño DBL 5006.
Orquesta Aragon, »*Aragon Vol. II*«, Areito LD-3984 (EGREM, Cuba).
Jose Fajardo, »*Selecciones Clasicas*«. Coco CLP 141X.
Mongo Santamaria, »*Mas Sabroso*«. Fantasy F-8071.

Charanga (New style)
The new style of the Cuban Orquestras is often called »*Onda Areito*«.
Orquesta Ritmo Oriental, »*Ritmo Oriental*«. Areito LD-3622 (EGREM, Cuba).
Orquesta Ritmo Oriental, »*Se Baila Asi*«. Areito LD-3536 (EGREM, Cuba).
Tipica 73, »*Charangueando*« (incl. sax and trumpet). Fania JM 560 Series 0798.
Tipica Ideal, *Fuera del Mundo — Out of this World*« (incl. trumpets). Coco CLP 142 X.

Popular dance orchestras
Tito Puente and his Orchestra, »*Dance Mania*«. Cariño DBL 1-5017.
Tito Puente and his Orchestra, »*No Hay Mejor — There is no better*«. Tico TSLP 1401.
Machito and his Afro-Cuban Salseros, »*Mucho Macho*«. Pablo 2625714.
Machito Orchestra, »*Fireworks*«. Coco CLP 141X.
Tito Rodrigues, »*Hits*«. WS-Latino WSLA 4060. (Available in New York.)
Beny Moré & Perez Prado, »*La Epoca de Oro de...*« *(The golden Era of...)* Cariño DBL 1-5003.
»*Beny Moré*«, Areito LD-3974 (EGREM, Cuba).

Modern groups and orchestras
Tipica 73, »*Tipica 73 - En Cuba*«. Fania JM 542 Series 698.
»*Irakere*«, Columbia 35655 (Live recording).
Salsa Na Ma, »*Diferente*«. Edition Wilhelm Hansen LPWH 116 (Denmark).
Tommy Olivencia, »*La Primerisima*«. Inca JMIS 1061.
Ray Barretto, »*Rican/Struction*«. Fania JM 552.
Ray Barretto, »*Barretto Power*«. Fania SLP 391.
Ray Reyes & La Orquesta Refrán, »*El Clave*«. Criollo C-472.
»*Eddie Palmieri*«. Barbarro B 205.
Eddie Palmieri, »*The Sun of Latin Music*«. Coco CLP 109XX.
»*Grupo Irakere*«. Areito LD-3926 (EGREM, Cuba).
Son 14, »*A Bayamo en Coche*«. Areito LD-3834 (EGREM, Cuba).
»*Los Bocucos*«. Areito LD-3720 (EGREM, Cuba).
Mongo Santamaria, »*Mongo, Mongo*«. Vaya JMVS 76.
Libre, »*Con Salsa ... Con Ritmo — Vol. 1*«. Salsoul SAL 4109.
Cortijo y su Combo Original, »*Juntos Otra Vez*«. Coco CLP 113XX (Contains rhythms from Puerto Rico).
Various records by: Willie Colon, Ruben Blades, Johnny Pacheco, Fania all Stars, Joe Cuba, Luis »Perico« Ortiz.

Jazz-Latin & Latin-Jazz
Various records by Dizzy Gillespie, Mongo Santamaria, Cal Tjader, Stan Kenton.
José Mangual, »*Buyú*«. *Turnstyle T-433.*
Chucho Valdes, »*Con su Piano*«. Areito LD-4013 (EGREM, Cuba).
Latin Percussion Jazz Ensemble »*Just Like Magic*«. Latin Percussion Ventures LPV 470.
Johnny »Dandy« Rodriguez, Jr. & other musicians from New York, »*Dandy's Dandy,* a Latin Affair«. Latin Percussion Ventures LPV-469.
Ray Barretto, »*The Other Road*«. Fania SLP 00448.

Latin-Rock
Various records by Santana, Malo, El Chicano, Fania All Stars.

Descarga — Jam Session
»*Estrellas de Areíto*« *Vol 1-5,* Areito 1: PRD-046, 2: PRD-047, 3: PRD-048, 4: PRD-049, 5: PRD-050.
Cachao y su Ritmo Caliente, »*Cuban Jam Sessions in Miniature — Descargas*«. Panart 2092.
Emiliano Salvador, Tata Güienes..., »*Descargas*«. Areito LD-4022 (EGREM, Cuba).
»*Cuban Jam Session — Vol. 1*«. Panart CLP 8000.

For practicing rhythms and solos
Eddie Montalvo & Charlie Santiago, »*Drum solos — featuring: Conga, bongo, timbales and full rhythm section*«.
(The A-side is recorded with rhythm section and soli. The B-side is with the rhythm section alone.)
Latin Percussion Ventures, Vol. 1: LPV 445, Vol. 2: LPV 450, Vol. 3: LPV 451.

Brazil

All the records mentioned are imported for Europe. The Brazilian records include records from U.S.A. and Europe.

Folk music
»*Atabaque e Berimbau — Eu, Bahia*«. Philips 6470 003 (Brazil).
»*Berimbau e Percussao*«. Polydor MP 2649 (Japan).
»*Afro-Brazilian Religious Songs*«. Lyrichord LLST 7315 (New York).

Samba Batucada
»*Sambas de Enredo das Escolas de Samba do Grupo 1*«. Top Tape (Brazil) 85070. (With vocals.)
»*G. R. Mocidade Independente de Padre Miguel*«. Copacabana (Brazil) COLP 11975. (Instrumental.)
Mocidade Independente Padre Miguel, »*Alma Brasileira*«. Warner Bros. (Brazil) 88.007.
Escola de Samba da Cidade, »*Batucada brasileira*«. Philips (Brazil) 2493. 012.

Various (Batucada, Moderno, Bossa Nova etc.)
»*Orfeo Negro*« (film score). Fontana 64 24 026.
»*Folkdances of Brazil*«. Audio International AIR 205.
»*Brasil Original*« (various groups and solists). RCA FJL2 7208.
Amaro de Souza & Haraldo de Oliveira, »*Saudades do Brasil*«. Arion 6.23002 (W. Germany).
Sergio Mendes & Brasil 77, »*Primal Roots*«. A&M AMLS 64353.

Samba (various types)
Cuarteto em Cy, »*Antoligia do Samba-Canção*«. Philips (Brazil) 6349133.
»*João Gilberto*«, EMI (Brazil) 31C 062 421006 (Moderno).
»*Martino da Viola*«, RCA (Brazil) FPL 1 0076 (Moderno).
Jair Rodriguez, »*Minha hora e Vez*«. Philips (Brazil) 6349 192 (Moderno).
Dorival Caymmi, »*Série Coletanea Vol. 6*«. EMI (Brazil) SC 10093 (Moderno).
»*Cartola*«. Discos Marcus Pereira MPL 9325 (Old style).
(Orchestra), »*A Musica de Donga*«. Discos Marcus Pereira (Brazil) MPL 9333 (Old style instrumental).
Gilberto Gil & Germano Mathias, »*Antologia do Samba-Choro*«. Philips (Brazil) 6349 361. (Gil: modern style, Mathias: old style).
»*Clementina de Jesus*«. Odeon (Brazil) 962 421115 (Old style).
Elis Regina e Jair Rodriguez, »*Edicao Histórica — Dois na Bossa Vol. 2*«. Fontana special (Brazil) 6470 514 (Moderno).
Sivuca, »*Live at the Village Gate*«. Vanguard VSD 79352 (Modern style).
Various records with Paulinho da Viola, Gal Costa, Baden Powell.

Bossa Nova
Various records with Antonio Carlos Jobim (Tom Jobim).
João Gilberto, »*Chega de Saudade*«. Odeon (Brazil) 62 421003.
Caymmi & Jobim, »*Caymmi visita Tom*«. Fontana (Brazil) 6470 528.
Various with Sergio Mendes & Brasil 66 (and 77).
João Gilberto, »*Brazil*«. Warner Bros. (New York) BSK 3613.

Choro
»*Festival de Choros — de Ernesto Nazareth a Waldir Azvedo*«. Premier (Brazil) 307 3307.
Paulinho da Viola, »*Memorias Chorando*«. Odeon (Brazil) 162 82435.

Baion
Luiz Gonzaga, »*Asa branca*«. RCA 1070216.
Luiz Gonzaga, »*O Fole Roncou*«. Odeon (Brazil) SC 10034.
»*Os Caçulas do Baião*«. AMC (Brazil) LP5 015.

New Styles — Modern artists
The artists mentioned here have their roots in the traditional music.
Elis Regina, »*Elis*«. EMI (Brazil) 31C 064 422 882.
Sergio Mendes, »*Alegria*«. WEA (W. Germany) 99 096.
Djavan, »*Seduzir*«. EMI (Brazil) 31C 064422888D.
Airto Moreira, »*Identity*«. Arista (New York) AL 4068.
Airto Moreira, »*Seeds on the Ground*«. Buddah (U.S.A.) BDS 5058.
Gilberto Gil, »*Realce*«. Elektra (Brazil) BR 32 038.
Milton Nascimento, »*Milton*«. A&M (U.S.A.) SP 4611.
Alcev Valenca, »*Cinco Sentidos*«. Ariola (Brazil) 201 622.
Edu Lobo & Tom Jobim, »*Edu & Tom — Tom & Edu*«. Philips (Brazil) 6328378.
»*Nana Vasconcelos*«. ECM (W. Germany) 1147. (A Berimbau-specialist.)
Dom Um Romao, »*Spirit of the Times*«. Muse (New York) MR 5049.
Flora Purim, »*500 Miles High — Live at Montreux*«. Milestone (U.S.A.) M 9070.
Paulinho da Costa, »*Agora*«. Pablo (U.S.A.) 2310 785.
Gal Costa, »*Gal Tropical*«. Philips (Brazil) 6349 412.
Various records with Egberto Gismonti, Hermeto Pascoal, Jorge Ben, Luiz Gonzaga Jr., Maria Bethania, Chico Buarque and Caetano Veloso.

Guide books for drumset
(Books about training of technique, note reading and coordination)

Ed Thigpen, »*Rhythm analysis and basic co-ordination*«, 1978.
Kenny Clarke & Dante Agostini, »*Méthode de Batterie*«, Vol. 1: note reading & Vol. 2: technique, 1971.

Guide-books for drumset concerning Latin rhythms

Frank »Chico« Guerrero, »*Latin Sounds from the Drumset*«, 1974.
Paulinho, »*Rhythms and Instruments of Brazil*«, 1965.
Ron Fink, »*Latin American Rhythms for the Drumset*«, 1971.
Ted Reed, »*Latin Rhythms for Drums and Timbales*«, 1957.
Joel Rothman, »*Beats and Variations for Dance Band Drummers*«, 1972.

Index of terms with phonetic pronunciation and references

This list does not include names and expressions from the record list.
The use of »h« after a vowel means that the syllable is pronounced short – as if stopping the breath.

Abanico, pron. *ah-bah-NEE-co*, 55, 104
Accentuated (loud) stroke, 10
Acordeon, pron. *ah-cor-deh-UNG*, (ung as in young), 144
Afoxé, pron. *ah-foh-SHE*, 77
Afro-Cuban (orchestra and type of music), 97, 108, 122
Afro-Cuban 6/8, 138
Ago-go, pron. *ah-goh-GOH*, 71
Alla breve, 9
Apito, pron. *ah-PEE-toh*, 84
Arcaño y sus Maravillas, 108
Atabaque, pron. *ah-tah-BAH-kee*, 85

Bahia, pron. *bah-EE-ah*, 144
Baião, pron. *bah-YA-ow*, 164
Baion, pron. *bah-YUNG*, 164
Balance rhythm, 61, 146
Bamboo reco-reco, 66
Banda, pron. *BAHN-dah*, 97
Bandolim, pron. *bahn-doe-LEEN*, 145
Banjo, 145
Basic pulse, 61, 146
Basic rhythm, 61, 146
Batuque, pron. *bah-TOO-kee*, 85, 145
Batucada, pron. *bah-too-CAH-dah*, 61, 148
Berimbau, pron. *beh-reem-BOW* (as in »bow of a ship«), 93, 145
Big Bands, 97
Bolero, pron. *bo-LEH-roh*, 118, 122
Bolero Cha, 104, 118
Bolero Ritmico, 104, 118
Bongó, pron. *bon-GO*, 29
Bongos, 29
Bongosero, pron. *bongo-SEH-roh*, 29
Bossa Nova, 148, 160
Botija, pron. *boh-TEE-yah*, 96
Box Rumba, 96
Break drum, 96
Breaks, 98, 103, 114, 131, 137, 153
Brushes, 161
B-section, 97
Byrd, Charlie, 160

Cabasa, pron. *kah-BAH-sah*, 77
Caixa, pron. *GUY-shah*, 82
Caixa de Fósforos, pron. *-dee - FOS-four-rus*, 92
Caixeta, pron. *guy-SHEH-tah*, 83
Cajón, pron. *kah-HUNG*, 96, 122
Call and answer section, 96
Calypso, 172
Campana, pron. *kam-PAH-nah*, 24
Campesino, pron. *calm-peh-SEE-noh*, 116
Candomblé, pron. *kan-dom-BLEH*, 144, 158
(El) Canto, pron. *KAHN-toh*, 96, 122
Capoeira, pron. *kah-poh-AEE-rah*, 93, 145, 158

Caribbean Islands, 8, 172
Carnival, 96, 144
Cascara, pron. *KAS-kah-rah*, 52, 122, 132
Cavaquinho, pron. *kah-vah-KEEN-yoh*, 144
Caxixi, pron. *ka-SHEE-shee*, 93
Cencerro, pron. *sen-SEH-roh*, 24
Cha-cha-cha, 100
Cha-cha-cha cowbell, 52
Chapottin, Felix, 97
Charanga, pron. *cha-RAHNG-gah*, 97
Charanga orchestra, 97, 100
Chinese temple block, 83
Chocalho, pron. *sho-CAHL-yoh*, 64
Choro, pron. *CHO-roh*, 145
Choro conjunto, 145
Cierre, pron. *SIEH-reh*, 98, 103, 114, 131, 137
Clarinet, 145
Claves, pron. *KLAH-ves*, 16
Clave rhythm, 17
Clave rhythm – Rumba style, 128
Comparsa, pron. *kom-PAHR-sah*, 96
Conga, 35
(La) Conga (rhythm/style), 96
Conga, basic rhythm, 41, 44, 45
Conguero, pron. *kong-GEH-roh*, 35
Conjunto, pron. *kon-HOON-toh*, 97
Cornet, 96
Coro, 96, 122
Coro-solo, 96, 116, 122
Cowbell, 24, 52, 158
Cross-rim, 53, 160
Cuban flute, 97
Cue, 99, 147
Cuica, pron. *koo-EE-kah*, 74

Danzón, pron. *dan-SONG*, 97, 108
»Desafinado«, 160
Descarga, pron. *deh-SKAR-gah*, 98, 107
Donga, 148
Drumset, 161

Ebony flute, 145
Escola de Samba, 144, 148

Flute (apito), 84
Foot, 9
Folklorico, pron. *fohlk-LOH-ri-coh*, 96, 122, 132
Frying pan, 96

Ganza, pron. *GAHN-sah*, 64
Getz, Stan, 160
Gilberto, João, 160
Gonzaga, Luiz, 164
Guagua, pron. *WAH-wah*, 122, 132
Guaguancó, pron. *wah-wang-KOH*, 122
Guajéo, pron. *wah-HEH-oh*, 97, 108

Guajira, pron. *wah-HEE-rah*, 116
Guajira Son, 116
Guajiro, pron. *wah-HE-roh*, 116
Guiro, pron. *WEE-roh* or *GWEE-roh*, 18
Guitar, 96, 144, 160

Hammer (martillo), 31
Hembra, pron. *EHM-brah*, 29, 35
Hi-hat, 156, 161

Jaw-bone, 28
Jazzband Cubana, 97
»Jazz Samba«, 160
Jobim, Antonio Carlos (Tom), 160

Kalimba, 96

Lopez, Orestes, 108

Machito (Frank Grillo), 108
Macho, pron. *MAH-choh*, 29, 35
Macumba, pron. *mah-KUM-bah*, 144, 158
Mambo, 108
Mambo cowbell, 52
Mambo section, 108
Maracas, 21
Maracatú, pron. *mah-rah-ka-TOO*, 169
Marcha Carnavalesca, 144
Marcha de Carnaval, 144
Marcha Rancho, pron. *– han-CHU*, 144
Marching band, 76, 82, 144
Marching cymbals, 76
Marching drum, 82
Marimbula, pron. *mah-RIM-boh-lah*, 96
Martillo, pron. *mahr-TEE-yoh*, 31
Matamoros, Miguel, 97
Match-box, 92
Matched grip, 52
Maxixe, pron. *mah-SHEE-she*, 145
Modern rhythm section, 97
Montuno, pron. *mon-TU-noh*, 97
Moreira, Airto, 169
Morros, pron. *MOH-hos*, 144
Mule jaw-bone, 28
Musica Campesina, 116
Musica Guajira, 116

»One note Samba«, 160
Open »slap« stroke, 40
«Orfeo Negro«, 160
Oriente province, 97
Orquesta tipica, 97

Pachanga, pron. *pah-CHANG-gah*, 97
Paila, pron. *PAEE-lah*, 52, 54
Pailas, 52
Palitos, pron. *pah-LEE-tos*, 122, 132
Pandeiro, pron. *PON-DAEE-roh*, 68
»Pelo Telefone«, 148
Percussion: rhythm instruments.
Polka, 145
Popular, pron. *poh-puh-LAR*, 96, 122

Prado, (Dámaso) Perez, 108
Pratos, pron. *PRAH-tos*, 76
Prato e Faca, pron. *PRAH-toh ee FAH-kah*, 67
Puente, Tito, 108
Punto Guajiro, 116

Quijada, pron. *Kee-HAH-dah*, 28
Quinto, pron. *KEEN-toh*, 35, 51, 134

Reco-reco, pron. *reh-koh-REH-koh* or *heh-koh-HEH-koh*, 66
Reverse clave, 17
Rim, 176
Rim-shot, 54, 55, 82
Rio de Janeiro, 61, 144
Ritmo doble, 26, 104
Rock, 9, 47, 89, 100, 142, 172
Rodriguez, Arsenio, 97, 108
Rodriguez, Tito, 108
Rumba (Rhumba), 122
Rumba Abierta, pron. *ah-bee-AIR-tah*, 122, 132
Rumba Columbia, 122, 132
Rumba de Cajón, pron. *– de ka-HUNG*, 96, 122
Rumba Folklorico, 132
Rumba Popular, 123
Rumbón, pron. *ruum-BONG*, 96, 122

Salsa, 98
Samba, 148
Samba basic pulse, 61, 146
Samba Batucada, 61, 148
Samba Canção, pron. *– kan-SAOH*, 148, 155, 160
Samba Carnavalesco, pron. *kar-nah-vahl-LES-koh*, 148
Samba Choro, pron. *SHO-roh*, 148, 155
Samba de Morro, pron. *– dee-MOH-hoh*, 148
Samba do Salão, pron. *doh-sah-LAAOH*, 156
»Samba de uma nota so«, 160
Samba flute, 84
Samba basic pulse, 61, 146
Samba Moderno, 156
Samba Schools, 144
Sanfona, 144, 164
Santana, 100
Santos, Ernesto dos, 148
Saxofon, 97, 108, 144
Schottisch, 145
Segunda, pron. *se-GOON-dah*, 35, 122, 132
Septeto, 96
Septeto Habanero, 96
Septeto Nacional, 96
6/8, 138
Slap-stroke, 39
Snare, 82
Snare drum, 82, 144, 160, 161
Son, 96
Son groups, 96
Son Montuno, pron. *– mon-TU-noh*, 116
Sonido, pron. *so-NEE-doh*, 35, 37
Spring reco-reco, 66
Surdo, pron. *SOOR-doh*, 62

Tamborim, pron. *tam-boh-RIM*, 70
Timbales, pron. *tim-BAH-les*, 52
Timbalero, pron. *tim-bah-LEH-roh*, 52
Timbalitos, pron. *tim-bah-LEE-tos*, 52
Tipica, pron. *TEE-pee-kah*, 97
Tres, 96, 108
Tres golpes, pron. – *GOL-pes*, 35, 122, 132
Triangle, 79
Triangulo, pron. *tree-ANG-guloh*, 79
Trinidad, 172
Trumpet, 96, 144
Tumba, pron. *TUM-bah*, 35
Tumbadora, pron. *tum-bah-DOH-ra*, 35
Tumbadoras, 35-96
Tumbao, pron. *tum-BAA-oh*, 41, 97, 122, 132, 172
Tuning and maintenance of congas and bongos, 176

»v« = variation for conga rhythm, 44, 45
Vibra-slap, 28
Violão, pron. *veeo-LAOH*, 144
Wood-block, 83

Yambú, pron. *yam-BOOH* (Rumba), 122, 132

Zabumba, pron. *sa-BUM-bah*, 164